WOMEN
and
SOCIAL CHANGE

WOMEN
and
SOCIAL CHANGE

by

Afsar Bano

Reference Press

4831/24, Ansari Road
Darya Ganj
New Delhi - 110 002
Phone: 23260807
Fax: 23274173
E-mail: essess@del3.vsnl.net.in

First Published 2003

ISBN: 81-88583-20-0

Price Rs.800/

Published by
Reference Press
4831/24,Ansari Road
Darya Ganj
New Delhi - 110 002
Phone: 23260807
Fax: 23274173
E-mail: essess@del3.vsnl.net.in

Printed in India by:
Print Line, Delhi

Contents

Preface

In our country. for thousands of years, our family life and our society have evolved and developed. Now, we , as a nation claim a strong presence of women in all walks of life, but the lot of the female community in our land has remained more or less same. They have suffered for centuries together, and they are suffering even now. But we must ensure that they, as a community should not suffer any more. At least, they deserve their rightful place in our social, economic and political setup, which is still male dominated. However, it wouldn't be fair to say that no body talks of the plight of women.

Movements for the women lib are about a hundred year old now, and there has been an awakening, regarding their problems and the injustice caused to them, for several decades, the world over, even in Asia. And in India all governments, the foreign one earlier and our own elected one, after independence, have devoted enough attention to the problems of women, resulting into numerous reforming measures and framing of laws. However, the ultimate output has not been satisfactory, at all. Hence, a genuine concern about the group of the deprived, known as women, among the academics, scholars and social activists.

This study is a modest effort with an aim of stirring the calm waters, making the society aware of women's problems and their pitiable state in our society and polity. In fact, the urge for the attainment of this goal has resulted in this work. It would certainly be an honour for this author, if this endeavour makes a breakthrough, by causing the people ponder over the issues, related to women and feel concerned really, about their fateful condition.

Author

One

Introduction

The world over, in contemporary feminist literature, the word 'women' has been replaced with the term 'gender' as a new category of analysis to assert that much of sexual differentiation is a social and political construct, related to but not determined by biological sex difference. It (Gender) "is seen as the process by which individuals who are born into biological categories of male or female become the social categories of men and women through the acquisition of locally defined attributes of masculinity and femininity". Therefore, the feminists argue that this replacement (from women to gender) provides deeper analysis of present inequalities, and thus challenges the structure of current social, economic and cultural processes.

In fact the invention of this new word 'gender' is the result of two decades of intensive thought and research. In its most recent usage, gender seems to have first appeared among American feminists who wanted to reject biological determinism implicit in the use of such terms as 'sex' or 'sexual difference'. Two major theories of gender are prevalent today- the psychologically focused theory of gender, and the historically and anthropologically focused explanation of gender.

The former is represented in the writings of Simone de Behaviour, who says: "One is not born but rather becomes a woman." She claims that it is a whole process by which femininity is manufactured in society. To quote her, she is defied and differentiated with reference to men and not he with reference to her; she is the incidental, the inessential as opposed to the essential. He is the subject, he is the absolute - She is the Other.

Simon Behaviour argues that it is the child-bearing role, of women which excluded them from the productive process, and prevented her from seeing themselves as subjects in their own right. Thus, an artificial idea of womanhood was created by the society. She exhorts: "No biological. psychological or economic fate determines the figure that the human female presents in society, it is civilization as a whole that produces this creation, intermediate between male and eunuch who is described female."

Nancy Chodorow also subscribes to the above viewpoint and substantiates her argument from a psycho-analytical point of view. She argues that since women have always been assigned the responsibility of primary parenting and nurturing, she develops a psychology of being more suited to the task of nurturing and caring and thus herself chooses the role of a care-given and confinement to the private. On the other hand, man from the very beginning is encouraged for more and more individualisation and attaining status resulting into such personality traits impelling him to associate himself with the public.

The second theory of gender, based on historical and anthropological explanation, proclaims that in most of the societies so far, gender has been a socially constructed category rather than biologically determined. However, the proponents of this theory have also stressed that the nature of this social construction differs from one society to the other. So, there cannot be any uncausal, unavailable and a historical explanations of it. Anthropologist Michelle A Rosaldo supports this theory on the basis of her cross cultural research which reveals that women are subjected to the authority due to the existing dichotomy between the public and the private.

Historian Linda J Nicholson also rejects the unicausal explorations of inequality of sexes. She also emphasises, that it has been affected by various causal factors in different social contexts. She stresses the need to fight against the powerful tendency present in political theory to reify the public-private distinction and to perceive it as rigid. She believes that one can comprehend this distinction only through the study of history for the gender structure irregular time and place is less affected by other contemporary stressors, such as political, economic, than by the previous history of gender. Joan W Scott also stresses the centrality of history in analysing different aspects of the construction of gender. She explains (a) how cultural myths and symbols justify the suppression of woman: (b) how these symbols create the 'binary opposition of masculine and feminine, male and female; (c) how social institutions family, labour markets, educational instructions, and polity reinforce this dichotomy-, and (d) how the subjective identity formation of individuals is psychologically determined.' She, therefore, emphasizes the need to expose the social construction of gender by deconstructing it. 'Ibis calls for:

> "....a refusal of the fixed and permanent quality of binary opposition, a genuine historicization and deconstruction terminism cannot be monolithic in its issues, goals and strategies, since it constitutes the political expression of the concerns of women from different regions, classes, nationalities and ethnic backgrounds. There Is and must be a diversity of feminisms, responsive to the different needs and concerns of different women and defined by them for themselves.

The most positive part of the whole discourse is that these concerns are reflected in practice also. Women involved in different social movements are fighting against injustices on their own cultural terms. Environmental activists, such as Vandana Shiva are speaking of the need to decolonize northern assumptions such as the concept of sustainable development and appeal to save environment through knowledge based on poor women's experience.

Thus, feminist scholarship has brought sweeping changes to social and political theory. It has cautioned us against constituting gender as a super-ordinate category of analysis. It should neither be an automatic starting point of analysis of adjustment, nor should it be ignored as a potential starting point. We must avoid approaches that are gender-blinded or gender-blind. Then only we can have true meaning of democracy and participation.

This has eventually led to the dichotomy between morality and power. Women in the name of being more moral have been excluded from the public realm. Even the suffragists argued in favour of women's franchise by claiming women's superior morality as it would usher the state in a reign of peace. This is why Elshtain alleges that suffragist instead of challenging the separation of the public and private, merely "perpetuated the very mystifications and unexamines presumptions which served to rig the system against them."

Against this background, one can understand the significance of the feminist slogan; The personal is the political.

The feminists argue that public realm of politics can be rational, noble and universal as the messy content of the body, meeting its needs providing for production, caretaking and attending to birth and death, are taken care of elsewhere.

So a modern reflective political theory should recognize that the glory of the public is dialectically, entwined with the exploitation and repression of the private and the people restricted to that sphere so that they can take care of people's needs. In view of this, feminists conclude that 21st century politics requires a basic rethinking of this distinction and its meaning for politics.

Feminists are tying to develop a theory, of social practice on the following premises: First, there should be no sexual division of labour in workplace and in political organizations of all ideological persuasions: second, it believes in a differentiated social order within which various dimensions are distinct but not separate or opposed, and which rests on social conception of individuality, which includes both women and men as biologically differentiated but not unequal creatures.

We must expand conception of politics, based on the

understanding that power relations between men and women are not confined to the 'public' world of law, the state and economics, but that they pervade all areas of life. This means that, contrary to the assumptions of traditional political theory, the family, reproduction and sexuality must be included in political analysis.

The question arises how far this public/private dichotomy and its deconstruction is relevant to the women of the Third World? Can this empowerment epistemology be rooted In White women's experiences, subjectivity and identity fulfil the interest of Third World women?

However, in the post colonial discourse, women of North have themselves understood the significance of Third World women's realities and they have themselves rejected the monolithic nature of earlier feminist discourse on the grounds that it ignores difference, indigenous knowledge, and local expertise. For example, modernity is equated with Westernization, industrialization, and superiority, whereas non-modernity is equated with non-Western countries, tradition and inferiority. In the 1970s, Ester Boserup's pioneering work Women's Role in Economic Development asserted that modernization had marginalized women and their contributions in the Third World. Chandra Mohanty also questions the Western approach. How, she asks:

> "...is it possible to refer to 'the' sexual division of labour when the content of this division changes radically from one environment to the next, and from one historical juncture to another? At Its most abstract level... concepts such as the sexual division of labour can be useful only if they are generated through local, contextual analysis. If such concepts are assumed to be universally applicable, the resultant homogenisation of class, race, religious, 'and daily material practices of women in the Third World can create a false sense of the commonality of oppressions, interests, and struggles between and among women globally."

Sen and crown too cautions against adopting a concept of

gender that ignores difference and diversities. They believe this diversity is built on gender oppression and hierarchy. He exclaims:

"The most fundamental and general of these opposition associates women with nature and men with culture. Nature is always seen as of a lower order than culture. The feminists like Ortner argue that the opposition between women/nature and men/ culture is itself a cultural construct and not given in nature. Firestone in her work Dialectic of Sex argues against this separation of private and public. Women necessarily suffer from a fundamentally oppressive biological conditions. It is their role as reproducers that has handicapped women over the centuries and made possible men's patriarchal power." The consequences of the public-private dichotomy are disastrous. Due to this, only women have been deprived of political power and effective participation. Citizenship for women is always seen as "an elaboration of their private domestic task."

Part - I

Background

Two

The Change in Past

The woman has been the subject of study, in all ages — from the ancient to the modern times. Comments on the nature of women their ambitions and aspirations, desires and wishes, birth and upbringing, relations with husband, paramour, children and other relatives have been the subject of discussion, comments, conversations and investigations throughout the history of mankind. The woman has been branded as a mysterious creature as well as a devoted mother and self-sacrificing wife during various periods of time through which the human civilization has evolved out from its primitive roots to an advanced scientific and technical culture.

The changing status and position of the woman in different periods and in different civilizations have very greatly influenced her upbringing and education. If during one period of time or in one civilization she was brought up as a prized possession of the parents, in some others she was completely neglected and was accepted only as a provider of sexual pleasure to man and as a producer of his offspring. As a provider of pleasure and producer of children, her education was completely neglected but whenever and wherever she was given high prestige in society, her education became the primary concern of the social order. Thus, the education of the woman has been completely limited to her sociological status and psychological make up. In the present book the focus is on the social psychological dimensions of a women education in India.

For better understanding of the socio-psychological dimensions of women education in India one may look into the background out of which the role, position and education of women have emerged from the past to the present. In the following pages the authors have presented a brief description of women's role, position and education in the religious and historical perspectives. The authors have confined their description mainly to the Indian women but have also focused attention on the women in the West in the context of their struggle for emancipation and empowerment in order to visualize its influence on the Indian womanhood.

In Ancient India

Ironically, very little information is available about the civilization in pre-Aryan India. However, opinion of some, archaeologists is that the non-Aryans had originated in India as early as around 2500 B.C. and were of mixed origin and diverse ethnic composition. Later, their intellectual bent of mind influenced the Aryan thought process. The law of karma, reincarnation, animal veneration, female or earth-mother goddesses, deity worship and male and female fertility symbols might have been imbibed by the Aryans from them.

It seems that to begin with the Aryans overwhelmed the non-Aryans, suppressed their religion and culture and imposed their own values. However, as time passed the Aryans became progressively Indianized, they absorbed the customs of the original inhabitants and modified their religion assimilating the existing culture. The Aryans' own religious and social customs were fused with theirs and Indianized by the native people. Thus, fusing together of incoming concepts and prevailing customs became the tradition of India and of Hinduism.

The Aryans produced vedic literature. The philosophies of Vedanta and Upanishads are their contributions.

Aryan family life was stable. The society was founded on the institutions of home and family. The women were assigned prestigious position in the social order. The Rig Vedic expression "the wife is the home"-shows how domestic life was woven around the woman.

The pre-vedic society was basically matriarchal. It worshipped a goddess of earth-mother type. The Aryan society was patriarchal but the worship of the goddess prevailed. Earlier the mother goddess was worshipped in the form of icons but the Aryans almost replaced the icons with matronly women real mothers who were human and humane. The mother was given a high status in all the spheres of life.

There was attached great importance to the goddess Aditi who typified the motherhood. She was considered the ideal mother like Maat of the Egyptians and Themis of the Greeks. Her function has been described to tenderly the living beings.

Rig Vedic Aryans loved their wives and children. They had a desire for male child but the birth of a daughter as potential mother was also accepted and welcomed. However, in Rig Veda no desire for a daughter is expressed, while in Atharva Veda the birth of a daughter is even deprecated. In Upanishads there are prescribed certain rituals to be performed by a man who wants a learned daughter to be born.

In the Rig Vedic period the son and daughter were not discriminated in their upbringing. The son was to take to the profession of the father, while the daughter was to inherit the glory and honour of her mother. The wife as mother was given the dignity and respect in the household. She was expected to perform duties which were both of celestial as well as terrestial in nature. She participated in all sacrifices instituted by her husband.

Women were educated both in the spiritual as well as temporal subjects. They were given training in the religious lore, in the historical tradition and mythology. They were also given training in the fine arts as well as in the military science in certain cases. As a qualification for marriage, the education of a girl was considered as important as that of a boy.

The education of the women mainly centred round the acquisition of language and literature, the fine arts and the military science. The ancient literature records that there were scores of women, eligible to become Rishis and composed very effective poetry. The name of Ghosa, the wife of the great seer Kaksivan can be mentioned. In Rig Veda she has been mentioned many a time. Two long, hymns, 39 and

40 of the tenth mandala stand to her credit. Lopamundra is another lady Rishi who is credited with having composed a hymn jointly with her husband Agastya.

Music was a necessary equipment for women of the period. Songs were sung on all important occasions and functions. Dancing as an art was also learnt by the women. The women were also trained in self-defence. They knew how to use bow and arrow.

The paternal and maternal tie was very strong among the early Aryans. The father was respected as the earner and protector, the mother was loved for providing daily nourishment and maintaining the household. The daughter was caressed and fondled by her parents and brothers who gave her lavish presents at the time of her marriage. She was considered the breath and life of the family.

The women had liberty of movement. There was no Parda. Indo-Aryans recognized the truth embodied in the dictums, "Ignorance is weakness," "Knowledge is power".

The number of Upanishads is estimated to be around fifty. In most of them, we do not find any reference to women. It is only in Chandogya and Brihadaranyaka Upanishads that we find that women were admitted into philosophical groups and were allowed to discuss the highest spiritual truths of life. They enjoyed a position on a par with men. The men and women were considered as the 'two wheels of the same chariot'.

From the account of this period we find that women were free from social constraints. Girls were free to choose their own husbands. They married only after attaining puberty. The women were even exalted to the position of goddess and given different celestial names like Prithvi, a vague personification of the earth, Usha, the goddess of dawn, Ratri, the spirit of night, etc.

The concept of Ardhanarishwara was propagated. The concept was that of a figure image of half Shiva and the other half as Parvati. This image signified the interdependence of men and women. It conveyed the message that separately men and women are incomplete.

Only jointly they are complete. The figure image depicted the masculine and the feminine functions of the Supreme being.

It may be noted that in the Upanishadic texts woman was not eulogized as a person in herself but first and foremost her role as wife and mother was given high status and value. The women were idealized and glorified as mothers. The girl as a potential perpetuator of a family line was valued as much as a son.

Since Rig Vedic age education of women was given much importance. There is evidence that the discipline of brahamacharya was also required to be observed by the girl. The stage of brahamacharya in all probability may be the period of studentship of the girl preceding her married life. The girls were taught that marriage was not for lust, but for perfect domestic life and for producing illustrious progeny. They were given training in the art of house-keeping and house management. Their education was to prepare them to conduct themselves properly in the married life. They learnt the art of some handicrafts, the elements of hygiene, physiology and nutrition.

The pattern of education in the Upanishadic period became more philosophical in nature. The men and women shifted their attention from Vedic ritualism to more intricate problems of life. The women engaged themselves freely in debates and philosophical symposia.

Education helped the women to become more balanced and lead a regulated good life. It was directed towards the development of their natural virtues and latent capabilities and aimed at all round development of their character and personality. Eminent women scholars of this period, like Sulabha, Vadya, Maitreyi and Gargi made significant contributions to the advancement of knowledge.

A description of status, position and education of the women of ancient India is incomplete without the mention of Manu's views. *Manusmriti* (about 200 B.C.) prescribes duties and obligations of a woman. For Manu, woman is a perpetual minor and has to lead whole of her life under the guardianship of either the father, the husband or the son.

Manu prescribes that the wife must always worship her husband as God even if he is debauch, immoral and lacks good qualities. It is the bounden duty of the wife to obey and follow the dictates of her husband. The woman's salvation lies only in the devoted service to her husband. He refers to her duties in the following words:

> "She must always be cheerful, clever in the management of her household affairs, careful in cleaning her utensils, and economical in expenditure"

Manu favoured only the domestic and religious education for women. He also favoured the giving of training in music and dance to the woman in order that she may be able to please her man.

The society in the Epic period was completely patriarchal and patrilineal, so the husband was considered the senior partner in the home. But the wife was also given the dignity in the household because of her vocation of motherhood. Her virtues were recognized. Her abilities in the maintenance of the household were appreciated. She was considered to be a true friend of man given by God. She was man's half, his religious partner, giver of joy and sons.

The epics *Ramayana* and *Mahabharata* contain the description of women who presented ideal conduct and models for the womenhood to be adopted by the lesser mortals. But these models also have ingrained in themselves the subordination of the women. Thus the epics trace the story of the rise and fall of the status of women in Hindu society. Mentioned below are a few highly revered and illustrious ladies who form the central theme of these epics.

The foremost among all the ladies mentioned in epics is Devi Sita. Sita is a paragon of virtue. She is an ideal wife who serves her husband with complete devotion, who is an embodiment of the spiritual sublimity of feminine character. She suffers great hardships but remains unperturbed by them. Her only wish is to serve her husband with all her capabilities. She has to suffer the ordeal of fire but at no occasion she expresses any doubt in her loyalty, fidelity, devotion, love and sacrifice for the well being of her husband. She is learned. She can quote moral tales and smrities. She had religious education.

No doubt the ideal of Sita has inspired Indian women for ages. But in the modern times some are raising doubts about the complete subordination to the husband eulogised in the character of Sita. For educationists, it is a dilemma. Should the women education be directed towards the flowering of the women as devoted as Sita to her husband or teach them for independent outlook. For a proper answer all the aspects of Sita's personality as portrayed in the epic have to be carefully examined. One thing stands out that as Sita had her own will and determination and even when she had to undergo torture her determination did not waver.

She was one of the strong-willed women of the Epic Period. She possessed not only physical charm but also a brilliant mind. She was exposed to the brutalities of men when she was forced to discard her clothes before the men of the Kauravas court. But she did not lose the balance of her mind and reasoning power. The arguments presented by her in the Kaurava court were so perfect that nobody except Vidura and Vikarna possessed the courage to reply to her question. In the midst of her humiliation, she still showed good manners and saluted those Kuru elders who did not dare to check the evil. She was deeply learned and had comprehensive knowledge of old traditions, history and the Puranas. She did not hesitate in condemning her husbands when they failed in the performance of their duties. She did not tolerate her insult and inspired even a peace loving man like Yudhistira to war.

Draupadi presents to us an ideal of womanhood who was learned, iron willed, revengeful, intolerant towards undignified behaviour, loving and affectionate and also forgiving. She was a perfect wife, wise counsellor and dear companion to her husbands.

Among the other learned ladies of the Epic period we may name Gandhari, Kunti, Kaushalya, Sumitra, Kaikeyi, Gautami, Sulabha, Mandodri, Trigata and many others.

Gandhari was the noblest of mothers. She had understanding, judgment, intellect and good sense. She remained attached to the cause of justice and righteousness even when her sons were on the verge of being annihilated and their empire destroyed. She had a high sense of justice, possessed great intellectual qualities and depicted in her conduct both human virtues and frailties. She was jealous of Kunti's motherhood and had a longing for a daughter and son-in-law in order to attain Heaven. She spent her life in penance, self denial and righteousness. But she had weaknesses which make her character real and thus presents ideals which are attainable by ordinary human beings.

Kunti was an ideal wife and mother. She was also of strong will. She taught her sons to die gloriously in war than live in infamy. She was an unwed mother of Karna whom she threw in the river. But her love for her son was irresistible, sublime and pure. Kunti presents an ideal of womanhood which is unflinching in love, righteousness yet not so bold as to face the hostile society for her begetting a son out of wedlock.

The three queens of king Dashratha-Kaushalya, Kaikeyi, Sumitra were well-versed in household affairs but were also involved in the state craft. They had many virtues but also sufferred from human frailties. Kaushalya was the ordinary human being but served her husband, as a slave, friend, sister, wife, and mother. Sumitra was calm, steady and balanced. For her the path of duty and righteousness was more important than any material possession. Kaikeyi was dominating, bold and resourceful. Her life shows that she was over-ambitious and wished, to control the kingdom through her husband, and, later through her son. She is by and large portrayed as a negative character.

There are many other women whose lives and exploits are presented as the ideals of Hindu womanhood. These ladies were highly cultured and were prepared to sacrifice personal good for the social good. The education of the Indian women, particularly the Hindu women has been very greatly influenced by the ideals propagated through the study of their lives and exhortations. However, in the modern times some questions are being asked about the ideals so propagated. In the various chapters of this book we will examine these doubts and try to arrive at some conclusions regarding their validity in the twenty-first century.

Buddha inculcated in his followers a reverence for learning. He conveyed the Dharma or Truth to his first disciples at his teaching sessions at Varanasi. These disciples became the first members of the Sangha. Among his first Upasikas or followers there, were two women. Initially, he was reluctant to incorporate women into the Sangha and this attitude resulted in the subsequent neglect of female education by his followers.

Buddha believed that seven factors lead to wisdom: inner mindfulness, searching of the norms, energy, zest, serenity, concentration, and mental balance. These thoughts were installed in the young Buddhist males but were ignored in the case of sisters of the Sangha. As indicated above Buddha initially was averse to the admission of women into his Sangha system but later on agreed to the formation of the order of the nuns-these nuns were imparted religious and spiritual education. A life of celibacy, austerity and strict mental discipline was expected of them. The education for the women was also introduced at the later stage in order to help them to acquire the knowledge that would enable them to lead a fuller life. But the end of Buddhist era in India also resulted in the end of female education for many generations.

In Jainism, there was given great importance to self-denial, restrains of passion and a life of renunciation. A life of restraint and devoid of passion was expected from men and women. The women were also admitted into monasteries and given full facilities to get the best possible education. The Jaina system of education had depth, was universal in nature and applicable to all alike, irrespective of caste, creed or sex.

The spiritually trained Jaina women attained a high degree of academic education and involved themselves in preaching their faith of universal love and brotherhood. They dedicated themselves to social service.

Jainism was divided into two main sects-Digambaras and Shwetambaras. The Digambaras were of the opinion that women were incapable of attaining salvation and so did not admit them into their order. The Shwetambaras, on the other hand, made no distinction between the sexes and freely admitted aspirants of both the sexes into their order.

Theoretically, Jaina believed that man and women both had the right to attain perfection or perfect liberation of the highest order. But in practice Jaina felt that there were very few women who had the strength of mind and body to endure the hard life of an ascetic. The women were considered weak and so unfit to undertake a course of self-mortification and self-effacement. Thus in the spiritual order women had secondary position.

Sikhism considers woman as worthy of respect as man's helpmate and a partner in his domestic life. Women are not looked upon as evil or perpetrator of sin, nor simply the objects of men's pleasure. A woman's roles as mother, wife, sister and daughter are praised and the qualities which the women are expected to develop are love, obedience, contentment and sweet temper.

Sikhism advocated equality among all the human beings. The social equality of the women is ungrudgingly recognised. The militant brotherhood of the Sikhs, the Khalsa founded by Guru Gobind Singh in the seventeenth century was open to both sexes and all classes. The women were initiated into the Khalsa by taking the name of Kaur and were expected to perform the same duties as men.

Since in Sikhism the equality of sexes was recognized, very few restrictions were put on womens' education.

Christian View

In Christianity, women are considered as the harbinger of evil. No doubt Catholics give a high respectful place to Virgin Mary but both Protestants and Catholics feel that the women brought the evil to the earth. The fall of Adam is attributed to the evil design of Eve. Hence the pious and saintly Christians like St. Bernard, St. Antony, St. Bonaventure, St. George the great, all cursed women. The woman was described by them as the organ of the devil', 'a scorpion ever ready to sting', 'the poison of an asp', 'the malice of the dragon' and 'the instrument which the devil uses to get possession of our souls'.

The position of the woman in the Jewish faith was very low but in Christianity it was further lowered. They charge her with the crime of disobeying God, causing the fall of Adam and her guilt being transmitted to the whole mankind so that every child is born in sin. Since God had to send, Jesus to be sacrificed because of the first crime of the woman, so she is considered responsible for the crucification of Jesus. The Christian saints and priests considered women to be unclean and so gave much importance to a life of celibacy. It is because of this attitude that the Christian women were denied those rights and privileges which Christian men enjoyed. It is only in twentieth century that the movements of women liberation have resulted in their recognition as equals to men. The women had to wage a severe and persistent battle to achieve those rights which should have been their on the basis of their recognition as a part of humanity.

It is true that women have now been given rights. But they obtained these by their own struggle and by the slackening of the hold of priests over western societies and laws.

Education, historically, was the sole privilege of the rich and the priestly class. The priests dominated the transmission of knowledge throughout Christiandom. They controlled the access to institutions of learning. In all the Christian countries education was the monopoly of the religious orders. The governing priests did not consider the education of women essential. They were of the view that women were incapable of absorbing the same amount of education or the same in-depth knowledge as men. Besides this they thought that women's minds were weaker than men's and did not require that intellectual exercise which the men needed. They had spread the myth that women should be restrained from speaking in church and from getting education.

The Christian priests' disregard for women education was rooted in their belief in women's inferiority. This disregard was further reinforced by the fear of female emancipation. They were afraid that free education may lead to the deployment of women's full potential.

This in their view was going to upset the natural order between men and women and God and women and the church. They emphatically pointed out that the women are modest, obedient and docile and as such do not require as thorough an education as men do.

Later the missionaries started giving education to women but they segregated boys and girls and prescribed different courses of study to the two sexes. The boys were taught useful subjects in the vocational, mechanical and scientific spheres. The girls were taught domesticity, cooking, knitting, etc. The idea was that boys should be prepared for life outside home and the girls for life inside the home.

As we have already pointed out that the situation has very much changed now in almost all the Christian countries but still the stigma attached of being a woman has not been completely wiped out. And whatever women have achieved in raising their status and position and in attaining prestige has been the fruits of their own struggle for emancipation and empowerment.

Islamic View

In Islam straight forward directions regarding the status and the position of the women have been laid down. It is the only religion in which the universal laws for all walks of human life are laid down including that for women. There are directions regarding social and political rights of women. There are laws regarding their claims to property and their privileges for the custody of children and their religious duties.

Islam gives equality to women in relation to men in many respects. It makes a case for the dignity of women. In holy Quran it is mentioned that "women are the twin halves of men". "The world and all things in it are valuable but the most valuable thing in the world is a virtuous wife", God enjoins upon you to treat women well for they are your mothers, daughters and aunts''.

There are also many aspects which present seeds of discrimination between men and women. Islam gives rights of inheritance of property to women as a daughter, a wife, a mother, a sister and in some cases even to more distantly related. But when a man has a son and a daughter both, the share of the daughter is, half that of the son.

The inequality between men and women is also evident in Islam when we find that women are put in seclusion in Islam. They are put behind parda and debarred from any male company besides their immediate and near relations. Other areas of discrimination are man's right of divorce, the right of men to practice polygamy, have four wives at a time and similar other provisions like "the testimonies of two women are equal to one man". Parda system isolated women from the outer world and confined them to the four walls of their house.

In the holy Quran the women are exhorted to be modest, chaste, lead a life of decorum and decency which was interpreted by the religious leaders in terms of putting the women in Parda, put a veil or burkha on their bodies. This resulted in losing their right to participate in communal activities. Thus Islam differentiated between the man's world and the woman's world.

In early Islam, female education was highly restricted. Only in the families in which the father was educated, the girls learnt to recite the verses of Quran. But her learning was totally dependent on the approval of the father

In the medieval period women education was by and large ignored. The women were excluded from public gatherings or in any intellectual deliberations. The result was that most of the women remained illiterate and unlettered. Some females had access to tutors and libraries but they were not engaged by men-folk in any intellectual discussion. Hence they could learn through their own individual efforts. By and large women remained in status as inferior, unequal, submissive and ignorant beings. Females were denied access to learning. They were also excluded from the mosques where most of the education occurred. They could not attend the Kuttabs and the Madrasah.

Some of the women who were fortunate to receive education usually came from affluent, prestigious families that could afford to hire private tutors and successfully face the criticism of the community for educating their females.

It is worth noticing that despite Islam giving equality to sexes and permitting men and women to acquire success, education and honour and in spite of it giving equal religious and spiritual rights, the Islamic clergy interpreted it in terms of equality in their own natural sphere of being men and women. They propagated that the roles of men and women are different and so they have to be isolated from each other. While man needs education woman has to stay at home and involve herself in house keeping for which the training in the house craft is only needed, which can be provided in the home itself.

A Long Journey

Above we have described the role, status and education of Indian women as determined by the religious order to which they belonged. Let us now look into the status, etc., of the Indian women in historical perspective.

We have already emphasized that from the very beginning of the history of civilization society has been male dominated and the status and the position of the woman depended on how man conceived her in his relationship with her. In India the Rig Vedic society was founded on the home and family and so assigned a place of importance to her. The Rig Vedic sages focus the domestic life on the sentiments centred round the women. The women of the Vedic and Brahmanic literature. The learned lady was held in high esteem.

In the Epic age the woman was considered to be a true friend of man. She was regarded as man's half, his religious partner, giver of joy and sons. Through her man was able to attain immortality. Sita, Savitri, Damyanti, Draupadi born in royal families and in luxury followed their husbands to the wilderness of the forests and endured a life of much hardships along with them. They embodied in themselves extreme love, devotion and selfless service to their spouses. They served without expectations of any return from them. Women of this period were also ideal mothers and true teachers of their offspring.

There is evidence that the Muslim invasion brought about the deterioration of women's position. Restrictions on her rights and freedom were imposed. Muslims adherence to Polygamy and Parda also influenced the Hindus. Restrictions of the rights and privileges of the women were imposed. The women were considered inferior to men and so began to be ill-treated. The women, both among Hindus and Muslims were confined to their homes and their duties, rights or obligations all were interpreted in terms of devoted wife and sacrificing mother.

The position of the medieval Muslim women, according to Muslim law was somewhat better than that of contemporary Hindu women. But in practice it was similar or in many instances inferior than Hindu women because of the rigidity of the Parda system and the denial of education to Muslim women.

There is no authentic account of the prevalence of education among Muslim women of various classes and masses. However, it seems that the majority of Muslim women were illiterate and those few who were educated learnt through oral and non-formal instructions. There were ladies of the noble families who had the privilege of learning the religious texts and various arts and crafts but those they learnt by their own persistence and in their own homes. History reveals that there were highly learned and accomplished Muslim ladies like Razia Sultan, Chand Bibi, Nur Jahan, Jahanara, etc. These ladies could learn and attain dominance by sheer strength of their personality. Thus, we may conclude that during Muslim period while the women from royal families enjoyed much respect and freedom and were interested in learning, the women of lower and middle strata of society were largely ignorant and illiterate.

Modern Era

At the advent of the British Empire the status and the position of the Indian women were very low. From the ideological point of view women were considered a complete or inferior species. They were inferior to males having no personality, no significance. From the social point of view they were kept in a state of utter subjection, denied any right, suppressed and oppressed.

The customs of polygamy, the parda, the denial of woman's rights over property, child marriage, Sati Pratha and denial of remarriage to widows - all these practices in this period resulted in the development of a very weak personality of the woman. She was not only considered an inferior by the male members of the society but she in herself became rooted to the idea that she was weak, helpless, subordinate and inferior - a non entity, a slave. Hence women themselves became great perpetuators of tyranny on the women over whom they could exercise their sadism. So dowry demands, forcing of the widows to burn or to lead a life of misery and toil, a dominant mother-in-law and subservient daughter-in-law, all such acts were initiated, perpetuated and committed by the women or in connivance with the women.

The British influence was in the positive direction. The close contacts with western cultural tradition, literature and education affected very deeply the minds of the Indian leaders. The result of it was the social movements for reforms in those evils which were prevalent in the society. The reformist movements started in the 19th century. The leaders and the social reformers who were in the forefront of the struggle for women emancipation were Raja Ram Mohun Roy, Ishwar Chandra Vidhyasagar, Swami Dayanand Saraswati, Swami Vivekanand, Mahatma Gandhi, Jawaharlal Nehru and many others.

To Raja Ram Mohun Roy goes the credit of laying the foundations of all the principle reformist movements which subsequently became instruments for modernization of the country. He devoted whole of his life for raising the status and position of the women in India. He propagated his own democratic, rational and human conception of womanhood.

It is said that while Raja Ram Mohun Roy saved the widow from self-immolation or becoming Sati on the funeral pyre of her husband, Ishwar Chandra Vidyasagar released her from a living death, by helping to legalize the Widow Remarriage. He wrote a book on widow remarriage which was published in 1853. It was through his efforts that the widow remarriage Act of 1856 was passed which permitted the legitimacy of the issues born of such marriages. He also gave much importance to the education of the girls which was considered essential for the development of their personality. Swami Dayanand Saraswati felt that the woman's status must be raised. He sought to create equal status for the women in the field of Sacred Thread Ceremony. He considered that education must aim at making women capable of performing her duties in home as well as outside the home. He founded Arya Samaj in 1875 at Bombay. It started Gurukuls for widows, rescue homes for destitutes, etc.

Another social reformer was Swami Vivekanand. He was greatly pained at the miserable condition of women in India. He, therefore, recommended that women should be supported and educated as men. He said, "It is only in the hands of educated and pious mothers the great men are born. The ideal woman in India is that mother, the mother first and the mother last." He suggested that the women should be made ambitious through a sound system of education. For him the ideal of womanhood was not only Sita or

Savitri but that of an ideal mother. He said, "Motherhood is the beginning. Motherhood is the end of Indian womanhood."

Mahatma Gandhi considered that if a husband is a God, the wife is a Goddess. Wife is not a slave but a friend and companian with equal rights. Gandhi held the view that women have a right to education. But he was of this view that men and women are not identical but complementary to one another. Education for them should be such that it makes of them capable of performing their duties. Gandhiji's efforts led to the elevation of the woman's status an involved her in the struggle for social progrtess and political independence. The women were able to develop their latent powers. Women like Sarojini Naidu, Kasturba Gandhi, Kamla Nehru, Aruna Asaf Ali participated in the political arena with all their might and potentials. Indeed India witnessed the rise of many great women.

India gained freedom in 1947. Her Constitution was adopted on 26th January, 1950. The Constitution gave full and equal rights to women as compared to men. Thereafter we are witnessing a strong, persistent and unrelenting struggle for the emancipation, empowerment and dignity led by women activists, enlightened political leaders, educationists and social reformers.

The western countries being mostly Christianity dominated gave the status and the position to the women as indicated by their religion. Hence in most of them till quite recently women were given a very low status in comparison to men. The Christians considered the women as temptations of the world of flesh and of the devil. The fathers of the church believed in the myth that Eve led Adam into sin.

Earlier, before the advent of Christianity, the women of Greece enjoyed much better status and position than later Christian women. Plato, the Greek philosopher made no distinction of the sexes in his ideal 'Republic'. He, no doubt, admits that women are generally inferior to men but in his view they have similar, if lower, capacities and power. He emphasized that there is no occupation or art for which they may not be fitted by nature and education. He, therefore, wants them to share in government and war as well as in the various mechanical trades. Still the Greek opinion was that women are best suited for household chores. Aristotle had unshakable faith in the value of household and the family and considered man as its natural ruler.

The Romans held women in greatest honour as the words of Cato the Censor show: "All men, rule over women, we Romans rule over all men, and our wives rule over us."

In law, however, the women had an inferior status in that they did not have freedom. They were always put under the control of some male member of the family. Before marriage she was entirely under the control of father, on her marriage she passed into a similar position towards her husband, and if she remained unmarried, she was under the control of her nearest male relative. In spite of this legal position, the position of the women in their family was an honoured one. Roman girls did not, as a rule, go to school. They were taught all that they were to know of book learning at home by their mothers.

When Christianity came a new set of virtues began to be propagated in place of the vices which had engulfed the later Roman social order. It is to be noted that the Roman society, in the beginning of the Christian era, had become a completely debunked society in which ethical and moral values were completely eroded. Christianity combined and harmonized an ideal of personal morality, sincerity, honesty, chastity, love, loyalty, kindness and unselfishness. Womanhood was elevated and given a new dignity. Before the establishment of Christianity, divorce became frequent, infanticide, child exposure, cruel and bloody gladiatorial shows licentiousness in private life were the evils which had deformed the society. Christianity fought against these evils and created a better and just order. Women, even though remained under the subjection of male members, yet were given an honoured place in home.

In the early middle ages, from the sixth to the tenth centuries, the creeds and dogmas established by the church were accepted without any doubts or questions. But after tenth century, particularly, during the eleventh and twelfth centuries, Christian scholars started questioning the dogmas spread by the church. They adopted logical methods of discussion and analysed the various beliefs and faiths on the anvil of rationality. This period is, therefore, known as the period of Scholasticism. "The aim of Scholasticism was to support the doctrines of the Church by rational argument, to show essential harmony between reason and faith." The thirteenth century was the Golden Age of Scholasticism. In this age, Scholasticism projected two high peaks. One was that of the doctrine of St. Thomas, who along with Albert built Aristotelianism into a Christian system of thought. The other was that of St. Bonaventure. At this peak, the Augustinian thought of the middle ages reached its highest development , St. Thomas and St. Bonaventure were two sages who led to the construction of Scholastic synthesis middle ages.

We find in general in the doctrines of the church of the middle ages that woman was represented as the source of all evils in the world. St. Franciscan Bonaventure wrote.

> "Woman is an embarrassment to man, a beast in his quarters, a continual worry, a never ending trouble, a daily annoyance, the destruction of the household, a hinderance to solitude, the undoing of a virtuous man, an oppressive burden, an insatiable bee, man's property and possession ."

The view of St. Thomas Aquinas (1225-1274) about women were almost similar in that he also considered women inferior to men. He might be greatly influenced by the opinion of the age. In his opinion man represents in himself perfection, while woman stands for the imperfect. He also depreciates the functions of the woman. Woman is dependent on man for procreation and for guidance throughout her life whereas man needs woman only for procreation. Man is thus master and woman a mere helper. The woman has weaker body, the smaller growth and weaker intellect and lesser will-power.

During Scholastic period it was not compulsory for girls to go to the school. To them domestic education was given in their homes. The University rules did not allow the admission of women in the Universities.

Martin Luther (1483-1546) criticised and protested against certain practices of the established church of his times. He tried to combine the best ideals of the past with religious morality and a new idealistic approach to Christian religion developed in Protestantism. The Protestants advocated an honourable and equal status for women like men. According to them the man is the embodiment of the strength, power and greatness while woman is the embodiment of the smooth, gentle, softness and beauty Man and woman are complements of each other. Their relationship is not that of a master and a slave. The Protestant reformers also advocated universal compulsory and free education for all classes and for both men and women.

The Protestant revolt was accompanied and followed by the humanists who initiated the period known as Renaissance. These humanists rejoiced the theological dialectic of Scholasticism. In this period the emphasis was laid on the popular and universal education for both men and women. The woman was now not given an inferior status but was recognized as an active partner of man in bringing progress and Prosperity to the society. Comenius demanded education for all children rich and poor, boys and girls, in all cities and towns, villages and hamlets. John Locke and Hobbes recognized that familial authority belonged to the mother as well as to the father.

The Protestant revolt did not put equal influence in all the countries of Europe. However, in France, the State, church and the government achieved a considerable degree of independence from Rome. At this time Jean Jacques Rousseau introduced the philosophy of Naturalism in education. However, his philosophy of education did not follow the principle of equality in the education of men and women. For him the procreative role of the woman makes her unlike man. Functionally the women are determined by their reproductive role. He also implied in his attitude towards women education that they are the source of evil. Modesty is the only virtue of a woman and man has the absolute right over his wife.

He gave a long list of women characteristics like shame, stupidity, weakness and ignorance. He was of the view that intellectual pursuits are not for the women. Nature intended women for domestic functions mainly. For him the woman was only required to please man. So woman has to learn singing, dancing, embroidery and designing. She may receive an early education in morals and religion so that she can provide a good home for her family.

The psychological developmentalists like Pestalozzi and Herbert and Froebal were however of a different view that the woman is neither physically weak nor morally inferior to man. She is the active sharer of sorrows and sufferings of life with man. Pestalozzi believed that it was possible to improve the status and position of woman only through education. Herbert emphasized that the aim of the education of the woman should be to analyse her interests, to discover which are best for her and for society and apply these interests in the various situations in life. His emphasis was that education of woman should develop the will to be good and the desire to make good moral choices resulting in a high degree of personal character and social morality. According to Froebel, "Education must be controlled development by which both man and woman come into realization of the life of the all encompassing, unity of which both of them are a part a development by which their lives broaden until it has related itself to nature until it enters sympathetically into all the activities of the society, until it enters into the achievements of the race and the aspirations of humanity". Thus it may be concluded that the developmentalists consider woman having equal position like that of man. They are the active members of the society who help to make a better home and society.

Jeremy Bentham was a covert feminist. He wanted to put untapped brains and energies of women to use. He believed that the sensibility of women is greater than men. The woman is more fit for a family life and man for outside life. But Bentham did not want to exclude women altogether from public life.

James Stuart Mill emphasized that the emancipation of women has a two way effect: "they themselves be happy, they will add to the happiness of society". Hence he laid stress on the women education as the surest way to cultivate them and to free them from the bonds of domesticity by opening up careers for them. Mill criticized the theory of inner inferiority of women as supported by Aristotle and Rouseau. But Mill did not question the traditional family system and its demands on women.

Among the socialists Marx and Engels are predominant. They were the forerunners of the doctrine of communism. According to this doctrine they preached that through the institution of family, the children became private heirs which meant the women's reproductive labour like their productive work underwent a transformation from social to private. And this led to the subordination of women in terms of the emergence of the private property.

The description given above about the status, position and education of the women both in India and western countries indicate that women, by and large, were given much inferior status and position in most of the periods of history and by most of the thinkers with a few exceptions. The great philosophers like Plato, Aristotle, St. Thomas Aquinas, Rousseau and others talked much of equality and goodness of mankind but did not acknowledge the same goodness and equality to women. John Stuart Mill may be taken as an exception. The social theorists considered that institution of private property was the root cause of relegating women to a secondary position.

The situation so far presented started to change in the later part of the nineteenth century and the beginning of twentieth century. The women education began to spread. The Industrial Revolution, American Independence and the world wars awakened the western women. Further the political upheavals and revolutions in USSR, France, India and China made the women aware of their enslavement by the male members of the society. The women began to demand equal rights with men.

The Industrial Revolution in Europe ushered a new era in the emergence of women from their homes to engage various other vocations. It inspired the women's movement for bringing change in their status and position. The First World War brought dramatic alteration in the image of woman. At the end of it the opportunities of women's employment increased many-fold. The women also asserted in their freedom of dress and in smoking and drinking in public.

The Second World War brought almost four million new women workers. There was an upsurge in the demand of women's equal rights with men. The women education spread rapidly. The women now entered in all types of professions along with the right to speak in public, to vote for and hold office. There was a revolt against the double standards of morality and against puritanism. As twentieth century advanced the women adopted swim suits, short skirts, started taking part in sports, driving cars, etc. The women got greater leisure by the introduction of mechanized kitchens. By the middle of the twentieth century women's liberation movements became more vigorous and involved more and more women's organizations, in Europe, in general and in America, in particular. The women now presented the cult of new feminism. It demanded full social equality for women. The women fought for more independence and discarded the traditional triangular roles for themselves that of children, kitchen and the church. The women's organizations rejected the 'Barbi-doll' stereotypical model of woman. The middle class educated women were in the forefront of the struggle for women's rights and for presenting a new image of feminism. They protest against a passive, conforming, dependent female stereotyped roles and a future which ties them down to the home and family.

The women's movements have achieved much. Still, even in the west the women have not yet attained that position and status which they consider is equivalent to men. They are still fighting for equal pay, status, position and security like that of men. They have become intolerant to any discrimination in their service conditions because of their sex. The battle is going on.

Struggle for Emancipation

We have traced very briefly the history of women movements for empowerment, equality and recognition and worthy members of the society in the west. Let us now peep into the situation as it exists with respect to Indian women.

The Indian women have fallen from the high position and status held by them in Vedic times to a very degrading position in the medieval period and in the earlier decades of the modern period. It was for the enlightened Indians educated in the western tradition and culture that brought a change in the outlook of the Indian males and females regarding their mutual relationship. In Indian situation the movement for female emancipation was led in the beginning by the male members of the society. These Indian males who fought for a higher status and the position of women were those who were impressed by the regards and considerations which western women enjoyed but they made the case of women emancipation on the basis of the reinterpretation of Indian religious texts and exposing the gimmicks of the half literate clergy which advocated sati system and approved the ill treatment of widows, parda, system, confining of the women to homes, child marriages and calling any women as Kulta or corrupt if she deviated slightly from the norms of conduct laid by them for women. For the ill-treatment of women they were drawing support from a perverted interpretation of the religious texts and religious precepts. The enlightened Indians exposed their misinterpretation and based their argument for women liberation on their own very well studied and expressed interpretation.

The movement for women emancipation was also undertaken by enlightened women like Pandita Rama Bai and others. They set the trend which was followed by hundreds of women. The freedom movement launched by Gandhiji drew women into the central field of struggle. Women fought for the freedom of the country as well, as for their own emancipation. According to *Manusmriti* Hindu women were given a right to Stridhan properties but not to the joint family property on which she had only the right to maintenance. She was given an inferior position in the law of adoption. The status of the woman was determined according to the nature of relationship she had with a man. She was a "Sarvainini" as a wanton woman, "Veshya" as a prostitute, "Kishkashirii" as a woman discarded by her paramour or a "base" as a woman kept exclusively by the man.

According to Justice Bhandare "It was only later that during the time of Vijanesvera that the archaic Smriti law was freed from religious fetters and changed for the benefit of women". But it took a long time and centuries of oppression that women got some legal rights over their property. It was only in 1937 that the concept of widow's estate was developed in respect of property inherited by her from her husband.

The freedom struggle created an urge in the Indian male and female to ameliorate the conditions of the downtrodden and neglected sections of the society. The women, Scheduled Castes and Scheduled Tribes were some such sections. Hence when the constitution for an independent India was drawn, the emphasis was put on the development of an egalitarian society. For the elimination of discriminatory and derogatory practices against women Articles 14, 150, 16, 39(e) and 51 were introduced. These guarantee equality and special protection for women.

The Article 14 provided for equality of all before the law. Article 15 emphasized that the "State shall not discriminate against any citizen on grounds only of religion, race, caste, sex, place of birth or any of them." Article 15(3) stated that "Nothing in this article shall prevent the state from making any special provision for women and children." Article 16 mentioned that (1) there shall be equality of opportunity for all citizens in matters relating to employment or appointment to any office under State. (2) No citizen shall, on grounds only of religion, race, caste, sex, descent, place of birth, residence or any of them be ineligible for, or discriminated against in respect of any employment or office under the State.

Article 39 States: The State shall, in particular, direct its policy towards securing: (1)that the citizens, men and women equally, have the right to an adequate means of livelihood (2) that there is equal pay for equal work for both men and women (3) that the health and strength of workers, men and women and the tender age of children are not abused and that the citizens are not forced by economic necessity to enter avocations unsuited to their age or strength."

Article 51 A States: "It shall be the duty of every citizen of India to promote harmony and the spirit of common brotherhood amongst all the people of India transcending linguistic, logistic and regional or sectional diversities, to renounce practices derogatory to the dignity of women."

When the Universal Declaration of Human Rights was adopted on 10th December. 1948 its Article I provided that "all human beings are born free and equal in dignity and rights". Article 2 provided for equality of sexes. It states that "everyone is entitled to all the rights and freedoms without distinction of sex."

The International covenant on Civil and Political Rights, 1966 urges every covenant State to respect and ensure to all individuals within its territory the rights recognized by that covenant without distinction of sex. Article 3 of this document emphasize that covenant States should undertake to ensure equal rights of men and women in 1979 the convention on the Elimination of All Forms of Discrimination Against Women reiterated "that discrimination against women violates the principles of equality of rights and respect for women's dignity and is an obstacle to the participation of women on equal terms with men in the political, social, economic and cultural life of their countries, hampers the growth of prosperity of society and the family and makes more difficult the full development of the potentialities of women in the service of their countries and of humanity and urges that change in the traditional role of women as well as role of women in society and in the family is needed to achieve full equality between men and women".

Justice Bhandare writes "In spite of the enshrinement of these provisions, equality between men and women continue to be an elusive goal, not only in our country but all over the world. A wide gap exists between the ideal and the practical in our country, partly due to historical reasons. However, the main reason why such discrimination continues in our country is the attitude, of inferiority and bondage-towards women and an atmosphere in which women are deprived of all basic freedoms, starting with that of education, and are thereby exposed to easy exploitation".

This book concentrates on women's education and its impact on male-female discrimination and on the female psyche. In almost all the chapters, the book highlights the importance of education to the girl child as well as to the grown up woman.

Justice Bhandare raises some questions regarding disparity between man and woman and says that several of those questions do not have an adequate and satisfactory answer. An attempt is made to seek answers to these and similar questions by focussing our attention on the triad of sociological, psychological and educational aspects of female development in our country. The questions raised by Justice Bhandare are: (a)How is it that in public life-professions, business and services-women are not adequately represented? (b)How is it that women put in longer hours of work compared to men and yet do not enjoy equal status or opportunities? (c)Why is it that property owned by women constitutes a very small fraction of the property owned by men? (d)Why is it that maternity is not recognized as an essential social function? (e)Why is the rate of suicide so high among women? (f)Why is it that fairness vanishes when it comes to giving a fair deal to the 'fair' sex.

The struggle for the emancipation of western women had its impact on the emancipation movements in India. But in India the feminist movement did not take the aggressive and militant form which it took in some European countries. In India the feminist movements were not vehemently or violently opposed by the male members, or clergy or politicians. Rather they were supported by enlightened political and religious thinkers. The agitations for female liberation in India began in the later part of the nineteenth century and were carried on with zeal till the Constitution of India in 1950 gave them equality in terms of their lawful existence. Those agitations were largely spearheaded by women reformists and male thinkers who had the best of western education. These movements emphasized on the need of the small middle class educated and privileged women. The real breakthrough in the recognition of male-female equalities was made only when the Constitution of the Indian Republic was adapted in 1950.

Before that in 1949 the University Education Commission which was set up under the Chairmanship of Dr. S. Radhakrishnan has observed:

> 'There cannot be educated people without educated women. If general education had to be limited to men or to women, the opportunity should be given to women, for then it would more surely be passed on to the next generation".

The secondary education commission (1952-53) emphasized that:

"Every type of education open to men should also be open to women". Thus this commission did not make any distinction between the education of men and women and so the era of equality of educational opportunities to women began.

The Report of the National Committee on Women's Education (1958-59) made a strong case for the education .of women. Its important recommendation was:

> "The education of women should be regarded as a major and a special problem in education for a good many years to come and a bold and determined effort should be made to face its difficulties and magnitude and to close the existing gap between the education of men and women in as short a time as possible".

As has been specified earlier the movements for women emancipation in India were largely initiated by the Government on the insistence of the educated and reform-oriented women leaders. These leaders by and large did not lead independent movements but were more dependent on the government help, funding and the initiatives in framing laws and rules for women's upliftment. The National Council for Women's Education played an important role in spearheading the movements for women education and their upliftment. The Council set up a committee to examine comprehensively the problem of curricula for girls at all stages of education. This committee was set up on November 1 1961 under the chairmanship of Smt. Hansa Mehta.

The committee after carefully examining all the evidences produced before it came to the following conclusions:

> "Our enquiry has not imbued with any conviction that there are clear and ascertained differences between the two sexes on which an educational policy may readily be based. We have encountered a number of facile generalizations about the mental differences between boys and girls: we have found few, if any, which we are able to accept. Men and women have existed for centuries; but either sex is still a problem to the other and indeed to itself, nor is there any third sex to discriminate dispassionately between the two. In the mean time it is the part of wisdom neither to assume difference nor to postulate identity, but to leave the field free to both to show themselves".

The above mentioned conclusions show the confusion in the thinking of the women leaders who failed to arrive at definite conclusions regarding the differences between two sexes. We have endeavoured to point out, that, such conclusions have left the field wide open for discrimination particularly in education. The last words 'but to leave the field free to both to show themselves', sound quite traditional which emphasizes that woman's field is home and the man's work. The committee's observation may lead to the conclusion that both males and females should work freely in their own fields. However, the committee tries to refute traditional view by emphasizing that "the traditional view assumes that there are two different personalities-masculine and feminine, with widely different and complementary traits and that they owe their origin to sex. This view also has however been proved to be incorrect. Recent scientific studies have shown that the differences in the psychological traits of men and women are due, not to innate sex differences but to social conditioning".

The committee on the basis of such observations as above, recommend, for the education of girls and women that "Education is a great levelling force and one sure way to raising the status of women to real equality with men is to eliminate, or to reduce to a minimum, the existing wide gap in the education of girls and women."

The Education Commission (1964-66) endorsed the views of the National Committee on Women's Education and emphasized:

> "The education of women should be regarded as a major programme in education for some years to come and a bold and determined effort should be made to face difficulties involved and to close the existing gap between the education of men and women in as short a time as possible".

Thus we see that year after year various committees and commissions emphasized the education of the women for raising their social status. But besides some progress in the quantitative expansion of women education no significant developments took place in raising the status of rural, downtrodden, Schedule Castes and Schedule Tribes women. Hence the committee on the Status of Women (1971-74) concentrated on this anomaly.

It observes:

> "The deep foundations of the inequality of the sexes are built in the minds of men and women through a socialization process which continues to be extremely powerful. Right

> from their earliest years boys and girls are brought up to know that they are different from each other and this differentiation is strengthened in every way possible-through language forms, modes of behaviour of labour etc. They begin to learn very early what is proper or not proper for boys and girls and all attempts at deviation are noticed, discouraged and sometimes punished. The sissy and the tom boy are equal objects of derision. There is nothing wrong in this if it were merely a question of distinction. But it soon gets inextricably tied up with the traditional concepts of the roles of men and women and their mutual relationships which are based on inequality. The process of indoctrination affects the development of individual personalities.
>
> The only institution which can counteract the effect of the process is the educational system. If education is to promote equality for women, it must make a deliberate, planned and sustained effort so that the new value of equality of the sexes can replace the traditional value system of inequality".

The committee comes to the conclusion that the reasons for the variation of social attitudes and the consequent slow progress of women's education are both social and economic.

It found that a substantial number of girls are engaged in contributing to the family income by their own labour. The prevalence of child labour has been admitted as the greatest deterrent to the spread of education among children of the poor. The committee was appalled by the extent and degree of use of young girls of five to fourteen years in work for twelve hours a day.

The committee also found that large majority of girls by the time they reach the age of eight, are required at home to do various domestic chores, e.g., collecting fire wood, coal waste, cow dung, fetching water, at times from long distances, washing, cleaning, cooling, taking food and water to parents in their places of work, etc.

About the girls education in the rural areas it observed that:

> "education in the rural areas often results in alienation of the girls from their habitat. While this criticism was voiced in many places, the most vocal opinion was expressed by women in the villages of Himachal Pradesh. Since the development of the state and the standard of living of its people depended on the continued efforts of women in agriculture, education in their opinion was becoming an adversary of progress. Girls who completed their formal education in the villages, did not want to continue living in villages or take part in agricultural activities. The problem became more acute when, owing to absence of secondary schools in the villages, they had to study outside, in urban or semi-urban areas. Many of them found village life with its hardships intolerable afterwards .... Most girls who complete secondary school develop a desire for white collared jobs, or urban life in some forms".

The National Policy on Education (1986) considered that "Education will be used as an agent of basic change in the status of women." It suggested that "the National Education System will play a possible, interventionist role in the empowerment of women. It will foster the development of new values through redesigned curriculum, text books, the training and orientation of teachers, decision-makers and administrators, and the active involvement of educational institutions. This will be an act of faith and social engineering".

National Commission on Self-Employed Women and Women in the Informal Sector (1987-88) has emphasized:

> "Education is both an important instrument for increasing and bettering the chances of women's employability and for empowering women as they learn to think for themselves, become confident and also develop the capability of recognising more acutely the areas of exploitation."

The National Commission for Women, a statutory body was

set up under the National Commission Act, 1990 to safeguard the rights and interests of women. This commission reviews legislations, intervenes in specific individual complaints of atrocities and takes remedial action to safeguard the interests of women where appropriate and feasible.

In Indian situation the women's movement has not been in terms of radicalism or the violent assertion of the female rights. The reason for it seems to be the sensivity of both the males and female towards the necessity of the upliftment of the women from their miserable existence. The Government and NGOs all laid great emphasis on the empowerment of women for which they all recommended crash programmes for women education.

The feminist movement in India can be characterized by its sensible approach. In this movement almost all political parties except those who have leanings towards fundamentalism and orthodoxy in their outlook lend their support. By and large it is non-commercial and non-sectarian; But this movement has failed to break away, from the traditional approach of motherhood, housewife and kitchen queen. The movement has not yet reached a large section of rural and slum area women. It is the movement essentially spearheaded by urban, educated middle class. This class is in a typical paradoxical situation. It wants the best of both worlds. It wants to secure independence from male domination but is not willing to think in terms of a life pattern in which the male does not figure as a key person in the role of a father, brother or husband or in any other form.

In spite of the feminist movements, political support and increasing awareness of evil influences on national progress of the neglect of women, we find that Indian women's status and position has not undergone any revolutionary change. No doubt the urban middle class women have become more assertive, better educated and economically independent by involving themselves in all types of jobs, some of which were so far under the special male prerogatives like those in the army, police or as airline pilots. But the majority of the women of rural and poor classes are suffering from various types of disabilities. The main reason for such a situation seems to be the woefully low percentage of female literacy. According to Prof Moegiadi, UNESCO's representative in India "four South Asian countries — Bangladesh, India, Pakistan and Nepal account for the largest number of out of school girls and Illiterate women."

Addressing a national workshop on State Policies on Incentive Schemes in Primary Schools and their Contribution to Girls Participation, jointly organised by NCERT and UNESCO, he said:

> "Though progress has been made, we are all aware that according to, the 1991 census of India we have 50.2 per cent literacy, and now according to the latest information we have 64 per cent literacy rate. It is estimated that in near future it can be 70-80 per cent" .

The number of females in the work force is also very limited. The 1991 census figures tell us that the working population was 317 million out of the total population of the country as being 846.3 (males 439.3 and females 407.0) million. The males were 226.4 (71.4 per cent) and females 90.6 (28.6 per cent) million who were working. The males in the organized sector were 23.0 million while women were, only 3.8 million. The respective percentages were 85.8 and 14.2. In the unorganized sector there were 290.2 million persons out of which 203.4 were males and 86.8 million women. The respective percentages were 70.0 and 30.0. Hence the women working in organised sector were very few as compared to men.

The National Commission on Self Employed Women and Women Engaged in Informal Sector observed that the women could be found to be largely confined to strenuous and monotonous work that might be irregular and seasonal and women workers could be rarely benefited from the introduction of mechanization and new technology. About eighty per cent of the total female work-force continues to work as agricultural labour. It may be said that one of the basic hurdles to the development of employment opportunities for the women has been lack of adequate training to women workers.

The percentage of Agricultural labourers according to 1991 census was 21.01 per cent for males and 44.83 per cent for females.

Indian women are also being increasingly victimized. Crimes against women are increasing. Crimes such as rape, bride burning, wife battering and ragging of girls are also on the increase. Emotional violence against females at work is a new phenomenon. The rape cases increased from 3,945 in 1982 to 9,752 in 1989. These figures are on the basis of the National Crime Records Bureau, Ministry of Home Affairs, Government of India. But the Marie Stopes Institute, Delhi thinks that these official figures are not correct. According to it on an average, two million women and girls are raped in India every year.

Thus we find that even now there is much discrimination against women and they are a neglected lot. Rajbala says that "A basic statistics paints a grim picture. Over 400 million women with 75 per cent illiteracy work 10-14 hours daily, undergo 4-6 pregnancies and run low income households".

In India, women have been surrounded in a web of myth and reality. She has been considered as a goddess as well as an evil incarnate. At one stage if she was put on a very high pedestal and at another stage she was thrown into the pits of filth and guilt. The casualty has been the reality of her existence. It is only recently that the emphasis has been put on the understanding of the women as she is, as also on the understanding of her relations with man in the light of the recognition of the fact that both are the equal parts of humanity. In this context her education is now considered as important and worthwhile as that of man.

Historically, in the Indian situation the rearing of the girl child and her education has always been taken with indifference. The only exception may be the Vedic period. The birth of a male child is celebrated with joy and happiness while the birth of a girl child is a matter of sorrow and gloom for whole of the family. This trend is changing in the enlightened households but by and large in majority of the families the situation has hardly changed.

The ambivalence with which the Indian women were viewed. has created a typical situation in the relationship between men and women. It was believed that since energy resided in women, they were objects of worship. The Devi cult assigned all the creative and protective powers to women. But at the same time the women were considered as the promoters of evil, seductress who destroyed men if given freedom and the power to exercise their free will. Thus the women's will power had to be controlled. The husbands were given their absolute rights over her body, soul and mind. The women accepted their subordinate status for centuries. It is only in the later half of the twentieth century that the Indian women started revolting against the stipulations that the women are inferior to men. The empowerment of the Indian women is the battle cry of the feminists of today The enlightened men are offering their help in the emancipation of the women.

At the advent of the new millennium we find that the Indian women are joining the world of work in increasing numbers. In many cases it is creating stresses in the family life particularly in those homes in which the womens' role is confined to being housewives. The pressing economic demands make it obligatory for women to seek employment in various fields but the old conservative notions that the women's rightful place is in homes, create situations of stress, and conflict. Under the shadows of conflict and stress the education of the women is being planned, propagated and provided. This book highlights the conflicts and the stresses of the working as well as non-working women and also the influence of socio-psychological factors on women education.

In India, there is growing realization that the women education is of great importance to the healthy development of the social and national life. Efforts are being made to provide schools, for all the girls of school-going age and to give incentives to them to learn. Still the situation is far from satisfactory. The literacy percentage among Indian women is lawfully low. This may be due to the lower social status and the psychological make up of the women, particularly of the lower classes and castes.

The Dalit women and the women of the minority communities have by and large miserable existence. The Dalit women are exploited not only by the higher caste people but also by their own male relatives. Similar is the case with the women of the minority communities, especially in the case of lower class Muslim women. The reasons for their exploitation seem to lie in their ignorance. Most of them are Illiterate and so have neither the means nor the will to fight against their exploitation. Hence their education is a matter which has to be given top priority.

What will be the futuristic trends of women education? Whether women education should be of the same pattern as the education of men? If not then why and what type of education is required for them? Should women be trained for joining the world of work or only for the household work as the housewives? These are some of the questions which are being raised about women education. In the present book an attempt is being made to discuss these and some other vital issues concerning women education so that some appropriate measures may be taken for organizing it thus ushering in an era of equality, dignity, esteem, self-respect and self-confidence for the Indian women.

It may be emphasized that the issues in women education are not only confined to quantitative development. Equally important are qualitative aspects. In an article "The Burning of Roop Kanwar - Madhu Kishwar, who visited Deorala where bride burning of Roop Kanwar took place, reported that "the fascination with the sati cult has been attributed to the superstitious ignorance of illiterate village women, but it is noteworthy that the entire cult being created at Deorala is in the hands of educated men". When we think of women education we are concerned with the development of progressive outlook in them. We will not like to provide that type of education to our women which the menfolk of Deorala got, which led them to close their minds rather than broadening their vision. The leaders of the pro-sati campaign were urban, educated men in their twenties and thirties.

The main premise on which the argument throughout is based is that Indian women are by nature not docile, nor are they devoid of a mind of their own. It is due to four fold major factors that we find them in the state in which they are. These factors are: 1.Religious precepts from some eminent sages motivated by the desire to subordinate the assertive women. 2.The physical weakness perpetuated by multiple pregnancies and childhood marriages. 3.Women's own desire for showering motherly affection on their own men and for maintaining domestic peace at their own cost. 4.Lastly their complete economic dependence on malefolk.

Three

Role in Freedom Movement

Around the globe, the Women have been known to participate in national liberation movements. Although they have not been found to be politically very conscious or involved in day-to-day political issues, women have mobilised themselves during crisis situations. In India, women have participated in the national freedom struggle. However, a clear picture has not emerged. There have been debates and counter debates about the magnitude of women's participation in national struggle as to: (a) Which section of women did participate? (b) Did it help in the emergence of female political leadership? (c) Were women able to create some niche for themselves in the political sphere? (d) Was their participation in some way a reinforcement of patriarchy or it created and acknowledged the separate identity of women as individuals?

In attempting to analyse the role of women in Indian Freedom Struggle, one is beset by a series of problems at the very outset For. one, the political role of women as a subject of research is of recent origin in India. There are very few comprehensive studies on women's participation in the Freedom Struggle. Studies published between 1968-88 do touch upon various aspects and dimensions of women's participation. Some date has also been generated, some factual accounts made such as most standard histories of The National Movement mention women's participation and role in the Civil Disobedience Movement. Women in revolutionary terrorism have also been described. Some accounts of contemporaries who participated in the movement refer to the strength and broad base acquired by it as a whole through women's participation.

However information on women in the writings prior to 1975 have been mainly on women of elite sections of society. Large majority of women have not figured in these accounts, and their role has remained Unexplored and marginlined. Except some accounts by some elite women participants not much is known about the lives or the social background of the mass of women, who entered the movement in different regions of the country. But recently some work has been done in this area.

Further most of the accounts of women's participation have been mainly descriptive and not analytical. They do not examine either the reason or the implications of this spontaneous upsurge of political activity by women of all classes. The elite perspective is dominant, which relates women's participation to reform movement and education but ignores the role of peasant women. Women from different sections including even prostitutes or thousands of housewives, who directly or indirectly supported the freedom fighters by shouldering family responsibilities have not been discussed. The impact of colonialism on women's lives and beliefs, created a source for radicalism among Bengali youth. Strangely, it was recorded by an English as early as 1907, and repeatedly mentioned by Mahatma Gandhi.

Some have described existing research on women's participation in national struggle as non-comprehensive, cursory in nature and generally a history from above. Thus, one has to start with caution and carefulness in recording and analysing women's participation in national liberation movement.

Base for Awakening

Generally, one starts with the presumption that the social reform movement from the mid 19th century prepared the base for women's awakening and their entry in the movement later on. The elite class-led social movement of the 19th century, was a movement run by men on women's issues. Pandita Ramabai stands solitary in the galaxy of names like Raja Ram Mohan Roy, Agarkar, Ishwar Chandra Vidyasagar and Veerasalengam. Their efforts rallied round issues affecting women's life adversely such as the practice of sati, female infanticide, plight of the widow, child marriage, polygamy, etc. Raja Ram Mohun Roy championed the ban of the practice of sati. His campaigns resulted in the governmental resolution of 1829, banning the practice of sati. Raja Ram Mohun Roy was trained in western liberal education. He founded the Brahmo, Samaj in 1929, which by the second half of the century practiced a Christianised version of Hinduism. The Brahmo Samaj split in 1886 into Adi Brahmo Samaj led by Devendra Nath Tagore, and Brahmo Samaj of India led by Keshav Chandra Sen. This faction opened schools for girls, started a women's magazine in 1863 and founded the Brahmitra Samaj in 1867. This Samaj taught Brahmo religion, handicrafts and social skills to the female relatives of the Brahmo Samaj members. Keshav Chandra Sen exhibited a mixture of reformist, revivalist and traditional ideas about women. On the one hand, he pressed for a law to legalise cross-caste marriage within the Brahmo community, and to raise the minimum age for marriage of girls to 14, on the other hand, got his daughter married at the age of 13. The Brahmo Samaj was further split in 1878 into liberal and conservative factions. The liberal Sadharan Samaj sponsored women's education, but the Nava Vedhan Brahmo Samaj did not favour higher education for women. Vidyasagar took up the cause of widows, and started a movement in support for widow remarriage in the 1850s. It resulted in Hindu Widows Marriage Act of 1865, but in actuality not much was achieved. It met with strong opposition from the Bengali orthodoxy. There were signature campaigns but most effective was the social pressure from the reform leaders, ranging from social out-casting to threats of violence.

The real explosion came with the campaign against child marriage and the debate over age of consent bill, initiated by Behramji Malabari in 1884, who started a nationwide debate. It met with strong opposition from the orthodox. The attack was spearheaded by Lokmanya Tilak, who defined the legislation as an attack on religion. The orthodox were not wrong in connecting the issues of reform and religion. Throughout the 19th century, the conservative Brahman elite class was making a very successful attempt. It remains the major factor in Indian politics even today to define Indian culture and Indian nationality in terms of reconstituted Hinduism. There was no way the reformers could avoid the issue. This 'Hindu identity' had to be challenged to make active even a consistent democratic liberalism or liberal feminism because it had remained caste ridden and patriarchal. Numerous low-caste radicals were willing to meet this challenge, but only few of the elites were eager. As a result, the movement was almost totally overwhelmed by Hindu revivalism by the end of the 19th century. The new revivalism was embodied in powerful organisations such as Dayanand Saraswati's Arya Samaj (1875), Vivekananda's Ramkrishna Mission (1897) and Annie Besant's Madras Hindu Association (1904). These new organisations attacked the reformers, but supported some reforms of the Hindu society. They did incorporate a good deal of the programme of reformers such as educating women, raising the age of marriage, remarriage of child widows etc, but all this was to be done within the framework of Hinduism. The ideal of Sita, the subordinate and oppressed 'Pativrate', defined the limits of Indian women's advance.

Barring a few exceptions, the modernists and the revivalists were not really concerned with gender equality, women's own desires or their perspectives on dignity and justice. Nor were they aware of the inter-relationship between patriarchal control over women's freedom, roles and behaviour and the carefully preserved pluralist hierarchical Organisation of the Indian society.

Some regard the reform movement as a failure, but Gail Omvedt maintains that it helped to lay some of the foundations for the women's movement that emerged in the 1920s. Though men kept control within the family and within public life, the slow movement of women out of the home and the women's groups sponsored by male reformers and later the nationalists helped to 'extend the female space' for action.

One generation later Jyotiba Phule spearheaded the middle class and low caste movement for their rights all over India in the mid 19th century. He pushed the analysis of the inter-relationship between women's sub-ordination and maintenance of caste hierarchy far beyond the point that Vidyasagar had managed to articulate. Phule identified women's subordination as an instrument to perpetuate existing models of hierarchy. Periyar called for rejection of the mangalputra and wrote, "our ladies must come forward to compete with males in all spheres." The main social organisations founded by men centred round ceremonies. 'Satyashodhak marriages' dramatised the defiance of caste ideology by refusing the use of Brahmin priests or traditional rituals and by institutionalising women's equality. The ceremony concludes with the mangalashataka and garlanding. Periyar also emphasised garlanding and equality. In this respect, both were ahead of even the best laws of today - the reformed Hindu 'Civil Code' includes the patriarchal saptapadi ritual and even registered marriages make not even a rhetoric mention of women's equality.

The ideology of Phule and Periyar had a strong feminist element in it. They definitely connected women's oppression and exploitation with other forms of social inequality and called rigorously for a fully liberated society.

However, in the long run, the reform movements strengthened women's "socialisation for inequality" within the middle class as a whole and heightened the growth of institutions like dowry and the supremacy of the patriarchal family in women's lives. Instead of its expected liberating influence, education became a powerful force in strengthening the sanskritisation process, which manifests the integral links and mutually supportive relationship between patriarchy and heirarchy.

The First Step

Women's participation in the Freedom Struggle dates back to 1905. The Swadeshi movement, which was triggered by the British decision to partition Bengal in 1905, saw women's entry into the movement, and the skilful tactics of several women leaders contributed to increase the participation of women in public life. Attempts at mass mobilisation also facilitated this participation. Pamphlets were written in Bengali and widely distributed. One of those was a pamphlet by Ramendrasundari Trivedi entitled 'a vow for Bengali Women', which tried to explain the Swadeshi movement in simple language for a village woman to understand. The pamphlet called upon women to participate in the ritual of Rakhi bandhan and arandhan (not lighting cooking fires), and to boycott foreign goods. Nirod Choudhary reported that the Swadeshi movement aroused a strong sense of patriotism in his mother who smashed the family's foreign made cooking pots. The traditions of Hindu mela were revived and exhibitions became a regular part of Congress meetings. Meetings were regularly held by women, although there was strong opposition, especially against the young unmarried girls in the leadership. Sarla Devi, daughter of Swarna Kumari Devi, started physical culture clubs, began a Swadeshi store for Women's work and organised festivals which celebrated Bengali traditions. She played an important role in the Swadeshi movement until she moved to Lahore in 1905 after marrying Arya Samaj leader Ram Bhoj Dutt Choudhary. Some British women who made Indian nationalism their own cause, played important roles as helpers as well as 'catalysts'. such as Annie Besant, Dorethy Jinaragadasa, Margaret Cousins, an Irish feminist and Sister Nivedita.

The Swadeshi movement also marked the formation of several women's organisations. Mahila Shilpa Samiti (19061908) was clearly inspired by the Swadeshi movement. Earlier, in 1901, Sarla Devi Choudhrani had formed the Bharat Stri Mahamandal after serious differences with the male leadership of the National Social Conference (NSC). In fact, women's associations had started coming up in the latter half of the previous century. In the Presidency of Bombay a women's magazine 'Stress Bodh' was started in 1857 by the Parsies. The 'Prasthana Samaj' which had organised Arya Mahila. Samaj in 1882 under the leadership of Pandita Ramabai Ranade associated with the modern faction sought government funds for a girls' high school and legal authority to discourage child marriage. She formed NSC to provide an all-India forum for discussion of social reform after the leaders of the National Congress had decided to eliminate this subject from their agenda in order to present a united front to the British. Tilak was bitterly opposed to Ranade's action. In 1895, Tilak's opposition to NSC forced the holding of separate sessions by the Congress and NSC.

Female relatives of the reform oriented leaders began forming local women's organisations, justified by revivalist ideals, and there were no campaigns for social legislation. The Hindu ladies social and literacy 'cell' was started in 1902, Gujarati Street Mandal in 1903 and Women's Zoroastrian Association in 1903. In 1908, Seva Sadan was started by the reform oriented leaders of the different communities. In 1904, the leaders of Maharashtra Social Conference (MSC) organised a women's section which held an annual conference during MSC sessions. This conference, the Bharat Mahila Parishad (BMP) organised educational and inspirational programmes in which women of distinction - Ramabai, Annie Besant, Sarojini Naidu and several others - gave speeches before women.

In the Madras Presidency, a women's magazine was started by Kamala, wife of Indian Christians' social reformer Satlinadhan. A Brahmin widows' home was founded in 1913 by Subhalakshmi Annal, and a Mahila Seva Samaj in Mysore in 1913.

Local Muslim women's associations were found in the early 20th century by upper class Muslim women in several cities. In 1916, the Begum of Bhopal formed the All India Muslim Women's Conference, at which papers on social reform and education were read and resolutions passed. In 1917, Abu Begum proposed a resolution against polygamy that provoked opposition from Muslims. However, Gail Minault points out that in other cases Muslim women skilfully utilised religious themes and anti-British feelings to justify their activities during the Khilafat and Non-cooperation Movement.

After 1910, women experienced in organising and working in local women's associations, and convinced that women should take the leadership into their own hands, started provincial and national women's organisations. There associations were inevitably elite, bourgeois and urban, consisting of women from the upper class with the advantage of social status, education and privilege, but redeemed by their desire to serve all women. The Young Women's Christian Association of India (YMCA) had become national in 1896. The Women's India Association (WIA) was formed in 1917 in Madras (now called Chennai). In the same year, Sarojini Naidu led a delegation of women formed by Margaret Cousins to the Constitutional Reforms Committee, demanding universal adult franchise women.

The National Council of Women in India (NCWI) was formed in 1925, All India Women's Conference (AIWC) in 1927. By mid-1935, WIA and AIWC claimed membership of over 10,000 women. NCWI developed eight provincial councils by 1934 and had 180 affiliated societies with a membership of over 8000. WIA did not limit itself to fund raising, social service and women's education, but also sought to influence government policy on equal rights for women in some areas, and was involved with the issue of suffrage, education and social reform. WIA founders included women like Margaret Cousins and Annie Besant who were not only suffragists, but political radicals and critics of imperialism in their own country.

AIWC, which had originally convened only to discuss women's education, became a permanent body which succeeded in developing branches all over India. It called itself a political, even had a clause in its constitution prohibiting its engagement in party politics. But by 1932, however, AIMC had involved itself with political rights of women. Although its major focus and priority remained women's question and elimination of women's backwardness, the future of India gradually became and important concern. From the beginning, WIA had an interest in home rule and women's suffrage, which was clearly patriotic. Yet, even in troubled time of 1928-29, the WIA insisted that their policy was to work for reform through the Legislative Council. They were not prepared to accept Civil Disobedience, for this would jeopardise the relation they had so carefully worked out with the government to secure for women, positions of magistrates on various councils and committees and to urge the legislation for the improvement of women's status. However, when the Civil Disobedience Movement started in 1930, WIA was faced with a dilemma. Dr Muthulakshmi Reddi, a founder member of WIA and later as Vice-President signed a protest in 1928 against the all British Composition of the Simon Commission. The choice was between aligning with the national movement or adopting an apolitical stance. Situations caused leaders of these organisations to redefine their aims, amend bylaws, argue with each other, and finally end up with organisations which were somewhere between autonomous women's associations and women's auxiliary of the Indian National Congress.

Kamala Devi Chattopadhyay observed, though the Women's Conference had originally stated it would not participate in politics, it realised that it would have to concern itself with public in its wide term, without alignment to any particular political party. It also accepted women as members from any party. It took a strong nationalist stand, and demanded equal rights for women to enable them to play their full and legitimate role in the national affairs. Otherwise, all other rights might become illusory.

Many members of WTA were also members of AIWC, and many such members were members of the Indian National Congress, and leaders in the National movement as well. This factor led to close relations between women and the national movement.

Although women's associations could never decide their stand on the involvement of women in politics, the women in general were ultimately drawn into the vortex of the Freedom Struggle by Mahatma Gandhi. In South Africa, his stayagrah 'army' had women in it. With his experience of South Africa behind him, Gandhi was aware of the potentialities of women as passive resistance. As he experimented with his weapon of satyagrah in India, he realised that women could participate in it together with men.

With the belief that for the Freedom Movement to be successful it had to be a movement of masses, Gandhi felt that swaraj would be meaningless without reform of social structures and upliftment of the weaker sections, namely the women and the lower social strata, to a position of equality with others. While lending support to the cause of improving women's condition through education and reform of marriage laws, he declared himself to be uncompromising in the matter of women's right. He remarked, "woman has been suppressed under custom and law for which man was responsible and in the shaping of which she had no hand .... Woman has as much right to shape her own destiny as man has to shape his .... It is upto men to see that they enable them to realise their full status and play their part as equal of men." He differed from the early reformers by his revolutionary approach to women's role in society and their right to personal dignity as individuals. Without belittling their roles as mothers and wives, he insisted that they must play an equal role with men in the achievement of freedom and social justice. In his opinion, women had natural abilities to lead in a non-violent struggle for human liberation. The most significant aspect of Gandhi's ideas lies in the remarkable similarity between them and the demands now voiced by the women's liberation movement all over the world - equality in the family and society, the right to one's own body; the opening of wider opportunities for self development; and, a refusal to be treated as sex symbol.

Equal Rights

As president of the Indian National Congress in 1931, Pandit Nehru accepted equal political and legal rights of women, and introduced the concept of equal obligations along with equal rights in the Fundamental Rights resolution passed by the Congress that year. Along with adult suffrage, the resolution emphasised the need for protecting women workers, particularly granting them maternity leave. He asserted that "women must be trained to participate in every department of human activity and play an active part in all professions and sphere. For this purpose, they must fight social institutions like pudah, untouchability, caste system and marriage laws. But above all, they must participate in the struggle against the root cause of political subjugation and the economic system. The women's movement would suffer set back if it remained isolated from the general political and economic struggle for liberation in the country."

Some historians of the social reform movement have held that this merger of the women's movement in the political struggle diluted its strength, though perhaps it gained in legitimacy by the championship of national leaders. Some others, however, claim that the India perspective gave the women's movement in India an identity distinct from similar movement in other countries.

Thus, women and their associations were drawn inside the vortex of national struggle for freedom under the inspiration and guidance of national leaders like Gandhi and Nehru. During the Non-cooperation Movement, women in different parts of India joined processions, propagated the use of khadi and charkha; some of them left government schools and colleges. Renuka Ray in Calcutta gave up her studies along with her friends and joined the movement. So did Vijayalaxmi Pandit.

Basanti Devi, wife of C R Das, accompanied her husband in his tour of Bengal and asked women to boycott foreign goods. She was arrested on December 7, 1911, on the charge of obstracting the gentlemen of Calcutta, by selling khadi She presided over the Bengal provincial conference of Chittagong in April 1922, and Kasturba Gandhi presided over the Gujarat provincial conference appealing to women to take to spinning and weaving khadi. In Allahabad, Rameshwari Mehra formed a kumari sabha to encourage girls to take part in public discussions. There were women like Hemprablia Majumdar, who received lathi blows. Bee Amman, mother of the Ali Brothers, discarded her veil and addressed meetings all over India, advocating the use of khadi supporting Hindu Muslim unity.

In Borsad satyagrah of 1923-24, women turned out in large numbers. It is on record that women displayed greater courage than men, when police confiscated their house, buffaloes and other property.

In the Bardoli satyagrah of 1928, the women gradually outnumbered men in political gatherings. Sardar Patel commented that in stead-fastness of purpose, simplicity and purity, they were better than their men. Maniben Patel and Bhakti Desai fixed their tents and huts on the land declared to be sold by the government.

The salt satyagraha launched by Gandhiji in March 1930, was extended to a mass campaign at the beginning of April 1930. Gandhiji had initially exclude women from participating in 'salt satyagraha'. This was not taken lightly by women. Margaret Cousins sent a spirited reply on behalf of WIA, protesting against the division of work by sex, as women had been left in charge of the ashram of Sabarmati while men were to accompany Gandhi in the march to Dandi. Kamla Devi Chattopadhyay met Gandhi and expressed her desire to be involved in the satyagraha. Durgabai Desmukh met the local leaders of Madras and suggested that they be included in the movement.

On April 6, 1930, the salt laws were ceremoniously broken by Gandhi. Sarojini Naidu and Muthuben Patel were with him. Many women had walked to Dandi and the awakening in the villages was astonishing. Gandhi was arrested and in a statement to the press on 7 April, 1930, Gandhi said that he was becoming increasingly certain that in the struggle for swaraj, the women of this country could contribute a greater share than men.

Gandhi had nominated Sarojini Naidu to lead the raid on Dhasana salt fields. She declared that the "time has come when women can no longer seek immunity behind the shelter of their sex, but must face equally with their male comerades all the pains and sacrifices for the liberation of this country." Lilavati Mushi and Sarojini Naidu organised women and led them in different parts of Bombay (now called Mumbai) to make salt. Kamala Devi Chattopadhyay stood outside the law courts and sold salt at high prices.

Women's role in salt satyagrah was significant in two ways. First, among Congress women, this represented a shift from role of supportive auxiliaries to direct participation in the struggle, even when it involved defiance of the leadership. Secondly, the impact of the women's role resulted in the conversion of a section of the leadership, especially Gandhi and Nehru. Kamala Devi Chattopadhyay commented, "ancient prejudices melted, walls of tradition cracked and rays of new hope is creeping in." Nehru remarked, "our women came to the forefront and took charge of the struggle. Women had always been there of course, but now there was an avalanche of them which took not only the British government, but their own men folk by surprise. There were these women, of the upper or middle classes leading sheltered lives in their homes, peasant women, working class women, rich women coming out into tens of thousands in defiance of government orders and police lathis. It was not only the displays of courage and daring, but what was even more surprising was the organisational power they showed." Thus, the women had turned this struggle into a beautiful epic.

In July 1930, when Lord Irwin was to address the Central Assembly, it was decided that there should be picketing by a group of women volunteers on the first day, and 27 women from Lahore, Ambala and Simla were chosen for this purpose. Women went in groups of twos and threes and stood outside the Central Legislative assembly Hall. They had black flags hidden under the fold of their sarees. As soon as the viceroy came and got down from his car, they took out their flags and shouted "Irwin, go back." In Lahore, Manmohine Sehgal organised picketing in front of college gates and also student's strikes. Arrested women in Lahore jail were Zutshi, Kamala Nehru's mother Raspati Kaul, Parvati Devi, Asaf Ali and Satyavati from Delhi.

Same happened in Bihar, where a number of women were arrested. Hasan Imam addressed several meetings of students in Patna and Barh together with her daughter Sami, Suit. CC Das and some other women she organised a procession of women in Patna on July 15 to inaugurate an intensive campaign of boycott of British goods. During the week ending July 25 Patna witnessed two demonstrations, in which nearly 3000 women took part. Hasan Imam, Sami, Smt. C C Das, Gauri Das and Vindhyavasirii Devi were summoned to court. Imam formed a committee of women in Muzaffarpur to propagate spinning. Women leaders were also advocating non-payment of chowkidari tax.

In Karnataka women who took part in the struggle were Kamala Devi Chattopadhyay, Umabai Kundapur Krishnabai, Panjikar and Ballasi Seddama. Gowramma and her coworkers offered satyagarh in front of the house of the Patel of Akoriji in north Kanara. The police dragged women, beat them with canes and harassed them. Women gave food and shelter to Congressmen, often acted as messengers carrying secret information from one camp to another, and when the call for satyagrah came they had to be proved fervent satyagrahas.

Women in princely states did not keep aloof. In Viramgam satyagrah in May 1930, 700 women were lathicharged. In the Rajkot satyagrah of 1938-39 and the movement in Linodi, women were active. In Rajkot, Kasturba was jailed along with Manibelm Patel and Mridula Sarabhai. Kamala Devi organised agitation in Ram Durg state in Karnataka in 1930.

Civil Disobedience

In the Civil Disobedience Movement inaugurated by Gandhi in October 1940, women courted arrest in large numbers. One of the first to do so was Sucheta Kripalani, who had been in charge of the women's department of the All India Congress Committee since 1939.

In the 1942 'Quit India Movement' almost all the top leaders were immediately arrested, and the movement was practically leaderless. However, women joined in taking out processions, holding meetings and demonstrations and organising strikes. In Assam, a young girl, Kanaklata Barua, led a procession of 500 and was killed in the police firings. In Midnapur, Bengal, women played a notable role and were victims of police atrocities. In Bombay, Usha Mehta operated an underground radio station. The Congress Radio, broadcasted news at 7.30 P.M. from August to November 13th, 1942, till Usha Mehta along with her colleagues were arrested. She as sentenced to few years rigorous imprisonment and was sent to Yeraveda jail, where she found herself among 250 women political prisoners.

Aruna Asaf Ali was one of the most important figures of 1942. For four years she remained underground, avoiding arrest. She published bulletins and edited along with Ram Manohar Lohia 'The Inquilab'. A price of Rs 5,000 was announced as a reward for her capture.

Besides the women who joined the Freedom Movement on the call of Gandhi, there were a few who could not believe his creed of non-violence. They were revolutionary and in the 1930s such organisations sprang up rapidly. They were active in Bengal, Dakha, Commilla and Chittagong where the storm centres. Young college girls joined these secret societies. Kalpana Joshi, Preeti Waddadar were associated with Chittagong armoury raid. Preeti led a raid on the Pahartali railway officers' club. She later committed suicide. Shanti and Soniti shot dead Stevens, the district magistrate of Commilla in December 1931, and were given life sentences. The Chchatri Sangh started in Calcutta in 1928 was an important training and recruiting ground for future revolutionaries. In Delhi, Roopvati Jain, at the age of 17, was in charge of a bomb factory under Chandrashekhar Ajad. Sushila Devi cut her finger and put tilak on the forehead of Bhagat Singh and Batukeshwar Dutta on April 9, 1920. She was arrested and imprisoned. Durga Devi played the role of Bhagat Singh's wife. She shot a police sergeant at Hamilton Road, Bombay. She was elected president of the Delhi provincial Congress Cominittee in 1938.

In January 1942, the Indian Independence League was formed in Kualalampur and Indian women in Southeast Asia worked for the cause of India's freedom. In March 1943, a women section of the league was started and Indian women in Malaya, Thailand and Burma, enlisted as volunteers on the call of Subhash Chandra Bose. In July 1933, a women's regiment-the Rani of Jhansi Regiment was formed with Lakshmi Saligal as the captain.

The general idea or myth circulated for quite a long period has been that women's role in the national movement(s) against imperialism was male-dictated or male manipulated. Uma Rao and Ishani Mukherjee in their writings offer enough evidence against it.

Various writings in recent years indicate that once mobilised, women moved on their own, acquiring new confidence and articulating new priorities. The number of women directly involved in revolutionary movements in Bengal, Maharashtra, Punjab, in Uttar Pradesh and the erstwhile Madras Presidency in the turn of the century may have been small, but the inspirational support base of the revolutionaries included more women whose names will never feature in dictionaries of freedom fighters. The women who provided shelter and food, carried messages or arms, or instilled a passion to 'serve their country' among their children, telling them about the 'heroes' and 'martyrs' who sacrificed their lives for the country's freedom, did not belong to the elite class only. Many were uneducated and poor. They played such roles without waiting for any social sanction. They provided a communication channel for the message of nationalism when nationalist literature was under severe control. The stories continued to spread and the songs and poems were eagerly observed by young people, often from women in their homes. Women's invisible role, which provided greater force, has received little formal acknowledgement.

Similarly, women's active and even militant roles as participants and leaders in quasi-national peasants' and workers' struggles remained strongly invisible till recently. Recent attempts to reconstruct life stories of women activists and to obtain oral history from surviving women freedom fighters provide little substance to the theory of male direction, guidance or manipulation.

Some find it difficult to believe that leaders of the national movement were not aware of the growing base of women's support and feelings of national cause, and were 'surprised' at the intensity and the degree of their response to the Civil Disobedience Movement. The history of national movement records various instances when women defied the national leadership. It was evident during the salt satyagrah of 1930. Sarojini Naidu was defiant, Margaret Cousins wrote a spirited letter to Gandhiji, protesting against the division of work by sex, as women had been left in charge of the 'ashram' and Sabarmati, while men accompanied Gandhi in his famous Dandi

March. Despite the reluctance on the part of Gandhi, women participated in a big way in the satyagraha.

By and large, the leaders of the national movement envisaged a supportive role for women. They did not want women to involve in direct action. Gandhi himself described the difference between men and women as follows. "She is passive, he is active. She is essentially the mistress of the house. He is the breadearner." This sexual division of labour was perpetuated even during the National freedom Struggle. In fact, Gandhi inducted women in the Freedom Struggle because they were considered to be self-sacrificing, able to endure pain, and were essentially non-violent in nature. Gandhi did not visualise any fundamental change in the sexual division of labour, or any departure of women from their normal social roles as wife and mother. Madhu Kishwar remarks: "The symbols put forward to draw them into public life are those of ideal wives whose chief qualification was that they spent their lives in self-less service and unending devotion of husbands, following them to the end of the World. There was some inherent dichotomy in Gandhiji's thinking on women. On the one hand, he asserted that women had the same rights of freedom and liberty as men. On the other hand, he kept reforming to the mythical figures of Sita and Damayanti and their devotion to duty despite sufferings. The deduction- "participation in politics would be simply an extension of this duty." This approach has been criticised by Gail Omvedt and Maria Mies. Mies claims that Gandhi created a new myth of Indian womanhood, Sita-like in her devotion to service and self-sacrifice, weather to her family or her nation. As a consequence, Gandhi attracted women from well-to-do classes with "good education, well placed husbands and servants". For these women, family came first and concern with sociopolitical issues afterwards. May be Gandhi was not prepared for radical changes at the structural and institutional level. The status of women had to be improved, but institutions which impinged on and curtailed their freedom were to be retained.

However, in all fireness to Gandhiji, it has to be accepted that he has a broader vision in comparison to other leaders of the movement. Unlike social reformers, Gandhi had realised some of the negative consequences of colonial role on women's economic status. He decided to launch the khadi movement which would offer to the masses of women an immediate open channel for their participation in the national struggle. Even more, Gandhi used women's role in the khadi movement to convince men that women's participation as equals was essential if the swadeshi or boycott movement was to succeed - an argument that he extended later to the winning of full freedom for India and nation building. For women to provide leadership in the movement was not enough. They had to understand the dignity that came from being productive and independent. Such an understanding would help them to identify with poor women, emancipate themselves and achieve the new identity necessary for nation building.

Nehru's understanding of women's subordination was both limited and static. Though fully aware of the problems of building a democratic and eqalitarian society on the foundations of a social and cultural structure divided by multiple allegiance (or identities) - religious, linguistic, caste and tribal and hierarchical beliefs that prevented a "sense of equality", he did not understand the "critical connections between the control over women and the maintenance of that differentiated and hierarchical social structures. While he certainly accepted the emancipation of women as a value in itself, and claimed improvement in Indian women's status as his greatest achievement, some argue that his approach to women reflected the elitist vision of social reformers, relieved to some extent by his fascination for socialism, with little or no understanding of the deeper causes of women's subordination in India. While he introduced the emphasis on women's rights in the constitution, he did little to reduce the controls of the collectives that determined the boundaries of women's lives and behaviour - the family, community, caste, class, and religion.

Some argue that the issue of gender equality was given a back seat, and women's issue lost its appeal and fervour by being subsumed within nationalism. The new politics of nationalism glorified India's past and tended to defend everything traditional. Nationalism in this phase fostered conservatism in social beliefs and practices. Partha Chatterjee maintains, "the new patriarchy of nationalism gave women 'a new social responsibility' not to alienate men, but "to maintain the cohesiveness of family life and solidarity with the kin group. In addition, by associating the task of 'female emancipation' with 'sovereign nationhood', nationalism "bound them to a yet entirely legitimate subordination." Partha Chatterjee also explains the "disappearance of the women's question from the political domain by the end of the 19th century as the result of nationalism's "refusal to make the women's question an issue of political negotiation with the colonial state."

Some feel that this analysis suffers from the basic problem arising out of a tendency to find a linear connection between the reform movement, growth of nationalism and the roles prescribed for, or played by women in the Freedom Struggle. It neglects the fact that of women's own response to the challenges of colonial rule. Gail Minault and Geraldin Forber argue that women adapted the institution of purdah or seclusion, to form their own institutions, purdah, otherwise a hindrance to women's advancement, helped them through women's forums in which they could voice their concerns. Despite the restriction of purdah and without challenging patriarchal structures, it was possible for this rudimentary women's movement to acquire a unique strength.

Some opine that women's involvement in the national movement or the merger of women's movement with the Freedom Struggle diluted its strength, though perhaps it gained in legitimacy by the championship of national leaders. It has to be accepted that gender equality was not the main thrust, either of the social reform movement nor the National Freedom Movement. The social reform did help to improve the status of Indian women and placed great on education as the emancipator of women. However education never became the sole agent for gender equality, it suffered from the basic contradiction between upliftment of women and limited vision of that upliftment. Everything had to be done within the framework of patriarchal family. Women were not seen as individuals. Similarly, the national movement leaders envisaged an auxiliary role for women in the movement. It was by sheer hardwork and readiness for come what may, that women were able to prove their worth during the Civil Disobedience, salt satyagrah and the Quit India movements. The so-called extremist movement of Bengal witnessed a galaxy of brave young girls, who readily sacrificed their lives for the freedom movement. Innumerable number of women provided support to freedom fighters, looked after their families in the absence of their fathers, husbands and sons. Participation in the national movement was not limited to elite class women only. They did provide organisation base and ideas and vision to the masses of women. But once aroused, the common women surged forward and became the most solid base of the National movement, we salute those masses of invisible and unnamed women who added strength to the movement, which by many is termed as the 'elite agitational politics'. Recording the participation of such women is a mammoth task. Efforts in this direction are commendable. It is hoped, someday a new history will be written about the national struggle.

Four

After Independence

After the independence, the political scenario in India has been characterised by a rather curious feature with most of the political parties and combination of parties accusing one another of striving to subvert democratic institutions. The Narora document has done the right thing to focus on the central fact that politics in India today faces grave threats. It is also correct in underlining the fact that most of the political issues the country is agitating on, are directly or indirectly related to this central fact.

For a proper understanding, however, of the current turmoils and conflicts in this vast country of nearly 900 million population, into which gigantic social forces are being inexorably drawn, it is necessary to start with an analysis of the real nature of politics in India, and its active role in the course of sociopolitical development. Only an examination of the nature and role of the existing political institutions can lead to an understanding of the nature of subversive attacks on them and, consequently, of the imperatives for overcoming them. The debate on women's entry into politics in India is closely related to this analysis, In order to start this debate, one has to look at the nature and working of politics in India.

Nature of Political Power

The basic nature of a political system is judged not by the speed of its ways, nor even by the proclamations it may have chosen to make, it has to be judged by its actual working-by the resultant of the social processes it seeks to encourage, control and repress. Earlier, even before the transfer of power, on January 22, 1947, a resolution moved by Jawaharlal Nehru in the Constituent Assembly of India, which set the objective of framing a Constitution — "wherein shall be guaranteed and secured to all the people of Indian justice, social, economic and political; equality of status, of opportunity, and before the law; freedom of thought, expression, belief, faith, worship, vocation, association and action, subject to law and morality". The Preamble of the Constitution proclaims the resolution on the same lines. Devices like confided Fundamental rights, Directive Principles of State Policy, special safeguards for minorities, Scheduled Castes and Tribes and so on, have added to the attractive look of the Constitution. The democratic and egalitarian appearance of the political power in India has been further reinforced by the adoption of the socialistic pattern of society as the goal, still later by the full-threaded declaration of war against mass poverty----'garibi hatao' and, finally, by the 42nd amendment of the Constitution to declare the Indian Republic as a socialist and secular state. However, observers within the country and from abroad have refused to take these proclamations at their face value. They have clearly and categorically characterised the existing political power structure in India as exclusive and elitist.

For instance, Professor V K Rao, a former Union minister, identifies the locus of political power in India in "a political alliance of the intermediate classes with the upper classes, resorting to socialist ideology only to win mass support but using all levers of power to facilitate a type of capitalist development in the interest of a narrow section of Indian society". Another Indian analyst says, "whether in agriculture or industry or infrastructure or even scientific research, the advantage has invariably gone to that segment of power elite, which holds the political levers of parliamentary democracy. The present power structure constitutes the greatest stumbling block to any successful effort to relieve the poverty of the poor. According to Gunnar Myrdal, "India is ruled by a select group of upper class citizens who use their power to secure their privileged positions". He defines the elite groups as the product of a linking up of the vested interests of business, permanent officials and political leaders.

Caste Politics

The process of politics is one of identifying and manipulating existing structures in order to mobilise support and consolidate positions. When the caste structure provides one of the most important organisational clusters in which the population is found to live, politics must strive to organise through such a structure. The alleged casteism in politics is thus no more and no less than the politicisation of caste. Caste in contemporary Indian politics plays a very important role behind the facade of parliamentary democracy. The political behaviour of people is influenced by caste considerations as is quite evident at the time of distribution of tickets by political parties for elections and composition of ministries. As far as possible and practicable, the people prefer a candidate of their own caste, irrespective of his merits and demerits. Similar regard is paid when the list of party's office-bearers is prepared. When a single party is not in a position to have its own candidates, alliances are formed on the basis of caste to recommend the name of a person after arrangements of 'give and take' are made to the satisfaction of the constituents. The central discovery is that politics is more important to caste and castes are more important to politics than before. There is a widespread impression among educated Indians that caste is on its last legs and that, educated, urbanised and westernised members of the upper classes have already escaped its bond. Both these impressions are wrong. These people may observe very few dietetic restrictions, marry outside caste and even religion, but this does not mean that they have escaped the bonds of castes entirely. They show caste attitude in surprising context. That is the reason no political analysis of Indian politics that neglects caste is worthwhile. In fact, caste has become a factor to be reckoned with and none of the political parties, including Congress, Bharatiya Janata Party (EUP) and Communist, can ignore it. Some of the political parties are organised purely on caste basis. For example Dravida Munnetra Kazhagarn (DMK) and All-India Anna Dravida Munnetra Kazhagarn (ALADMK) are anti-Brahmin parties, National Democratic Party of Nair community, Socialist Republican Party of Ezhava community, Kerala Congress of Catholic community and Bahujan Samaj Party

(BSP) of lower caste communities are purely casteist parties. In Madhya Pradesh, it is a general observation that whenever there was Thakur Chief Minister, the Yadava, Kurmi and Brahmin legislators felt themselves neglected. Thakur officers were being promoted out of turn, despite the fact that some of them had adverse service records and inquiries were pending against them. Furthermore, few of the senior IAS Brahmin officers have been suspended. More or less, this has been observed all over the country.

To a limited extent, caste system was recognised by the framers of the constitution when they reserved seats for Scheduled Castes and Scheduled Tribes in the House of People and Legislative Assemblies of the states, made a provision for the appointment of a special officer for Scheduled Castes and Scheduled Tribes to investigate matters relating to the various safeguards provided for them in the Constitution and also by providing for a minister in charge to look after the welfare of Scheduled Castes, Scheduled Tribes and other backward classes in the states of Bihar, Madhya Pradesh and Orissa. There is also a provision which empowers the President/Parliament to indulge/exclude certain castes or groups therein in the category of Scheduled Castes. Subsequently, the Constitution was amended in 1951, and a provision was also made for protective discrimination in favour of Scheduled Castes, scheduled tribes and other socially and educationally backward classes of citizens in services. Keeping in view the social hierarchical caste based structure, which exploited the weaker sections of society, there was and is a justification for such a provision in the Constitution, but only to limited extent for a limited period. However, while doing so efficiency of administration should also not be blindly ignored, otherwise, their condition would become more miserable. It is important to note that the expression 'Scheduled Castes and Scheduled Tribes' as used in Article 338, include "such other backward classes as the President may, on receipt of the report of a commission appointed under clause (1) of Article 340, by order specify and also the Anglo-Indian community". About reservation, it should be remembered that reservation can neither be made on communal considerations nor more than 50 per cent seats be reserved. While caste has been politicised, in the process it has provided the Indian politics with processes and symbols of political articulation. Thus, within the new context of political democracy, caste remains a central element of Indian society even while adapting itself to the values and methods of democratic politics.

Class Conflict

In a literal sense, castes and classes have different implications. But in the politics of our country, they have come to be identified with each other. Even courts have accepted the view that in certain situations, the class as a whole may be taken as a caste and thus, caste may be entitled for the benefits of reservation that are available to a backward class.

We find that most of the tensions and conflicts have their source in social stratification and, for this reason, a possible solution to such political problems should be discovered in the rectification of the balance between different classes. The dialectics of Indian politics demand grappling with complex and contradictory trends in the country which has shown many positive and negative features during the past few years. Simply stated, the term 'class' signifies an aggregate of persons within a society possessing approximately the same status. It is a set of relationship constituted by the granting of deference of individual roles and institutions in the light of their place in the system of power and occupation. What really makes a class is the factor of economic interest. The factor of economic interest is so deep that, as suggested by Karl Marx, it differentiates between the rules and the ruled, the exploiters and the exploited. Marx, however, makes the meaning of the term 'class' very rigid by applying the criteria of ownership and control over the means of production and distribution of goods. It may also be added that in common parlance, this term is used in greatly varying senses as upper or middle classes, propertied and non-propertied classes, educated and uneducated classes, even productive and unproductive classes. Liberal writers dwell upon the doctrine of three broad stratas of society-upper, lower and middle-living in harmony and peace. Max Weber takes a middle view in this regard and while dealing with the objective and subjective dimension of this important issue, builds the concept of class on three factors-possession of economic means, external standard of living, and cultural and recreational possibilities.

The struggle of the members of different classes, for the sake of protecting and promoting their specific interest, leads to the creation of conflicts and crises that demand their solution, sooner the better, and thereby the relationship between social set up and political system is established. In the context of Indian politics, class cuts into caste and is also cut into sub-caste by it. Low standing in the social hierarchy has been commonly taken as a sufficient indicator of backwardness. The cause of most of the social conflicts and tensions lies in the want of economic justice.

Illiteracy and Backwardness

The socioeconomic analysis of educational advance in the post-independence period is available from a number of village surveys. From these, it is clear that the spread of literacy and education is much in evidence among the more affluent and socially advance sections of society than among the poorer and more backward sections. The traditionally upper castes are almost all literate and have progressed much further in higher education, the middle castes have registered significant educational progress; but the lower and other backward sections of the population are lagging considerably behind. Literacy is crawling at snail's pace, and female education has not even touched these sections of society particularly in rural areas. Thus, backwardness in education is closely related to the economic and social backwardness and bears the same hallmarks of a society divided against itself. The benefits of high agricultural productivity have not trickled down to the lower castes, the majority of whom work as agricultural labourers. The rigidity of social customs and the relatively poor bargaining power have kept the lower castes in their caste-ordained position.

The economic and political power essentially belongs to the propertied classes, mostly from the upper castes, who have continued to monopolise education and culture too. The vast masses at the base of the social pyramid are not only deprived of the real power, but the power mechanism so works as to perpetuate and intensify this deprivation of the masses lower down. Lower caste segments of population who have historically constituted the most oppressed and exploited mass of the Indian people, practically deprived of any share in the economic, political and educational cultural developments in the country, continue to live in almost the same socioeconomic conditions, some symbolic improvements in certain sectors notwithstanding. Can a nation of 960 million catch up with the rest of the world with nearly 48 per cent of its population totally illiterate? It cannot, if it does not take up bold measures to tackle the chronic problem within a timeframe. Though we have impressive statistics on education: 590,421 primary schools, 171,216 upper primary and 98,134 high schools, 6,596 colleges for general education, 1.354 professional colleges and 226 universities, for the 150.7 million children enrolled in the age group of 6-14 years, there are 2.90 million teachers. But India of 1999 is caught between the paradox of high technocrats. IIT professionals, MBA, graduates and other literate and another India overflowing with an illiterate population of more than 400 million.

Money Power

Economic power has paved the way for capturing political power and thereby using state apparatus for suppressing the opponents belonging to the poor and backward class. For instance, it is the power of money that purchases the vote bank and thereby manages to have the induction of legislators and administrators, who protect and promote the interests of the rich and upper class. Likewise, in rural areas, the rich peasants have established linkages with the administrative apparatus that work against the rural poor who are immensely vulnerable because they are non-owners and the power-wielders are supported by their ownership of land. Corruption breeds corruption. When it sets in, it grows like weeds in a garden. There is no known antidote for it except exposure and punishment.

Due to expensive elections, degeneration of moral values, and the desire to be rich overnight, political corruption has now become a great threat to our political system. It has diluted moral and ethical standards over the years, has seeped into all walks of life, and hampered the economic development of the country. Since Independence, all the Prime Ministers not only ignored, but actively helped some of the politicians who were very close to them in the matters of financial improprieties. This approach of Prime Ministers of not only shielding but also promoting the corrupt politicians, had its adverse impact on the Indian political system because it encouraged political corruption and hence, corruption started spreading from top to bottom. It is interesting to note that on the one hand Prime Ministers refused to appoint a commission of inquiry against their ministers or chief ministers, belonging to their party, but were quick in appointing such commission whenever a minister or chief minister belonging to some opposition party was involved. This shows that all the Prime Ministers have dragged their feet in appointing commissions of inquiry when their own kith and kin or lieutenants were involved. With the passage of time, links with the underworld of gamblers, smugglers and FERA violators on the one hand, and further deterioration in moral and political standards on the other, has further increased corruption in political life. When politicians indulge in corruption on a large scale, bureaucracy cannot remain far behind. The selling, of national secrets by officials occupying sensitive places is a sad commentary on the political and bureaucratic leadership of the country. Public Service Commissions and other recruiting agencies in some of the states have also become dens of corruption. One of the most disturbing developments which has encouraged corruption is that politicians have undermined the process of rule of law by withdrawing cases of corruption lying in the courts of law. It follows that when politicians who amass wealth by misusing their powers and position and are still not punished, then how can bureaucrats who are stunningly corrupt and serve their political masters, be punished? In fact, Indira Gandhi had once said that corruption is a worldwide phenomena. She had also admitted that it is not true that the Congress alone gets the money or gives the favours.... We do collect money, but everybody does". According to Viren Shah, the ex-president of the Indian Merchants' Chamber of Commerce, "Can we say that we have not contributed to corruption by bribing those in authority or making clandestine contributions to party funds?"

It is important to note that the history of many Third World countries tells us that when corruption and crime jointly act upon economic and political institutions and state power is employed for partisan political objectives, the result inevitably is both massive violence and authoritariatism and this is exactly the direction in which Indian polity is now heading which is very dangerous and unfortunate.

Nexus of Crime and Politics

Nani A Palkhivala, the eminent constitutional expert observes, "I do not think India, in its entire history of five thousand years has ever reached a lower level of degradation than it has reached now.... The picture that emerges is that of a great nation in a state of moral decay, of which crime, chaos and corruption are three of the several facets." In order to protect themselves, citizens in some parts of the country have begun to organise private armies. Sooner or later, all developing countries become difficult to govern, and over the past two decades, India has been moving in that direction.

The much talked report of the Vohra panel categorically points out that crime syndicates mafia. Organisations have developed muscle and money power and established linkages with government functionaries, political leaders and others. The CBI has reported that the nexus between the criminal gangs, police, bureaucracy and politicians has come out clearly in various parts of the country. There has been a rapid spread and growth of criminal gangs, armed sertas, drug mafia, smuggling gangs, drug peddlers and economic lobbies in the country, which have, over the years, developed an extensive network of contacts with the bureaucrats/government functionaries at the local levels, politicians, media persons and strategically located individuals in the non-state sector. In certain states like Bihar, Haryana and Uttar Pradesh, these gangs enjoy the patronage of local level politicians, cutting across party lines and protection of government functionaries.

The big smuggling syndicates with international linkages, have spread into and infected the various economic and financial activities including hawala. Transactions economy causing serious damage to the economic fibre of the country. The network of mafia is virtually running a parallel government, pushing the state apparatus into irrelevance. The cost of contesting elections has thrown the politicians into the lap of these elements. Another feature in the political culture of the ruling class is the politicisation of crime and of politics. Politicisation of crime involves competitive use of anti-social forces for the mobilisation of party funds, for managements of elections, for organising meetings and conferences and even for recruiting workers at lower levels from among anti-social elements. It also means the misuse of criminal intelligence as a political tool for black mailing political opponents.

Criminalisation of politics means direct entry of criminals into political parties and legislatures, including Parliament. Today politics is no longer decent: hooligans and hoodlums are gaining control of public life. The notorious criminals, history-shelters, smugglers and murderers are swarming into politics. Formerly, they were on the periphery of Indian political life, now they have moved considerably towards the centre to manipulate the gears and levers of political machine.

Kuldeep Nayyer wrote that according to the Chief Election Commissioner, 180 out of the 425 members of Uttar Pradesh Legislative Assembly had criminal records and the last general elections in Bihar were contested by as many as 243 candidates against whom charges were pending. According to India Today, "of the 424 members of the Vidhan Sabha, 132 are suspected criminals, 16 of them now actually sit in cabinet meetings. Election Commissioner G V G Krishnamurty, while addressing press persons on August 20, 1997, said as per records, 40 members of Parliament have criminal cases pending against them while nearly 700 members of state assemblies out of 4,072 are named in criminal cases, though It was an international accepted norm that 'law breakers cannot be allowed to be lawmakers", which India must also follow.

In a historic judgement on March 20, 1997, the then Chief Justice of India, A M Ahmadi, warned the nation of the emergence of new crime syndicates with a very strong nexus with politicians, bureaucrats, media, personalities and even members of the Judiciary. It is unfortunate that no counter moving force to check criminalisation of politics is emerging. The historic resolution passed by the Lok Sabha at the special session of Parliament on the occasion of the golden jubilee of Independence, August 26 to September 1 1997 observes: "The meaningful electoral reforms be carried out so that our Parliament and other legislative bodies be balanced and effective instruments of democracy and further that political life and processes be free of the adverse impact, on governance of undesirable extraneous factors including criminalisation."

Women of India are paying a heavy price in terms of a rising tide of violence and assent on their honour just because of distorted social values, a band of politicians, hand in glove with criminals and anti-social elements, caste conflicts, etc. Crimes against women are on rise despite all sacrosanct provisions in the Constitution, criminal law, Parliament, judiciary, police, media coverage, the National Human Rights Commission and the National Commission for Women. Perhaps every segment of India has to own the blame and should dip its head in shame for the continuing assault on womanhood in India.

State of Women

The women of India have been exposed to greater insecurity, to poverty, illiteracy, casteism, orthodoxy unhealthy living conditions, traditionalism, backwardness, corruption, criminalisation and male dominance in most of the fields. They have been affected by lack of opportunities and facilities owing to the innate discrimination prevalent in the society. In the last 20 years, there has been a global effort with a strong support from the United Nations to understand the discrimination and restore a status to women of the world. The slogan has been equality, development and peace.

The United Nations General Assembly declared the International Year of Women in 1975 followed by the International Women's Decade and organised three world conferences-Mexico in 1975, Copenhagen In 1980 and Nairobi in 1985. The Nairobi conference decided strategies for the advancement of women upto 2000 AD. The world has consciously marched forward with various instruments for eliminating discrimination against women during the 20 years. The fourth world conference on women held in Beijing in 1995, focused on the structural changes that are necessary in the society. It emphasised that no enduring solution to society's most threatening social, economic and political problems can be found without the full participation and full empowerment of the women. India's strategies and action plans are to eliminate all discrimination against women; remove the chasm between legal status and defect status; create an environment of harmony and partnership of men and women.

There are countries like Sweden, Finland and Norway, where women make up almost half of the national legislatures. Stories of smooth succession of power from husband to wife are in plenty. Commenting on how widows and daughters have been thrust into power by dynastic imperatives in Asian countries like Philippines, India and Indonesia. Rounaq Jahan, a Bangladeshi political scientist had observed, "They think that they can manipulate these women. But every time they were surprised that once in power, Women handled the men and mastered old style politics."

But behind most successful women leaders in India, there has been the hidden hand of a man. Just as Jawaharlal Nehru groomed Indira Gandhi, MG Ramchandran did for his screen partner Jayalalitha and Kanshi Ram is doing for his acolyte Mayavrati. Even Laloo Prasad Yadav is not far behind these veterans in propping up his wife Rabri Devi, who confidently faces the camera today instead of taking shelter in her kitchen. There may be a sharp variance in their life style, levels of political sophistication, in their dress sense, but they have one thing in common, that is, their valuable grooming in a political career by their mentors. Grooming Includes training in developing their ethos, political issues and marketing them to their selected audience (voters). Many of them would be raw, without a political or famed godfather to lend support. Like one-third reservation for women at rural and urban local bodies, 33 per cent quota may help women in increasing their numerical strength to 181 in the Lok Sabha, it certainly may not be enough in attaining empowerment in the real sense, which would still remain a far cry. After all the road to empowerment is circuitous. Attaining political power may not mean enjoying or utilising it for the betterment of the country or her constituents, till they are trained to cross the rough and tumble of Indian politics.

Therefore, the present political scenario and demand for women's quota have generated a need for starting grooming courses for women politicians in India. Just as the path of empowerment became easy for the American women by mastering political skills. The Indian women can also attain empowerment if only they are groomed well. For women in the West, there are no reservations on the road to political empowerment. But they have the 'primaries' and other sundry opportunities to make themselves hard enough for the long grind in the political arena. Strangely, the idea has not struck us, where women advancement in the political domain is just a matter of time. A politically ambitious woman in our country is just thrown in the thick of things, to fend for herself. As more and more women get into the thick of things there is an urgent need to evolve a system that will prepare them for this opportunity. Though there are many examples of women who have come through the system, they are seasoned, and experienced. But they have never been to any finishing school. What they have learnt is through sheer experience. There are no caucuses and no primaries where they can cut their political teeth. In effect, they have to behave, react and act as a politician from the word go. It is not an easy task. There are few women in public offices because few of them run for elections. The reservation in panchayats and municipalities will gradually bring more and more women into the political field. They will gather experience at a level, which will teach them the indispensability of a plural society. Among the women at the local institution level, those who want to adopt politics as a full-time career, will move up to the higher bodies in course of time, and their male colleagues will regard their ascent as a natural and legitimate progression. The training institutions or organisations will teach these political women not only the finer things of decision-making and use their power properly, but also the awareness, understanding of outer world, public dealings and if required, literacy, can also be taught to them. Such a process will not cause any political or social upheaval. The benefits of empowerment would also come in due course without the element of confrontation with other groups.

At present, like other Asian countries, there is very slow rise in the percentage of Indian women in Parliament, central ministry, administration, higher education and technical Institutions.

The Union government obviously thinks this call for affirmative action as is evident from its decision to introduce the Constitution (81st Amendment) Bill in the Lower House. If passed by Parliament, the amendment will have a third of the seats reserved for women in the Lok Sabha and the state assemblies. In this situation, the need for grooming institutions becomes very relevant.

Mohini Girl wrote, "the country is facing, as never before, a torrent of crime due to various socioeconomic reasons not to speak of infiltration of illegal migrants, besides other state sponsored terrorism ... much of these kinds of heinous crimes and atrocities have their roots in the drug mafia, foreign patronage and other country strategies to destabilise civilian population." Criminalisation is a big problem as most Asian cities are unsafe to live in despite the economic growth in the region. Compared to them, the law and order situation in Indian metros is better. The crime rate in Bangalore and Delhi is much lower than that in Seoul or Tokyo.

Apart from this situation, women's status in Asia is clearly in flux. Democracy seems to have helped by creating an environment in which autonomous women's groups could form, network and develop some political influence. Progress in terms of formal political representation of women has been much more gradual in most Asian nations. The practice of reserving parliamentary quotas for women seems to be spreading, although this obviously is a lengthy process. Women in Asia, therefore, face substantial political challenges with significant, but limited resources at their disposal.

Fortunately, in recent times, women have awakened to the fact that in order to break gender-barriers and overcome social bias, women's participation in the political process is essential. Though women constitute nearly half of the total population, politics has all along been men's domain. A February 1997 report on inter-Parliamentary unions says that Indian women hold only 7.2 per cent seats in the Lower House and 7.8 per cent seats in the Upper House. This can be called as token representation.

The percentage of women MLAs in state assemblies is also not very encouraging. Though in comparison to 1952, the percentage in the years from 1993 to 1998, has been certainly increased but still it is insignificant.

The truth is that except for mouthing political platitudes during elections, men are not prepared to give political space to women. One must realise that advancing the status of women is not only a moral imperative, but women's presence at the decision-making level is sine quanon for strengthening democratic traditions and fighting against injustice and oppression.

However, laws alone do not lead to social transformation unless followed by resolute action and socialite awareness of the wrong that have been perpetuated on women from time immemorial. But first of all there should be a revolution of consciousness in the minds of women-in the way they thought about themselves. Women must realise that gender deprivation is inconsistent with the basic human rights of women. They must realise that they have constitutional rights to equality, health care, economic security, access to education, employment opportunities, pay equity and political *power*. As India has celebrated more than 55 years of its Independence, this is a historic opportunity to invest in India's future for when a woman thrives, her family thrives, when families thrive, communities flourish and the nation reaps the benefits eventually.

Part -II

Evolution

Five

The Great Beginning

The nineteenth century, in India, may be noted for the most abominable conditions for women as well as the initiation of their emancipation. At the beginning of the century, the women were humiliated and tortured, kept illiterate, tradition bound and in complete subjugation to the men's will. As time passed, people began to rebel against this state of affairs.

The impact of western culture created a desire among many Indians to examine their beliefs and ideals. The scientific approach of the west initiated a search of Indian scriptures and mythologies for the causes of maladies that existed in society. A critical outlook among educated Indians aided the reinterpretation of religious texts and rational approaches replaced emotional reaction. These approaches led to the conclusion that blind faith, inability to discern right from wrong, and propagation of erroneous interpretations by decadent priestly class and immoral feudal lords had all been responsible for the existing web of subordination around women.

A Continued Movement

Reformers began their work in the direction of women's emancipation in the late nineteenth century, This work was continued in the twentieth century. In spite of great zeal and enthusiasm, the reformers achieved little success in breaking the strong notions of women's inferior status. However, the process of awakening to reality was initiated and India passed to an era in which myth around women began to be seriously questioned in terms of realities of human existence. Women started regaining their freedom of will and intellect. Still with the majority of women a major problem remained. They had for long believed that they were emotionally, morally, biologically and intellectually inferior to men and so were unable to contemplate their equal status with men. They failed to realise their full potential and high abilities. To alter this situation it was required that not only women, but the whole society should undergo a transition in its outlook towards them.

Let us now examine the movement for the emancipation of women, which was initiated in the nineteenth century.

It was largely through the efforts of Raja Ram Mohun Roy (1774-1833) that in 1829 Lord Bentinck decreed for the abolition of the sati system. He worked towards widow remarriages, inter-caste and inter-racial marriages, abolition of child marriages and polygamy. He founded a new religious order called the Brahmo Samaj. This reformed order became well known for the privileges it gave to women.

Keshab Chandra Sen (1838-1884) became Roy's spiritual successor and worked tirelessly for women's education. The Civil Marriage Act III of 1872 raised the minimum age for marriage to fourteen, gave permission for widow remarriage and inter-caste marriage and penalised polygamy. This reform was applicable only to members of the Brahmo Samaj and was brought about by Sen's courage and perseverance.

Many other prominent Indians were motivated by the example set by Keshab Chandra Sen. They led a vigorous struggle against child marriage and advocated widow remarriages. Ganga Ram at Lahore, along with others, started campaigns for women's emancipation. Mahadev Govinda Ranade (1842-1901) led a movement in Poona. He was a great patriot and social reformer who worked against existing Hindu customs, which made the life of the Indian women one of sorrow and hardship. It is notable that his reforms started with his own wife whom he taught himself.

In the north, Swami Dayanand Saraswati (1827-1883) founded

a religious order named Arya Samaj. The basic tenet of this order advocated equality of opportunity for all irrespective of caste, colour, or sex. In a very active manner, this society worked for women's education. Dayanand broadened the scope of women's education by emphasising education for self rather than linking it to their efficiency in familial roles. The curriculum for education devised by Dayanand was similar for both boys and girls. Hence Dayanand emerged as the first reformer who advocated and evolved a comprehensive scheme of education for raising women's status not only at the level of family and society but for her own development as an individual.

Another prominent person of the nineteenth century, Ishwar Chandra Vidyasagar (1820-1891) helped the British Government to establish the first girl's school in Calcutta in 1849. He was further responsible for the establishment of forty girls' schools in Bengal between 1855-1858. The Government Act of 1856, which legalised widow remarriage for Hindu women, was passed largely because of his efforts.

A brilliant national leader Gopala Krishna Gokhale (1866-1915) worked relentlessly towards raising the status of women in Indian society. He founded "Servants of India Society" in 1905 and established as its main objective the education of women. Two religious leaders who helped in bringing about the renaissance in the Hindu religion were Rama Krishna Paramahansa (1833-1866) and Swami Vivekananda (1862-1902).

Pandita Ramabai (1858-1922) was the most prominent of women of the nineteenth century who fought the battle for her own and her sisters' emancipation. Her book *The High Class Hindu Woman* was published in 1888 and highlighted the burdensome life of the caste Hindu women. She made a fervent appeal to the American (men and women) to render help for the enlightenment of Indian women and society. The last words of her book state:

> "In the name of humanity, in the name of your sacred responsibilities as workers in the cause of humanity, summon

> you, true women and men of America, to bestow your help quickly, regardless of nation, caste or creed."

American admirers sent Ramabai Rs.6000 to aid a widows' home, Sharda Sadan (home of learning), which she opened.

Another woman closely associated with education for women was Ramabai Ranade (1865-1922) who was the wife of Justice Ranade. She established an educational institution called Seva Sadan. Anandibai Joshi (1865-1887) was the first Hindu woman to take a Degree of Doctor of Medicine in America. Because she died very young, she could not provide a much-needed influence on education in medicine for Indian women. However, her life and work inspired women of late nineteenth and early twentieth centuries. Francina Sorabji (1833-1907) with her daughters, particularly her fifth daughter Cornelia planned and organised the establishment of schools for girls in the Western region of India. Cornelia was awarded a Law Degree from England.

Mahatma's Entry

Mohan Das Karamchand Gandhi, a shrewd politician and advocate of the righteous path, raised his voice against injustices to women of India in the 1920's. He took up many causes, including widow remarriage, and drew many women into his fight for freedom. His writings, speeches and private advocacy of the women's cause were attended to with great respect. In an article in a publication called *Young India* on November 18, 1926 he made it clear that if a man could remarry after the death of his spouse, a woman should also have this right: "What is considered desirable for man should be equally so for woman, and therefore, a widow should have the discretion as widowers about remarriage". In the same article he made the following comments:

> "I look to every youth in India to resolve not to marry a girl under sixteen. Let us tear down Purdah with one mighty effort. All that I have said about the wife applies equally to the husband-. She is a co-sharer with him of equal-rights and of equal duties."

Gandhi's approach towards women was idealistic. Though he was aware of their woes, he didn't think they had the same failings as men. He believed that their potential goodness incapacitated by years of bondage would, once freed, alleviate all the ills of society. He wrote that woman is sacrifice personified. His ideal of love was feminine as he identified that the greatest asset of a female was the ability to give motherly love. He saw the family as the nucleus of all Social Life and believed that women best functioned at home rather than in the work force. He saw the ideal of women with strong characters tending their families with peace and harmony and leading the world in this direction. He addressed a meeting of mill workers in 1920 at Ahmedabad:

> "It is not for women to work in factories. They have plenty of work in their own homes. They should attend to the bringing up of their children. If women go to work, our social life will be ruined and moral standards will decline".

Although Gandhi's efforts favoured the traditional role for women, he believed they deserved equal recognition for a job well done, just as men received. Gandhi's struggle for women's rights was that of dignity and humanity, rather than one of role differentiations. Certainly, in the tradition bound society into which his ideas were received they were quite revolutionary. His zeal led people to a realisation of injustices to women and prepared men to be more realistic in their attitudes towards women.

However, Gandhi still maintained the goddess image on a pedestal while exploding the myths about the witch like nature of women. He believed in the basic goodness of human nature and propagated the ideal of complete man and complete woman, both able to offer unconditional love while working for a common goal.

Gandhi's influence helped women assert their will. It was due to his leadership that women were given rights equal to men in India's Constitution. The history of the women's participation in the freedom struggle in response to Gandhi's call is one of the most fascinating stories of the rise of the Indian female, The Indian women of the late nineteenth century and early twentieth century who had led a life of drudgery behind purdah finally emerged free of the web that had held them captive for centuries.

Great reformers like Gandhi drew attention to the goodness inherent in women and made an appeal for an understanding of their human need. Men became aware of the love and affection which women were capable of bestowing. Many women realised that they were not inferior beings and were proud of the key role they played in the survival of human race. An important Muslim reformer of the early twentieth century, Sir Sayyid Ahmad Khan, began a movement for the education of Muslims under the western influence. However, he excluded women from his scheme and firmly opposed their education. In contrast Molvi Nazir Ahmad and Hali were in favour of education of women. Perhaps, because of the influence of his mother on his early life Sir Sayyid saw no need for women's education other than home learning. He opposed starting schools for girls but emphasised the education of Muslim boys at Aligarh. On the other hand, Hali had his women characters reflect on the backward condition of Muslim community, the stagnation of vernacular learning, and the need for girls to be educated in order to fulfil their household and family duties. He did not go to extremes; however, the reforms he advocated were justified in terms of women's traditional role. In a magnificent poem called *Homage to Silence* Hali versified the role of women and their right to education.

From the Foreign Lands

Among the foreign women who came to India to serve the cause of women's emancipation, the names of Margaret Noble, later known as Sister Nivedita, Annie Besant and Margaret Cousins stand out. These women of Irish origin and former participants in Irish Home Rule agitation took up the cause of the downtrodden and underprivileged in India.

In 1917 the question of women's franchise was mooted. A deputation of women headed by Sarojini Naidu as spokesperson presented a memorandum to the British Secretary of State in 1919.

The deputation demanded women's suffrage as well as increased educational and health facilities. The decision about the franchise was left to the Indian legislatures. With little opposition from these legislatures, thanks to the influence of the reformers, by 1929 women were enfranchised equally with men.

Although women were granted political rights equal to men, much reformative work was still needed to be done, as purdah and child marriages continued to be the dominant traditions. The laws of inheritance and divorce to assert their will legally restricted women. Illiteracy was predominant and so also the dowry customs. Women's organisations raised these issues for review. Enlightened Congress leaders like Nehru, Patel and Rajendra Prasad gave their full support for removing social and legal inequalities, which had been put upon women. Some of the women leaders who deserve acknowledgement for their efforts in achieving higher status for women in Indian society are chronologically: Annie Besant, Sarojini Naidu, Muthulakshmi Reddi and Raj Kumari Amrit Kaur.

Some interesting events occurred in 1929 when Gandhiji started Satyagraha, a freedom movement into which many women entered whole-heartedly. Mahatma's Dandi march which was in defiance to the salt law, had the full support of women. Within the next three years of this march, over five thousand women served terms of severe imprisonment suffered from lathi blows, cruelty, loss of livelihood and ill health. They picketed wine shops and shops that sold foreign clothes. They faced trials in law courts, suffered atrocities in prisons and were defamed for denouncing purdah and other evil social customs by the orthodox community leaders. Society came to realise, to some extent, the capacities of women as wilful responsible persons. Men and women began developing mutual respect. The prominent women of this period were neither an enigma nor a myth but were real people fighting for their independence. Sarojini Naidu, Kamla Nehru, Rukmani Lakhshmipathi, Hansa Mehta, Nellie Sen Gupta, Satyavati Devi, Miraben (Ms Slade), Durgabai and Kuttimala Amma all contributed richly to the destruction of the many strands of the web, which had dictated that women were either goddesses or witches. The above mentioned women were compassionate people who worked very hard for the good of all and for the betterment of their country.

The Power of Vote

In the general elections of February 1939, nearly five million women voters participated enthusiastically in electioneering. The majority of their votes were cast for Congress. It became clear that women could responsibly vote and the doubts of the orthodox men that the enfranchisement of women would bring their country to doom were quickly dispelled. The women who contested on the Congress ticket were extraordinarily successful. In ,one constituency, a woman elementary school teacher defeated the Vice-Chancellor of the University of her Province. In another, the wife of a doctor overthrew the President of a District Board who had represented the constituency in Parliament for twelve years. In thirty-nine years, India underwent such sweeping changes that by 1939, the political, educational and social position for women had risen so high that eight women were members of provincial and state legislatures. India ranked third among the nations of the world in regards to the political influence and position secured by its women. The United States and Russia were first and second respectively.

Viney Kirpal in her introduction to the edited book, *The Girl Child in 20th Century Indian Literature* writes about the depiction of the girl child in the literature of pre-independence period that "as in ancient literature, girl children are not presented as girl children. Their chronological age might place them as children but they appear in those works as 'miniature women-child brides, child wives, child widows'. The girls may be young in age but the responsibilities they are depicted to be taking up are those of grown up women." She further reports that "the period of adolescence and the transition to womanhood is like a blank page in these texts"

After Independence in 1947 most of the evils in Indian society were vigorously brought to the focus of attention of the nation. The principle of equality among the sexes was effectively put into law.

Those ideas were constitutionally accepted by the Indian people who had been prevalent in the advanced nations for a long time. When the Constitution of India was framed in November 1949. Its Preamble stated that equality among the sexes was a fundamental right. Many other laws were enacted, intense efforts were made to remove the long-standing legal disabilities around women. It is worth noting that equal voting rights for women were given the very day the Indian Constitution was adopted.

The State as Guarantor

Now, the government offers incentives to women to enable them to obtain education that will remove sex discriminations. No woman can now be refused employment because of sex. At present quite a number of women hold jobs in top administrative and managerial services. Almost all the services are open to women who are involved in serious competition with men for the topmost positions in foreign services, police and engineering. They have also found employment in areas such as nuclear engineering, flying and paratroops.

The Hindu Marriage Act of 1955 gave women the legal right to divorce. The daughter who was completely excluded from the inheritance of property among Hindus after the Vedic period now has this right which was granted by The Hindu Succession Act of 1956. In 1961 the Dowry Prohibition Act was passed. The Government began the family planning incentive programme as a social welfare measure to release women from unlimited child bearing responsibilities.

In spite of these measures to ensure equality, most women of India are sill tradition bound. Cormack, Rama Mehta, Promilla Kapur, Goldstein and others who have studied the thinking and the outlook of modern Indian women through questionnaire and Interview techniques found that the women, even the highly educated ones, are still completely rooted in their families. The unmarried still depend on their fathers for advice and guidance as well as for the choice of their husbands. The married depend on their husbands for advice about their careers, life-styles and future life plans. These women have identities, which have meaning only in terms of men in their lives. Independence as is found in Western women is lacking in most of Indian women who are willing to sacrifice their independence and identity for the family and for their men who get precedence over their own selves. Since society as a whole accepts this orientation, those who challenge this notion have a difficult time. Divorce is still a hated word in most of the Indian families. Nearly ninety per cent of all marriages among the middle classes are the arranged marriages. The choice of marriage partners depends on the parents.

The education of women is now considered as an essential feature of our national life. The point worth consideration is that: "should education strive to change this situation or strengthen these practices?" Many scholars are of the opinion that the stability of the Indian society is due to the prevalent practices while the exponents of the Women's Liberation Movement are very much against the undermining of women's position in any respect.

Six

An Equal Status

Notably, the word 'gender' means much more than 'sex'. The gender of a man is masculine and that of a woman feminine. Neither a man nor a woman is sex alone or a biological species. So, the concept of gender may be said to be more inclusive than that of sex. But this distinction as such says nothing as to which of the two is inferior or superior. A bigger circle is only bigger than - not necessarily superior to — the smaller one, which it may include. In other words, the word gender in my view is a value-free concept. Differences of value arise only when we take genders in relation to their functions in society and, what is more important, when our way of looking at the matter is merely external. The point may be brought out as follows:

When female child becomes a wife, she acquires the functions of a mother, similarly a male child becomes a father. Now the functions of a mother are mostly confined to activities which quietly take place within the house. The father, on the other hand, earns a living by working in the outer world. What takes place in the open is noticed easily. What happens at home does not strike the public eye. So by the average man, whose way of looking is confined to the externals - that is, whose *drishti* is *bahirmukhi*-the male is taken to be superior to the female. Those who are careful enough to take a comprehensive view of the human life, attach as much value to the mother's activities of producing and nursing children and keeping a family together as to the bread winners outdoor activity of earning a living. It is really a defect in our ways of looking at things, and not the fact of gender as such, which is at the root of prevailing bias against women.

However, in the contemporary feminist literature, gender is not a value-free concept. It is a value-loaded term. It has acquired new dimensions and greater significance. It now refers to the social institutionalisation of sexual difference . It aims at exposing the present masculinist hegemony in the name of natural sexual differences, and also at uncovering the male connotations of the existing vocabulary of reason, morality, autonomy, justice and history. It, therefore, aims at suggesting an alternative epistemology and methodology, which can uncover the present gender bias, and may reflect more accurately the experiences and needs of all human beings. Feminists assert that any discrimination based on the basis of sexual differences is unjust; the body differences do not warrant such discriminatory differentiation; and, that they are only socially produced. Catharine A Mackinnon says:

> "Our issue is not the gender difference, but the difference gender makes, the social meaning imposed upon our bodies - what it means to be a woman or man is a social process and, as such, a subject to change. Feminists do not seek sameness with men. We more criticise what men have made of themselves and the world that we, too, inhabit. We do not seek dominance over men. To us, it is a male notion that power means someone must dominate. We seek a transformation in the terms and conditions of power itself."

Past Theories

It would be relevant here to discuss how political theorists in the past have neglected gender. John Locke defines political power as distinct from the power relations operating within the household. Rousseau and Hegel have clearly contrasted the two spheres and have justified this contrast in legitimising male rule in the domestic sphere. Locke has categorically mentioned that when "women hold the helm of government, the state is at once in jeopardy". Rousseau believes that women pose a permanent threat to political order. The natural morality of women fits them only for the 'natural society' of domestic life. He argues in Politics and the Arts, "even if it could be denied that a special sentiment of chasteness was natural to women.

would it be less true that in society ... they ought to be raised in principles appropriate to it? If the timidity, chasteness and modesty, which are proper to them are social inventions, it is in society's interest that women acquire these qualities....."

Freud offers remarkably similar justification for women's confinement to domesticity. He writes, "for women the level of what is ethically normal is different from what it is in men. Their superego is never so inexorable, so impersonal, so independent of its emotional origins as we require it to be in men... They show less sense of justice than men, they are more often influenced in their judgements by feeling of affection of hostility..." Hence, Freud insists that the difference in moral capacity between the two sexes must be accepted.

Ironically, most contemporary political theorists continue the same neglect of gender by ignoring the family. Susan Moller Okin has rightly claimed, "the judgement that the family is 'non-political' is implicit in the very fact that it is not discussed in most works of political theory today". A number of examples can be cited.

However, there are a few exceptions. The works of Michael L Walzer, Philip Green, Allen Bloom and Michael J Sandel can be cited here.

Thoughts Today

Contemporary feminist scholars have used the word 'gender' after two decades of intensive thought and research. To them gender is a social and political construct, related to and not determined by, biological sex difference.

In its most recent usage, gender seems to have first appeared among American feminists, who wanted to reject biological determinism implicated in the use of such terms as 'sex' or 'sexual difference'. Two major theories of gender are prevalent today-the psychologically focused theory of gender; and the historically and anthropologically focused explanation of gender.

Simone de Beauvoir, in her work *The Second Sex*, a quintessential example of modern feminist inquiry and critique, claims that "one is not born but rather becomes a woman". She claims that It is a whole process by which femininity is manufactured in society. To quote her, "she is defined and differentiated with reference to men and not he with reference to her; she is the incidental, the inessential as opposed to the essential. He is the subject, he is the Absolute - she is the Other".

Beauvoir argues that it is the child-bearing role of women which excluded them from the productive process, and prevented them from seeing themselves as subjects in their own right. Thus, an artificial idea of womanhood was created by society. She exhorts: "No biological, psychological or economic fate determines the figure that the human female presents in society; it is civilisation as a whole that produces this creation, intermediate between male and eunuch, who is described female."

Nancy Chodorow also subscribes to the above viewpoint and substantiates her argument from a psychoanalytical point of view. She argues that since women have always been assigned the responsibility of primary parenting and nurturing, they develop a psychology of being more suited to the task of nurturing and caring. Thus she chooses the role of a caregiver and confinement to the private. On the other hand, man from the very beginning is encouraged for more and more individuation and attaining status leading to personality traits impelling him to associate himself with the pubic.

Chodorow's use of the notion of gender identity presupposes three major premises: First, everyone has a deep sense of self, which is constituted in early childhood through one's interaction with his/her primary parent, and which remains relatively constant thereafter. The second premise is that this deep self differs significantly for men and women, but is roughly similar among women and among men both across cultures and within cultures across lines of class, race and ethnicity The third premise is that, this deep self colours everything one does.

The second theory of gender proclaims that in most societies across cultures, so far, gender has been a socially constructed category rather than biologically determined. However the proponents of this theory have also stressed that the nature of this social construction differs from one society to the other. So, there cannot be any unicausal, universalist and a historical explanation of it. Anthropologist Michelle A Rosaldo supports this theory on the basis of her cross-cultural research, which reveals that women are subjected to the authority due to the existing dichotomy between the public and the private.

Historian Linda J Nicholson also rejects the unicausal explanation of inequality of the sexes. She emphasises that it has been affected by various causal factors in different social contexts. She stresses the need to fight against the powerful tendency present in political theory to rectify the public-private distinction and to perceive it as rigid. She believes that one can comprehend this distinctly only through the study of history, for the gender structure of a particular time and place is less affected by other contemporary structures, such as political, economic, etc., more by the previous history of gender. Joan W Scott also stresses the centrality of history in analysing different aspects of the social construction of gender. She explains (a)how cultural myths and symbols reify the suppression of women: (b)how these symbols create the 'binary opposition of masculine and feminine male and female; (c)how social institutions like family, labour markets, educational institutions and polity reinforce this dichotomy; and, (d)how the subjective identity formation of individuals is psychologically determined. She, therefore, emphasises the need to expose the social construction of gender by deconstructing it. This calls for:

> "a refusal of the fixed and permanent quality of binary opposition, a genuine historicization and deconstruction of the terms of sexual difference... (we must) reversel and displace its hierarchical construction, rather than accepting it as real or self-evident or in the nature of things."

In fact, all of them are unequivocal in proclaiming that the public sphere till today, has been constructed under the assumption of male superiority and dominance. It has avoided a number of compelling questions such as that of incorporating the responsibilities of child-bearing and child rearing into the fabric of job-structure.

The above analysis of gender has helped feminists in rejecting many of the existing dominant paradigms. First, they reject the claim that separation of the public and the private follows inevitably from the natural characteristics of the sexes. They argue that a proper understanding of social life is possible only when it is accepted that the two spheres, the private and the public, are inextricably interrelated. Unless the separation of the two worlds is not destroyed, the public life would always be conceptualised as the sphere of men. Carole Pateman has aptly remarked:

> "In popular (and academic) consciousness the duality of female and male often serves to encapsulate or represent the series (or circle) of liberal separations and oppositions: female, or-nature, personal, emotional love, private intuition, morality, ascription, particular, subjection; male, or-culture, political, reason, justice, public, philosophy, power, achievement, universal, freedom."

The most fundamental and general of these opinions associate women with nature and men with culture. Nature is always seen in a lower order than culture. The feminists like Ortner argue that the opposition between women/nature and men/culture is itself a cultural construct and does not exist in nature. S.Firestone in her work *Dialectic of Sex*, argues against this separation of private and public. Women necessarily suffer from a fundamentally oppressive biological condition. It is their role as reproducers that has handicapped women over the centuries and made possible men's patriarchal power.

The consequences of this public-private dichotomy are disastrous. Due to this, women have been deprived of political power and effective participation. Citizenship for women is always seen as 'an elaboration of their private domestic tasks'. Thinkers like Ruskin could argue that "man's duty as a member of the commonwealth, is to assist the maintenance, in the advance and in the defence of the state. The women's duty, as a member of the commonwealth, is to assist in the ordering, in the comforting, and in the beautiful adornment of the state."

This has eventually led to the dichotomy between morality and poor. Women, in the name of being more moral, have been excluded from the public realm. Even the suffragists argued in favour of women's franchise by claiming women's superior morality as it would usher the state in a reign of peace. This is why J B Elshtain alleges that suffragists instead of challenging the separation of the public and private, merely "perpetuated the very mystifications and unexamined presumptions, which served to rig the system against them."

Against this background, one can understand the significance of the feminist slogan:

The feminists argue that public realm of politics can be so rational, noble and universal only because like the messy content of the human body, meeting its needs for production, care-taking and attending to birth and death, as too in politics are taken care of elsewhere.

So, a modern reflective political theory should recognise that the glory of the public is dialectically entwined with exploitation and repression of the private and the people restricted to that sphere so that they can take care of the people's needs. In view of this, the feminist political theory concludes that the 20th century politics requires a basic rethinking of this distinction and its meaning for politics.

The feminists are trying to develop a theory of social practice on the following premises. First, there should be no sexual division of labour at work place and in political organisations of all ideological persuasions; second, there should be a differentiated social order within which various dimensions are distinct but not separate or opposed, and which rests on social conception of individuality, which includes both women and men as biologically differentiated but not unequal creatures.

Third, there is a need to base and expand the conception of politics on the understanding that power relations between men and women are not confined to the 'public' world of law, the state and economics, but pervade all areas of life. This means that contrary to the assumptions of traditional political theory, the family, reproduction and sexuality must be included in political analysis.

The question arises how far this public/private dichotomy and its deconstruction is relevant to the women of the Third World? Can this empowerment epistomology rooted in white women's experiences, subjectivity and identity, fulfil the interest of the Third World women?

However, in the post colonial discourse, women of the North have understood the significance of the Third World women's realities, and they themselves have rejected the monolithic nature of the earlier feminist discourse on the grounds that it ignores difference, indigenous knowledge, and local expertise. For example, modernity is equated with westernisation, industrialisation and superiority, whereas non-modernity is equated with non-western countries, tradition and inferiority. In the 1970s, Eshter Boserup's pioneering work *Women's Role in Economic Development*, asserted that modernisation had marginalised women and their contributions in the Third World. Chandra Mohanty also questions the western approach, when she asks:

> "Is it possible to refer to the sexual division of labour when the content of this division changes radically from one environment to the next, from one historical juncture to another? At its most abstract level ... concepts such as the sexual division of labour can be useful only if they are generated through local, contextual analyses. If such concepts are assumed to be universally applicable, the resultant homogenisation of class, race, religion, and daily material practices of women in the Third World can create a false sense of the commonality of oppressions, interests, and struggles between and among women globally.

G Sen, and Crown too, are cautious against adopting a concept of gender that ignores differences and diversities. They believe that this diversity is built on gender oppression and hierarchy. He exclaims:

> "Feminism cannot be monolithic in its issues, goals and strategies, since it constitutes the political expression of the concerns of women from different regions, classes, nationalities, and ethnic backgrounds. There is and must be a diversity of feminism, responsive to the different needs and concerns of different women, and defined by them for themselves."

The most positive part of the whole discourse is that these concerns are reflected in practice also. Women involved in different social movements are fighting against injustice on their own cultural terms. Environmental activists like Vandana Shival are speaking of the need to decolonise northern assumptions such as the concept of sustainable development, and appeal to save environment through knowledge based on poor women's experience.

Thus, feminist scholarship has brought sweeping changes to social and political theory. It has cautioned us against constituting gender as a superordinate category of analysis. It should neither be an automatic starting point of analysis of adjustment, nor should it be ignored as a potential starting point. We must avoid approaches that are gender-blinded or gender-blind.

Seven

Problems and Solutions

The planners agree that even with expanded employment opportunities, the poor will not be able, with their level of earnings, to buy for themselves all the essential goods and services which should figure in any reasonable concept of a minimum standard of living. The measures for providing larger employment and incomes to the poorer sections will, therefore, have to be supplemented up to at least certain minimum standard, by social consumption and investment in the form of education, health, nutrition, drinking water, housing, communications and electricity, and social welfare services. Social welfare services are intended to cater for the special needs of persons and groups, who by reason of some handicap-social, economic, physical or mental-are unable to avail of or are traditionally denied the amenities and services provided by the community. Women are handicapped by social customs and social values and therefore social welfare services have and should specially endeavour to rehabilitate them by inducing a change in the attitudes of society towards women, their role and contribution.

Major Issues

A statement of a plan of social welfare programmes relating to women, even if, it is within the purview of the overall social welfare programmes, will help in providing the correct emphasis on the problems and development needs of the weaker sections of women and provide voluntary organizations and voluntary effort "a certain" direction. The problems and consequently the developmental action required are, it appears, unlimited and the resources are limited. As such, priorities have necessarily to be assigned.

Among women, the following categories and some of the problems faced by them, call for special attention on a priority basis. The categories are:

(A) Working women. To include

(i) The low-income women living in tribal and backward rural areas and urban slums.

(ii) The migrant women.

(iii) The divorced /separated.

(B) Physically and mentally handicapped women.

(C) Widows with or without children.

(D) Destitute women.

(E) Women who come into conflict with law.

(F) Exploited women and unmarried mothers.

The problems faced by each of the above categories are numerous and some of them are common to other categories. To decide on action plan priorities, the handicaps and/or the factors which impose constraints need to be understood.

Working Women

According to 1971 Census, women workers constitute nearly 12 per cent of the total women population and well over 90 per cent of the women workers are found employed in rural areas. It should be recognized here that the problems faced by women workers in rural areas are altogether different from those in the urban areas.

Rural areas including tribal and backward areas: Women workers in rural areas are largely landless agricultural labourers; members of households with uneconomic holdings; those engaged in traditional household industries like hand-spinning, hand-weaving, oil pressing, rice pounding, leather, tobacco processing, etc. These household industries-which are predominantly female labour intensive and which have been a major source of employment in villages appear to have declined in importance during the post-independence period. This is also evidenced by the distinctly declining trend in employment of women workers in the rural areas between the decennial Censuses 1961 and 1971. It has not been possible to reverse this trend because:

(i) Almost all the women workers in the rural areas are handicapped by illiteracy and lack of mobility.

(ii) In addition to this, incessant child bearing coupled with hard domestic work does not provide them any time to go through formal education/training to acquire new skills. Facilities for acquiring new skills are still sparse.

Urban Areas: Women workers in the urban areas fall into three distinct categories:

(i) The first category consists largely of migrants from villages and members of families whose economic position has deteriorated to near starvation. The women of this class work mainly as domestic servants and as unskilled labour in various unorganized industries.

This category of women workers, who are largely slum dwellers, are below subsistence level. Their problems are to find a job which is secure or provides them regular income at least to subsist, a place for comfortable living, as most of them are away from their homes located in villages; and rehabilitation facilities for their families, particularly children and preparing them for better livelihood, through better education and training; in that order.

(ii) The second category consists of women, who need employment either to keep their families away from starvation or to ensure better standard of living. Most of such women are found employed in industries, services and professions. Some are even self-employed. In the case of this second category of women workers in urban areas, their existence ranges from subsistence to security. Some of these women, particularly those residing away from their families, are likely to be exposed to the dangers of exploitation from undesirable and anti-social elements. Personal security is therefore a major problem for them.

(iii) The third category consists of women who are highly educated and work in higher ranks of services and professions for personal satisfaction and independence. Belonging as they do at least to the upper middle-class families, they do not as group face any serious problems requiring immediate attention here.

Divorced/separated women are part of each of these categories.

Physically and Mentally Handicapped

There are several types of physical handicaps like blindness, deafness, orthopaedic handicap, leprosy, mental retardation, etc., which hinder two persons from even entertaining the hopes of equal participation in the overall social activity. These problems are common to both men and women.

Estimates of physically handicapped women are not separately available. To provide a basis for the formulation of Fifth Five-Year Plan, the working group on the Handicapped constituted for the purpose, estimated that "India may have well over 12 million blind, deaf and orthopaedically handicapped persons. In addition, an estimated 2 million suffer from moderate to severe retardation. The number of persons suffering from leprosy is believed to be around 2.5 million".

The basic problem concerning these physically handicapped persons is lack of adequate facilities for differential medical care, education, training and rehabilitation programmes and a lack of knowledge about these facilities by handicapped persons. Further, it is widely known that though the existing facilities are largely used by men, a majority of physically handicapped women are not coming forward to utilize the available facilities.

Widows with or without Children

The 1971 Census distribution of women according to marital status indicates that roughly about 9 per cent of the women are widows. Further, they are almost evenly distributed between the rural and urban areas.

Widowhood is a curse for most of the women in India for various reasons:

(i) It is almost invariably accompanied by economic disaster. This is because a large number of the families in India survive at below subsistence level and hence death of a male earning member pushes down the families concerned to near starvation. Also many of the females are voluntarily out of work force, and illiteracy remains the greatest barrier for the improvement of the economic position of widowed women, particularly in the rural areas.

(ii) Age-old traditions, social prejudices and cultural practices almost exclude widowed women from any socially productive work. Social acceptance of women is reduced with widowhood. In some communities/ regions. There is almost a sort of social boycott of widowed women.

Problems faced by Widows of Different Age Groups: The problems faced by widowed women are not all the same as between different age-groups; and as between rural and urban areas:

(a) For widows in the younger age group - particularly those belonging to 15-44 years of age - the problems are more - related to economic independence and rehabilitation in the society - preferably through remarriage.

(b) For widows in the age group 45 and above, the problem is more of social acceptance and security. Most of such women, if not previously employed, will be unfit for employment. Even in respect of employed women -widowed after 44 years of age - it is difficult to impart -of the needed training/skills for more remunerative jobs within the existing framework of education/ training facilities.

Problems of widowed women in the rural areas are even move severe than those in the urban areas. In addition to economic dependence and the social stigma attached to widowhood, there are no opportunities for their emancipation. Many of them are possibly not even aware of the efforts being made by the government agencies through voluntary organizations to redress their miseries.

Destitutes

These destitute women can be classified into three age-groups as their problems are different:

Below 15 years: Persons in this group can be categorized as children. They are mostly orphans and are, therefore, deprived of the tender parental care. They are also subjected to malnutrition and the consequent diseases. This age group, viz., below 15 years of age constitutes the formative years in a person's life, as the process of development and learning are most rapid during these young years. During these formative years, the effects of environment greatly influence the personality development, mental attitudes, moral character, etc. Often, destitute persons in this age group fall a prey to the environmental disadvantages.

15-44 years: This second group of women are both in the productive and reproductive age group. Their main problems are those pertaining to economic independence, social acceptance and security.

45 years and above: In the case of third group of destitute women, their major problem is social security. They are mostly unfit to be employed. They cannot even be trained to earn their livelihood.

Women who Come into Conflict with Law

Women who fall under this category are: (i) juvenile delinquents, (ii) women in moral and social danger - particularly those who indulge in immoral traffic and (iii) women prisoners.

Juvenile delinquents: are again a creation of the society and the environment in which they are brought up; the deprivation of proper nutrition and training/education which would enable them to earn a better livelihood, etc.

Prostitutes: Women subjected to severe economic distress and hardships often come into the clutches of persons who have vested interests in immoral traffic. Once they succumb, they do not receive proper health care - curative and preventive treatment for the diseases associated with immoral traffic; many of them are not aware of the existing health care facilities and added to it is the innate fear of being exposed to the general public and the resulting social reactions. The existing health facilities are also not adequate and are not perceived as being sympathetic towards their health problems.

Female Prisoners: Many of the problems faced by female prisoners are in common with male prisoners. However, some of the problems are peculiar to females alone. For example, women prisoners with children - particularly in case children are below five years - have problems in arranging for the care of their children. Also, problems in getting rehabilitated, after they are free, are more severe in the case of women prisoners than men prisoners.

Exploited and Unmarried Mothers

(i) Out-of-wedlock pregnancies are on the increase, judging from the number of abortions and live births among single women recorded at various institutions. Estimates of medical termination of pregnancies (MTP) in the case of single women alone range from 10 to 30 per cent of total MTP cases. In respect of live illegitimate births estimates based on hospital records range from 2 to 3 per cent of the total confinements. In reality many more clandestine live illegitimate births may be taking place which are not brought to public notice.

(ii) Premarital pregnancies, are as generally believed, no longer confined to the illiterate and depressed classes. According to some case-studies in this field, nearly 50 per cent of the pre-marital pregnancies were observed in the case of women who are at least matriculates. A few were graduates. Some of them were observed to be belonging to the privileged classes of the society. A more distressing feature, however, is that pre-marital pregnancies are being observed even in the case of school girls.

Among the reasons attributed to premarital pregnancies are: interactions between various social, psychological and economic forces like break down of joint families; overwhelming poverty, rapid urbanization bringing in its wake the social transformation which leads to increasing permissiveness, lack of communication between children and parents; emotional immaturity and craze for excitement among the youth; antipathy towards the introduction of basic sex education among school children, etc., are the most important reasons cited.

Permissiveness and promiscuity increase with rapid urbanization and measures to avoid such premarital pregnancies is a long drawn social education problem and cannot be expected to decline rapidly. However, the problems concomitant to premarital pregnancies can and should at least be tackled effectively.

The action plans should be directed primarily to solving the problems of these six target groups of women.

Broad Groups of Action

There is considerable overlap both in terms of the causes and programmes and agencies concerned with eliminating the problems and building rehabilitation/development plans for these target groups. As such, the action plans are classified under broad groups of actions rather than in terms of categories of women discussed above:

I. Provision of Services/Infrastructure.

II. Education/Training Programmes for the Target Groups.

III. Promoting Voluntary Effort: The Role of Women.

IV. Development of Human Resources.

V. Administrative Set-up and Coordination.

VI. Legislative Measures.

VII. Areas of Research.

The Fifth Five-Year Plan has rightly emphasized the need for a shift in the approach towards social welfare, from a mere provision of curative and rehabilitative services - the kind of approach adopted during the past two decades of planning - to promoting the needed preventive and developmental aspects of social welfare. The action plans should necessarily have such a preventive and development orientation.

Action Plans

Provision of Services/Infrastructure

(i) Services for the care of girls below 15;

(ii) Facilities for women in the productive age group, i.e. 15-45 years;

(iii) Programmes for the care of aged and infirm women; and

(iv) General welfare programmes.

Services for the Care of Girls below 15: There are three categories of children who need particular attention, viz., children of working women, destitute children particularly female children and juvenile delinquents. The following action plans are suggested:

(1) The child population below 6 years of working mothers in urban and rural areas is estimated to be around 20 lakh and 166 lakh, respectively. With a view to helping the working mother discharge her duties - both as a mother and worker better family aid services like Anganwadis, Balwadis, creches and day care centres might be launched in a big way.

Both in the rural and in the urban areas efforts should be made to cover more than 40 per cent of the children of working mothers.

(2) There are about 11 lakh destitute children in the country. The girls among them need particular attention, because they are likely to be exposed to social and moral dangers when they grow up. Efforts should be made to provide institutional facilities whether through the foster care programmes or otherwise for taking care of a majority of the destitute female children.

(3) It is impossible to discriminate between male and female juvenile delinquents, as the problems are common to both. However, the approach towards juvenile delinquency as such should be to provide the needed atmosphere for a child to develop personality, character and social conscience through setting up of clubs, play centres, juvenile guidance units, workshops, etc.

(4) Holiday homes schemes initiated earlier to provide organized and guided recreational facilities to children and be one of the measures to prevent juvenile delinquency. Such facilities should at least be extended to cover all the children residing in the slums of major cities.

Facilities for Women in the Productive Age Group: In some selected urban areas, hostel facilities are available for working women of the lower income groups earning Rs. 50 to Rs. 800 per month. However, the coverage of the programme in terms of the proportion of working women needs to be stepped up considerably. Similarly, district-wise investigation would be undertaken about the need for working women's hostels and appropriate facilities set up. The matching contribution for grants for construction/ addition/ alterations should be stepped up.

Socio-economic programmes were initiated in 1958 with the objective of providing full or part-time work to the needy/destitute women and the physically handicapped either through full wage or a wage sufficient to supplement the meagre income of their families. These programmes should be expanded considerably in both rural and urban areas, as they have the potential to provide the needed economic independence to women belonging to the weaker sections and thus act as a preventive measure to many of the social evils.

For effectively implementing these socio-economic programmes, active collaboration should be sought from agencies like Handicrafts Board, Handloom Board, Khadi and Village Industries Board, Small Industries Service Institutes, Small Industries Development Corporations at the State level and the nationalized banks.

To increase the employment potential for the following types of schemes additional steps should be undertaken within the purview of socio-economic programmes:

(i) Small-Scale industries.

(ii) Units as ancillary to large production of handicrafts.

(iii) Units for the procurement and production of handicrafts.

(iv) Handloom training-cum-production units.

(v) Agro-based industries like dairy, poultry farms, etc.

(vi) Traditional female labour intensive industries like rice pounding, oil-pressing, etc.

Attempts must be made to revitalize and activate the existing sick units falling under the purview of socio-economic programmes.

Ways to improve the working, efficiency and effectiveness of Mahila Mandals must be studied and necessary action taken. They should be reoriented to aim at increasing the earning power of women in the rural areas.

It is suggested that by the end of the Fifth Plan, about 10,000 Mahila Mandals, should be developed throughout the country to provide an effective media for organizing women welfare activities in the rural areas.

Scholarship programmes of the Central and State Governments for the handicapped should be expanded considerably and efforts should be made to encourage women to make use of the scholarships available.

Sheltered workshops should be organized.

Schemes for the welfare of destitute women between the ages 18-44 and 45-65 providing for basic amenities of food, shelter, clothing, basic education and training in crafts should be implemented through voluntary organizations who may be given grants to cover 75 per cent of the expenditure. It is suggested that this scheme should be revived and implemented in all the States.

Homes for the rehabilitation of rescued and released women prisoners should be started in all towns with a minimum of 5 lakh of population. Apart from providing shelter, food and clothing, the inmates should also be provided training in crafts like sewing, embroidery, knitting, etc. Efforts should, however, be made in the direction of making inmates self-sufficient and earn independent livelihood.

In some such protective homes, insane women are housed along with other women which is an unhealthy and undesirable practice and should be discontinued.

Programmes for the Care of Aged and Infirm Women: Women in the age group 65 years and over constitute roughly 85 lakh according to the 1971 Census. Many of the women lack absolutely any security They are mostly dependent on their children who often desert them. Thus, even women belonging to upper middle classes are sometimes reduced to the status of destitute. Efforts should therefore be made at least in a modest way to initiate social security measures through old age pension with the objective of providing economic independence to at least 25 per cent of women in the age group particularly in the rural areas.

For the women retired from active service and for those who are in need of some residential facilities, hostels should be started in all the major cities. If necessary, subsidies may also be extended under the grants-in-aid programmes.

General Welfare Programmes: Slum clearance programmes should be initiated in all the major cities and towns with a minimum of 5 lakh of population. People displaced should be provided alternative sites, with proper environmental sanitation, for building their homes.

Zila Parishads and youth in the districts should be entrusted with drinking water supply projects.

A vigorous campaign of education and action should be launched in favour of community sanitation and hygiene. Public utility services should be expanded. The practice of carrying night soil as headloads must be eradicated.

Education/Training Programmes for the Target Groups: Analysis of the problems faced by the target group of women indicated that illiteracy, inadequate education/training, lack of facilities for training in alternative skills and lack of knowledge about the existing facilities are some of the major problems that have hindered the progress of women in India. There is, therefore, the need for accelerating the efforts in this regard with renewed vigour. With this in view, the following action plans are recommended:

(1a) The Fourth Plan introduced a programme of functional literacy built round farmer's training in selected districts where high yielding varieties of crops were being cultivated. It is estimated that about 90,000 women received this training during the Fourth Plan and about 5 to 7 lakh of women are likely to be trained under this programmes during the Fifth Plan. This programme must be extended to all the rural areas.

(1b) Apart from imparting knowledge about farming, the curriculum for women should include courses of training, in occupational skills like kitchen gardening, food cultivation, poultry keeping, animal husbandry; household arts like cooking, nutritional values of foods locally available, sewing, knitting, etc.; and family planning.

(1c) Preference should be given to women belonging to Scheduled Castes, tribal women, widowed women and destitutes under this functional literacy programme.

(2a) For the non-student young girls without any education and school drop-outs - particularly for girls in the age group 11-14 years, the pre-vocational training programmes should be reviewed and strengthened by enlarging the scope of training and by increasing the number of trades.

(2b) In respect of girls in the age group 11-14 years, the objective of pre-vocational training should also be to train them to be self-sufficient in home management by organizing courses of training in sewing, cooking, nutrition, minor repairs of the house, motherhood, child care, etc.

(2c) Pre-vocational programmes should be extended to cover girls in this age group in the rural areas. In urban areas, preference should be given to girls in the slum areas and destitute girls.

(3) Condensed courses of education were started in 1958 with the twin objective of (a) opening new vistas of employment to a large number of deserving and needy women, and (b) creating a band of competent trained workers required to man the various projects in the rural areas in the shortest possible time. Under the scheme, women in the age group 18-30 who have studied up to classes IV and VI are trained for middle school/matriculation examinations within a period of two years. The scheme was found very useful but the statistics reveal that the beneficiaries have been mostly women belonging to the middle-class families. Preference should be given to women belonging to backward classes, widowed women and destitute women.

(4) Special efforts should be made to cover women belonging to Scheduled Castes and Scheduled Tribes through condensed courses. An incentive of Rs.1,000 (as recommended by the Review Committee), be given to the institution for every successful Scheduled Caste/Scheduled Tribe candidate trained.

(5a) The condensed courses should be organized in a big way and for smaller groups of say 5 to 7 with the help of high schools and colleges for girls. Efforts should be made to cover about 215 lakh women under the condensed course programmes, during the Fifth Plan period.

(5b) Apart from imparting general education, condensed courses should also aim at imparting job-oriented training with the active cooperation of existing vocational training institutions.

(5c) Under this programme of condensed courses, short-term courses should be organized to retain women who have been temporarily out of job-market to fulfil child bearing responsibilities.

(5d) For the failed candidates, short-term course of six months to one year should be organized.

(5e) Special efforts should be initiated to follow-up successful candidates with a view to helping them in securing jobs.

(6) Pre-examination training facilities should be offered to duly qualified poor women with the objective of equipping them to successfully compete in examinations for public jobs. It is suggested that about 80 lakh girls in the age group 14-17 may be covered under this programme during the Fifth Plan period.

(7) The school curricula in various States in India should encourage the doing away of traditional prejudices of inequality of the sexes.

(8) Sex education should be introduced at the appropriate stage

with the objective of also educating the young girls about the social and moral dangers they are likely to encounter.

(9) The value of physical training in the school curricula should be emphasized.

Promoting Voluntary Effort: The Role of Women: Voluntary welfare service organizations have been an integral part of the cultural and social traditions in India. Soon after independence, it was estimated that there were 10,000 voluntary organizations engaged in social welfare. In fact, all the schemes of Central Social Welfare Board are implemented only through voluntary organizations. The reorientation given to social welfare in the Fifth Plan calls for more effort on the part of both voluntary organizations and the State agencies involved. The following action plans are, therefore, warranted in this regard:

(a) Efforts should be made to promote a large number of voluntary organizations throughout the country. They have a critical role in mobilizing public opinion in favour of equality among men and women, and eradicating superstitions, social evils and waste. The motivational strategy for encouraging voluntary organizations needs to be well thought through and support facilities provided. Women should be promoted to take the initiative and responsibility for organizing voluntary effort, for not only can they bring to the tasks the necessary dedication commitment and empathy; but their very presence will provide their socially handicapped sisters a source of inspiration and set in a cycle of social rejuvenation. All voluntary organizations particularly those concerned with social welfare vis-a-vis women must be encouraged to have women members. Women Panchayats, Mahila Mandals, working women, etc., should be encouraged to spearhead such voluntary activities. Mahila Mandals should be promoted in every village so that they can function as field level agencies for social and economic transformation.

(b) Most of the voluntary organizations have been operating independently of each other. They have, therefore, not been able to fully benefit the community. The role of existing organizations should be determined and measures should be initiated to coordinate/supplement the efforts of various organizations at each district level.

(c) Many of the women's voluntary organizations are located in urban areas, while only a few organizations have endeavoured to work amongst rural women. Efforts should be made to promote a large number of voluntary women's organizations in the rural backward and tribal areas and urban slums to mobilize public support for different programmes and to implement them. This calls for liberation of the rules regarding the matching grant through voluntary contributions, simplification of the rules and procedures of obtaining the grant as well as administering the organizations, provision of trained staff, organization of leadership training programmes, etc.

Development of Human Resources: Administration of various social welfare programmes have become increasingly technical. During the past two decades of developmental planning, lack of technically competent workers has had an adverse impact on the quality and success of welfare programmes. With a view to provide the necessary support to various agencies, the following action plans are suggested:

(1) Training facilities for the workers attached to all the voluntary agencies, like Mahila Mandals should be initiated immediately. The training needs of workers, however, differ from organization to organization depending on the nature of tasks required to be performed.

(2) Through a proper investigation training requirements of workers in each district should be assessed and suitable training programmes designed.

(3) These training programmes should, as far as possible be organized at each district level.

(4) Trainees should preferably be local candidates.

(5) Effective implementation of the various socio-economic programmes require two cadres of workers: the grass-root workers and supervisory staff. The grass-root workers should be provided training in the latest techniques and methods of production with the active collaboration of well established industrial units and Industrial Training Institutes. The supervisory staff, on the other hand, should be trained in advanced techniques of production, business management, personnel management, etc.

(6) In the case of handicrafts units under the socio-economic programme, practising craftsmen should be trained as instructors and appointed.

(7) Short-term orientation should also be given to the members of the managing committees of the units - socio-economic programmes - about the general working of such units.

(8) Senior level officers in charge of the socio-economic programmes should also be exposed to short-term orientation courses in business management and allied fields through Small Industries Service Institutes, University departments of business management, etc.

***Administrative Set-Up and Coordination*:** Administrative traditions in India have tended to attach least importance to departments dealing with social welfare. This is reflected even in the training imparted to administrators. Only recently it has been realized that administration must also be welfare oriented. The federal nature of our policy vests a large responsibility for implementing social policy and programmes with State and local authorities. There is, therefore, the need for reorganizing the administrative set-up with a view to effectively implementing the various welfare programmes. The following action plans may be taken up for consideration:

(1) Orientation/training programmes should be organized for social welfare personnel, particularly at decision making levels, to sensitize them to social welfare needs and adopt the extension approach of reaching out to the clients. The new developmental and preventive concept, of welfare also needs to be imparted.

(2) Every State Department of Social Welfare should have a Women's Welfare Division with responsibility for planning, programming and monitoring the implementation of schemes of women welfare.

(3) The Central Social Welfare Board is one of the most important agencies for the implementation of social welfare activities. It should be reorganized and strengthened, and vested with larger funds and responsibilities for promoting and developing voluntary effort particularly in rural, backward and tribal areas and among the weaker sections of the community.

(4) The Central Social Welfare Board should launch a massive campaign for enlisting and developing a cadre of voluntary social workers who should be provided some normal assistance to enable them to carry out this work.

(5) State Social Welfare (Advisory) Boards should also be reorganized and strengthened.

(6) The State Board should also be made to function as liaison among the State Government and the local agencies.

(7) Suitable infrastructure should be developed at each district level and block level for implementing and expanding the programmes of Central Social Welfare Board.

(8) Trained social welfare workers should be associated with all the committees to be set-up by the Central Social Welfare Board.

Legislative Measures

(1) International experience indicates that evolving a sound social security system takes a long period of time. However, suitable enactment can be initiated to provide public assistance to select groups like destitute women and people above 65 years but without any means of livelihood. Assistance here need not be in the form of cash. It should be in the form of medical, housing, feeding and recreational facilities, etc.

(2) It should be open to the States and Union Territories to go in for taxation or special levy to finance such public assistance schemes without prejudice to any assistance made available to States and Union Territories from the Central Government under plan schemes.

(3) No child should be tried in adult courts nor should any child be sent to a jail.

(4) State Governments should enact legislation for apprehension, institutional treatment and rehabilitation of beggars, particularly women.

(5) Machinery should be set up for speedy and effective adjudication in all cases concerning the family, including the setting up of family welfare courts since the ordinary judicial procedure is not suited to handle such cases. Women, particularly in rural areas, should be protected against harassment.

(6) A vigorous campaign should be launched to educate women about their rights and the machinery through which they can seek their realization.

(7) Active public support should be mobilized by government agencies, voluntary organizations and public leaders against child marriage and dowry to support the legislative measures for the eradication of these undesirable practices. Ostentatious weddings and other wasteful social ceremonies should be banned.

Areas of Research

Primary data available with sources such as the Census and National Sample Survey, are insufficient and are very scanty for social welfare planning, particularly on the needs and requirements of handicapped women, destitute women, women under the purview of the suppression of Immoral Traffic Act, etc.: In view of this, the following areas of research are suggested:

(i) Studies on 'Social profiles' with district as unit' wherein information on the prevailing conditions of social needs and requirements, etc., are investigated.

(ii) Studies on the requirements of physically handicapped children and women.

(iii) Studies on the requirements of destitute children and women.

(iv) Studies on the training requirements of workers in voluntary welfare organizations.

(v) Studies on the socio-economic and psychological factors behind the problem of premarital pregnancies.

(vi) Studies on the magnitude of problems facing prostitutes and their children such as problems of children of prostitutes, particularly female children.

Voluntary Action

Voluntary action in India has always been an integral part of the cultural and social traditions. A variety of social services were provided by voluntary agencies prior to independence and in the first few decades' of planned development in India. Traditionally, voluntary agencies undertook a wide variety of activities in the areas of social reform in the pre-independence period. Independence resulted in government policy and commitment to support and strengthen voluntary agencies. Voluntary agencies have currently opted for several alternative roles depending on their objectives, location (rural/ urban) and resources available.

The role of voluntary agencies in national development has been considered vital due to their direct and first-hand experience and knowledge of local needs, problems and resources at the grass-roots. Further the commitment and zeal of the voluntary action movement is considered effective as it is not bound by rigid bureaucratic systems and is more responsive to people. The voluntary sector is observed to operate with great flexibility and bases its activities on felt needs. There is a process of continually learning from past experiences in programme planning and implementation, etc.

The essential strength of voluntary agencies derives from the fact that they are closer to the community and people. They represent in many cases the needs and aspirations of the people. Voluntary agencies often function more effectively than the government managed agencies in areas such as motivation, problem identification and analysis, project formulation, innovative methods of service delivery and involvement of the community, due to their spirit.

There are a number of lessons to be learned in such areas such as the demystification of technology; de-emphasizing formal educational qualification in favour of experience, capabilities, aptitude and ability to work with people; expansion of activities without adding on cumbersome bureaucracy; and reliance on community based and non-institutional approaches. The unique strength of the voluntary sector is its ability to pressurize the government without succumbing to it and losing its identity and lobbying on issues and ideas to make them acceptable to government and the people. The decentralized administration in the voluntary sector not only facilitates effective grass-roots, delivery mechanisms but also ensures the participation of the beneficiaries in the programmes.

Voluntary agencies in India have evolved as a result of a historical process that has brought them to their present status and role in the country's development. In the 1950s, most of the organizations provided either relief work or were involved in institutionalized programmes such as schools, destitute homes, hospitals as well as welfare activities. In the 1960s, many of these organizations realized that families with a weak economic base would be unable to procure the benefits of institutional welfare and relief services. It led them to the conclusion that services should enable beneficiaries to be productive and self-reliant through income generating programmes. In the 1970s, many of the voluntary organizations began to feel that economic inputs alone could not overcome poverty and a critical roadblock to development was the unequal social structure. A new type of education geared to raising the consciousness of weaker sections on their situation and rights so that they become active agents of their own development. and change was considered essential. Activist groups built around these considerations, subsequently came into existence in the voluntary sector.

The organization of women by voluntary organizations has acquired importance as the need has emerged for organizational structures to ensure women's participation in the development process. Many old established voluntary agencies have undertaken the task of setting up welfare development services for women in the country.

New Trends: From the mid 1970s onwards there was an emergence of many newly established organizations and activist groups. A large part of the activities of these groups have centered around combating atrocities and violence committed on women, dowry murder, brutal forms of maltreatment and exploitation. In many cases, women in distress have approached such groups for assistance in registering and follow up of cases, providing shelter, etc. These activist groups have identified themselves with oppressed, victimized, and harassed women and awakened new hopes, aspirations and consciousness among women on these issues. Recently many formal and informal groups have emerged throughout the country which have successfully mobilized women's awareness and have preferred to work directly with the women, relying less on material inputs from the outside and more on increasing the internal capabilities and resources-economic, social, cultural and political. These activist groups have also elicited the intervention of the State, especially of the judiciary and of the fourth estate, to project the rights of women and ameliorate their situations. At the same time, they have organized the women themselves for struggle.

Besides voluntary agencies and activist groups, there are many other functional groups such as Mahila Mandals, Youth Clubs, Nehru Yuvak Kendras, National Service Schemes, cooperatives and other people's institutions that have effectively taken up the issues of women in development with varying degrees of success.

Government's Stance on Voluntary Action: The Planning Commission has recognized the role of voluntary action in accelerating the process of social and economic development in most of its plans, particularly so in the Sixth and Seventh Five-Year Plans. Voluntary agencies at their best have played an important role in providing a basis for testing and devising innovative projects and new Models and approaches in programme implementation and in ensuring feedback, as well as in securing the participation of women living below the poverty line. They have developed competence in many non-traditional areas and played a vital role in supplementing governmental efforts so as to offer the rural poor choices and alternatives. They have often served as the eyes and ears of the people at the village level. By adopting simple, innovative, flexible and inexpensive means to suit their limited resources, they have tried to reach a larger number of beneficiaries with minimal overheads and with greater community participation. In the process they have successfully demonstrated how village and indigenous resources, rural skills and local knowledge are grossly underutilized at present, in a cost-effective manner. Voluntary agencies have also managed to mobilize and organize the poor to some extent and to generate in them the awareness to demand quality services and improve accountability of the local level functionaries. They have helped to train a cadre of grass root workers that believe in professionalizing voluntarism.

The increasing interest of the government in enhancing the role of voluntary agencies in the development of women is quite evident. Considering the magnitude of problems faced by women the government has rightly felt that it cannot assume the entire responsibility of service provision and development. It has sought to associate voluntary agencies in the various programmes aimed at women. The thrust of the current programmes is more towards development of women's potential and their productive participation in development rather than merely providing welfare services to them. A meaningful partnership with the voluntary sector has thus been an avowed goal and an essential variable in government's attempts to integrate women in development.

Women and the Voluntary Sector: Voluntary agencies have contributed immensely to the new directions and impetus provided to women's programmes during the decade for women. A number of innovative features in several government formulated schemes/ programmes are based on the experience of the projects run successfully by voluntary agencies.

The rationale for involvement of voluntary agencies in women's development is quite clear. Women in India suffer from multifarious constraints such as a low level of literacy, lack of access to resources and obstacles caused by the cultural and social customs and traditions that are discriminatory of women. In a situation such as this, the role of voluntary agencies in creating awareness among women of their rights and mobilizing women as well as developing in them appropriate motivation and leadership to realize those rights cannot be minimized.

The process of creating an environment conducive to the progress of women is dependent on a multitude of socio-economic factors, starting with a political will to enforce the development of women as a priority. The long-term objectives of the Seventh Plan spell out that raising the economic and social status of women is a critical goal of national development. The basic approach suggested is to inculcate confidence among women and bring about an awareness of their own potential for development. Within this framework, gainful employment to women is accorded the highest priority as an effective strategy. Various ministries and departments have formulated programmes for the development of women with an emphasis on the involvement of voluntary agencies as delivery mechanisms. The role of voluntary agencies in the mobilization of women in particular is seen as a critical factor for the development strategies of the future.

A higher involvement of voluntary agencies is thus envisaged in the implementation of such government programmes as the Integrated Rural Development Program (IRDP), Training of Rural Youth in Self-Employment (TRYSEM), Development of Women and Children in Rural Areas (DWCRA), Integrated Child Development Services Scheme (ICDS), and Adult Literacy programmes. Besides their involvement in these schemes, voluntary agencies can also assist in effective enforcement of minimum wages, supply of safe drinking water, afforestation, social forestry, consumer protection, promotion of science and technology, rural housing, legal education, etc. With the new focus on women, some funds should be earmarked for implementation of these programmes in the concerned ministries/departments for voluntary agencies. Further through the Central Social Welfare Board (CSWB), Council for Advancement of People's Action and Rural Technology (CAPART) and the National Rural Development Fund, the activities of and cooperation with voluntary agencies should be expanded and strengthened. To the extent that voluntary agencies are dependent on public funds, accountability has to be ensured but without cumbersome and rigid methods.

Voluntary Action in the Organization of Women: Empowerment of women cannot be ensured until they are enabled to organize themselves. Collective organizations spell strength. This is a prerequisite for initiating action, lobbying, pressurizing and bargaining. Grass roots organizations can greatly enhance the opportunities for poor women to participate in development programmes by providing an organizational base to operate from. By organizing, working together, sharing experiences and resources, building pressure groups and so forth, women can find independent access to opportunities for their betterment.

A large number of women are engaged in the unorganized sector working and living under precarious conditions and with no legal protection. The unorganized sector denies women all benefits of collective action. Dispersed and unorganized, they have no political power and no bargaining strength. As a result, it becomes much more difficult to implement protective labour laws relating to wages, conditions of work, insurance, provident fund, maternity leave, and creches, etc., and also to channelize economic inputs such as credit, technical training and marketing. In such a situation, the need for collective action becomes critical, and is dependent upon the organization of women in the unorganized sector. Many spontaneous and organized struggles have been launched by some voluntary organizations for the articulation of the needs of poor women, particularly the need to organize them for their interaction into the mainstream. For instance, the whole issue of women in the unorganized sector has been debated and seriously addressed through the awareness generated by certain organizations in different parts of the country.

Uncovered Territory: The issue of gender disparity at work is yet to be voiced effectively in the organized voluntary action movement. Of the vast masses in the category of the working poor, the unskilled ranks contain a larger proportion of females. These women are much less organized for any kind of market leverage or wage bargaining and even when organized, less inclined to redress gender inequalities at work sites. There is the need to replicate the success stories of voluntary action in organizing women in different parts of the country and to take up the issue to parity at work in a larger way.

The participation of women in development requires an all round transformation in the consciousness of both men and women as also in the socio-cultural norms, the mass media and pattern of education all of which at present tend to perpetuate a passive unequal role of women in social, economic and political affairs. There is a need for a strong voluntary action involvement in order to evolve a specific strategy based on the local situation, in this area, of women.

Any voluntary agency that is serious about promoting women's participation would have to seriously consider the challenge of recruiting and training women catalysts, extension agents and functionaries for reaching and eliciting women's participation.

Voluntary Action for Legal Aid: The majority of women have no knowledge about their rights and very few have resources to obtain legal redressal. It is now being strongly felt that laws by themselves cannot bring about the desirable change in the status of women unless women become aware of their rights. At the same time, it is also felt that since most of the women cannot afford legal representation in courts due to high financial costs and lack of access to knowledge pertaining to the legal process, the countrywide network of voluntary agencies can play an effective role in providing legal aid and legal education to women. One of the priority areas for the legal aid movement in the country should be the mobilization of women through voluntary agencies. Voluntary organizations also have an important role in providing counselling, para-legal support and rehabilitation of women in distress. In fact, in the absence of such help, neither police nor courts can effectively help women. In many such cases, women are compelled to withdraw cases under the dowry prohibition act and compromise with unjust situations due to lack of alternatives. This situation could be remedied if women could be assisted through counselling support, employment training, and rehabilitation and development support by voluntary agencies.

The upsurge of interest in women's issues which characterized the decade, has left its mark on the legal scene. Voluntary organizations and activist groups are beginning to initiate action on various legal issues. It is felt that the Government should provide financial assistance to women's organizations for setting up legal aid cells. Evidently, there is a need for many more voluntary agencies to take up the issues of women and provide necessary legal aid to women.

Environment and Women: It is well recognized that the management of the environment requires the participation of people as they are closest to it and have a stake in its preservation. Active involvement of women and their organizations in environment protection is of paramount significance since women are most affected by the issue. There is a serious threat to the environment due to its degradation and pollution arising from various factors such as policies of government as well as the private sector, unplanned discharge of residual and waste, handling of toxic chemicals, indiscriminate construction of dams, large-scale deforestation, expansion of settlements and unplanned mining and quarrying work. Such conditions have pushed great number of women into marginal environment where floods, droughts, shortage of fuel, and excessive utilization of grazing land have deprived women of their livelihood.

Many voluntary agencies have taken up the issue of environment protection. Among these agencies are the Dasholi Gram Swarajya Mandal that has started the Chipko Movement in which women play a very important role. This movement has received international acclaim and was initiated by hill women. Women embraced (Chipko) trees to prevent them being felled and some women were killed while thus protecting these with their own bodies. Trees to these women and others are the source of life. The impact of environmental degradation and of soil erosion is first felt by women. Many grass root level women's organizations have begun to take up environmental issues in addition to their continuing concern for rural poverty due to the intrinsic link among environment, poverty and gender.

The responsibility for creating awareness, mobilizing public opinion and building a strong people's movement lies mainly with the voluntary agencies. The awareness generated by individual women pioneers/leaders and all types of women's organizations on environmental issues has focused on the fact that women and men have the capacity to manage their environment, and their access to productive resources should be sustained and enhanced. It is also recognized that the requisite knowledge and information can be disseminated by voluntary organizations to reinforce the self-help potential of women in conserving and improving the environment.

Demystification of Technology: A number of voluntary agencies are involved in commendable work in the, demystification of appropriate technology for the advancement of rural women. The programmes implemented by voluntary agencies in this area include, providing opportunities for gainful employment and self-employment for women, reducing the drudgery in their lives, ensuring adequate medical and nutritional facilities, improving sanitation and environmental conditions and protecting women from occupational hazards. However, there is a need for further voluntary action in this direction that can develop and disseminate appropriate technology for women. Since the technological marginalization of female work is endemic in both the agricultural and the nonagricultural informal sector, voluntary agencies should be involved in overcoming gender differentials in the application and generation of technology. There is a need to actively deploy technology to reduce the drudgery of the poorest working women in back breaking tasks such as gathering of fuel, fodder and water.

Training constitutes another important input, particularly for upgradation of skill and augmentation of earning capacities of women. There is a strong need for a diversification of training undertaking by voluntary organizations. Their role should be particularly geared to the sensitization of administrators functionaries and catalysts on the issues and needs of women in development and in the delivery of comprehensive training programmes that have a component of knowledge, attitudes and skills for women's development.

Recommendations

The increase in the number, expansion and diversification of activities of the voluntary agencies has not necessarily equalized the disparities between them. There are not only regional imbalances in the growth of the voluntary sector but within a particular state, the growth of this sector has not been even. It is also well known that a majority of voluntary agencies are urban based and that relatively few have taken up the issues of women. It is recommended that the focus of voluntary agencies move from urban to rural areas, as the situation of rural women warrants immediate support. There is also need for the government to encourage voluntary action for the development of women by provision of adequate financial and structural support.

There is an urgent need to improve the effectiveness of voluntary action. Improvement will have to be brought about both in the organizational structures as also in the quality of services offered. Voluntary workers need to be professionals, equipped with appropriate skills for managing women's projects and sensitivity towards women's issues. National and State level institutions and training organizations should provide adequate facilities for research and training relating to women's issues. They should take up activities guided by the felt needs of women and those that can make a qualitative difference to women's lives, rather than be confined to traditional areas of support and action. Their work should be related to contemporary issues and thinking on women. As a caution, they should resist the temptation of initiating more work than they can effectively manage.

Voluntary action should be directed particularly towards preventive rather than purely curative measures. Efforts of voluntary agencies should also be geared towards generating self-reliance rather than to create dependencies. To improve their capabilities in planning and implementation of programmes, voluntary agencies are in need of expertise and technical guidance as much as financial assistance. Unfortunately, in the existing system of grants-in-aid, financial assistance to them assumes overriding importance vis-a-vis other forms of assistance such as technical guidance in the area of programme planning, project formulation, financial planning, administration, monitoring and evaluation. The proposed Resource Centre at the national level could also facilitate in the training needs of functionaries and in providing necessary managerial and technical assistance to voluntary agencies.

The process of grant-seeking and receiving is considered by a number of voluntary agencies as a frustrating experience. There is an urgent need to review the working of the grants-in-aid system. Wherever needed, modifications should be introduced to ensure that rules are simplified, grants released on-time and the amount provided is commensurate and proportionate to the needs of a particular programme. While a system of accountability for government funds is unavoidable, it need not be painful. Further, it should be ensured that financial assistance from the government does not seriously affect the basic character of voluntarism, its flexibility and innovativeness.

A number of programmes implemented by conventional voluntary agencies have emphasized imparting skills to improve the efficiency of women as housewives and mothers, and to improve their earning capacities. Voluntary agencies tend to neglect the participative potential of women in the development process as well as conscientizing women on their rights and roles. There is the need for such efforts that could increase the awareness of women and improve their participation as equal citizens in national development. Further, voluntary agencies should play a surveillance role and observe, explore and analyse the extent to which social legislations implemented for women have actually benefited them. They should also act as pressure groups to better enforcement of laws for women.

At present, there is no proper mechanism of coordination among different voluntary agencies working for the development of women. An effective mechanism for coordination between the government and the voluntary agencies is also to be ensured. CAPART and CSWB are appropriately situated to make efforts for more effective coordination and implementation of various programmes for women through voluntary organizations. For them to perform this role effectively, there should be a proper representation of grass roots women's organizations in CAPART and CSWB, that can serve as pressure groups. There is also the need for a continuous flow of information from government to voluntary agencies and vice versa through such mechanisms as a clearing house for information.

A focal point is desirable in the rural areas to encourage women's voluntary activities. Mahila Mandals and women's groups at the village or community level should be organized or revived and encouraged to register and function as women's institutions for undertaking socio-economic programmes. These institutions should be effectively linked with the various development and service agencies, offering training facilities for income generations as well as enhanced awareness among women. This linkage will enable women to absorb institutional finance for the development of viable economic activities. Particular attention will need to be given to the training of the Mahila Mandal functionaries and women's group organizers and provide them an orientation to development perspective rather than purely welfare approaches.

The CSWB which has been the coordinating agency for voluntary action for women and children, must respond to the new thrust of government policy meant for women and recast its own programmes.

Greater coordination and cooperation among NGOs is called for to avoid duplication of services. Greater funding for networking among NGOs must be provided. This will ensure more efficient utilization of funds and greater coverage of programmes. Government support to voluntary agencies for providing assistance to women in distress, including the running of crisis centres and short stay homes must be expanded. Para legal training must be an integral part of such efforts.

Voluntary agencies must be increasingly involved in the provision of employment and supportive services for women.

The National Literacy Mission must involve women's organizations in a big way.

The voluntary sector should increasingly be involved to act as a catalyst/intermediary in organizing women for collective action.

There is the need to document success stories of major NGOs in India and learn from their success and failures. Further, it is necessary to analyse the cost-benefit of NGO Projects versus governmental projects, i.e., both economic and social costs. It would also be critical to total the overall number of women reached by NGOs in India. The areas of activities and fields of success would also highlight their strengths and limitations.

In order to ensure that the security and integrity of the nation are preserved, there is a need to adopt suitable policies to ensure that voluntary agencies abide by the rules governing the receipt and utilization of foreign grants and submit audited accounts, returns and reports periodically.

Identity cards should be issued to workers of voluntary agencies who are dealing with cases of atrocities against women, as is already being done in some districts.

In order to have sufficient infrastructure and facilities, there is need to mobilize more resources for voluntary agencies which are engaged in welfare and development of women.

There is a need to decentralize the planning process to stimulate local people's participation in planning, implementation, monitoring and evaluation of development projects. A suitable mechanism should be evolved to involve voluntary agencies and other people's institutions at various stages of developmental programmes /projects. Voluntary agencies should further ensure the participation of poor women in the development process.

General Suggestions

In the preceding chapters recommendations have been made sectorally with a view to strengthening women's roles therein. Certain important issues, however, impinge on all spheres of women's lives and work. With a view to enhancing women's status and capacities to participate in the process of nation building, the following general recommendations are made:

The overall approach of this National Perspective Plan is to perceive women in a holistic manner. While the programmes for women will continue to be implemented by different ministries as part of their department plans, it is essential to have a strong inter-ministerial coordination and monitoring body along with its own supportive facilities service by the Department of Women and Child Development (Proposed infrastructure at Annexure 1).

All ministries must reflect the concern for the all round development of women. The concerned ministries must have women's cell which currently only exists in the Ministries of Labour, Small-Scale Industry, Science and Technology and Rural Development. It is essential that the new policy thrust for women's development should be reflected in the Planning Commission as well as the State Planning Boards. The National Commission on Self-Employed Women and Women in the Informal Sector, has also independently concluded that the Planning Commission and State Planning Boards need to focus their attention sharply on the realistic situation of (labouring) women.

An essential prerequisite for the implementation of these new policy directives would be a women's unit in the Planning Commission, to redefine categories of data collection for women, modify existing terminology and identify gaps in data collection relating to women and to give direction to plans and programmes for women's development. It is also essential to analyse the impact of the different macro policies on women while planning new endeavours.

Financial and fiscal resources should be apportioned and preferential allocations for women's employment in mainstream programmes and projects should be made. This would imply the rationalization on resource allocation within mainstream programmes so as to benefit women, rather than only seeking separate allocations for women. Critical emphasis must be placed on rate of investment in women preferred industries and occupations.

At the State level, the Departments/ Directorates of Women's Development should be initiated. Currently, there is no separate department of women in many States. Social welfare, handicapped, Scheduled Castes and Scheduled Tribes are subjects that are bracketed together with the development of women at the State level. This new department could also be the State level implementation body for the programmes/ policies of the Department of Women and Child Development of the Government of India.

In terms of programme implementation, the two major implementing bodies envisaged, are the Social Welfare Boards and the Women's Development Corporations. There can be a rationalization of service provision between these two bodies. The State Social Welfare Advisory Boards could eventually concentrate on implementing welfare/supportive programmes for women (homes for women in distress, working women's hostels, counselling centres for legal aid and paralegal training, condensed courses, etc.). Women Development Corporations would be responsible for the implementation of economic programmes through non-governmental and governmental agencies/ departments wherever necessary, concentrating on technical inputs like credit, marketing, design development, etc., and reaching out to women at the district and village levels.

Women should be entitled to a package of services at the block level created by the convergence of schemes such as Development of Women and Children in Rural Areas (DWCRA), Integrated Child Development Schemes (ICDS), Adult Education, Health Care, etc., at the grass roots administrative level. Every district should have a coordinator to assist in the integration of these programmes aimed at the development of women. The coordinator will also be responsible for motivating local planning of programmes and assist in their implementation and provide feedback for effective planning and evaluation. Since decentralization of planning monitoring and implementation of development programmes for women is suggested as also devolution of finance at district level, appointment of District coordinators for women's programmes would facilitate this process, and control over finance would empower them. The National Commission on Self-Employed Women and Women in the Informal Sector has also recommended the appointment of District Coordination Officers to be responsible for planning, monitoring, coordination and evaluation of the programmes affecting women. Rationalization of functionaries at the block and village levels to ensure coordination of programmes affecting women at the grass roots level also needs to be undertaken.

There are today sufficient number of programmes in the Government of India as well as innovative programmes in many States and sectors. What is needed is not merely larger resource allocation but technical inputs for greater effectiveness of these programmes, to guarantee better resource utilization. Emphasis has to be placed on more effective planning, monitoring and evaluation of existing programmes through a result oriented mechanism operating at different levels.

Recognizing that a critical input for women's development would be a new thrust to training and wider dissemination of information backed by research data and documentation. It is proposed to set up a National Resource Centre for Women. This resource centre would translate national developmental needs of women into a systematic grid of programmes and schemes for training at different levels in skills/ knowledge/ attitudes. The centre would identify and if necessary, strengthen existing governmental and non-governmental agencies including women's universities /women's centres and colleges through which the training, research/ dissemination could be carried out. The National Commission on Self-Employed Women and Women in Informal Sector has also recommended the need for a National Institute to cater to women's training as well as formulate guidelines and help the other constituent units at the State level, Divisional levels and district level to carry out training programmes.

Reorientation and sensitization of the administrative machinery at all levels in the Government of India, the States, as well as specialized technical agencies (both Government and Voluntary) to the issues of women in development is essential. Three levels of orientation are necessary, i.e., at the policy and planning levels, at the district or intermediary level, and at the block and village levels. The training of functionaries and their orientation to women's issues must also be in the right perspective, i.e., women should be perceived as producers and participants, not clients for welfare. The dynamic role of women's contribution to the national economy as partners and equal citizens must be reiterated and translated into programmes and projects. The National Resource Centre would be responsible for revamping the existing content/ methodology and monitoring of training at all levels.

A special division should be created in the Department of Women and Child Development for the enforcement of law for women. The officer in charge may be designated Commissioner for Women's Rights and must liaise with the various Special Cells for women created by the police, the CBI as well as with the Departments of Public Grievances at Centre and State levels as also the Women's Cell in the Home Ministry. This division will be concerned with the enforcement of law to ensure women's rights, to facilitate action oriented research in needs such as discrimination against women, protection at work, etc. The Census in future must take into account women's unpaid work in the household and outside as well as the value added in performing her many survival tasks for the family. A greater conceptual clarity has to emerge on 'work' and 'non-work' as well as a distinction between work that produces economic value and other activities that are consumption oriented.

Part - III

Emancipation

Eight

Share in the Process

Indian's as a nation, while granting equality of rights to men and women in society implicitly accept a sharp distinction between men's spheres and women's spheres and between masculine roles and feminine roles. Realization of true parity between the sexes granted by the Constitution will be possible only when conceptions and attitudes of the people are brought at par with it.

An overview of masculine and feminine spheres and roles in our society suggests that the inventory of activities considered proper for women and expected of them is not uniform all over India. Some basic notions about male and female roles, however, appear to be common.

The Primary Association

Women are primarily associated with the home and man with the outside world. As home-makers women are expected to look after domestic chores, such as cooking and serving food, processing and storage of food, and cleaning the house. Woman's contribution to productive activities or to actual earnings of the family varies at different socio-economic levels and in different regions. Thus women, whether they work in the fields, factories or mines, or work at construction sites, or those who are engaged in household industries, or in white collar jobs, all of them are expected to be home-makers along with those who confine themselves exclusively to home-making activities. Housewives and mothers are the feminine roles. In the cultural understanding of the people, homemaking like child-bearing and also child-rearing cannot be distinguished from femininity. In other words these are sex-linked roles for women.

According to convention, participation in decision making for the community and the exercise of political power is regarded exclusively as the man's sphere. This is clear from the entirely male composition of the traditional Panchayats, either of villages or of caste groups including caste-like groups among Muslims.

By and large manual work for one's own house is to be done by women, as they are considered derogatory for men. They may perform them only under special circumstances, for instance, men may cook when women are disabled by illness or confinement. For community feasts cooking by men from within the group is a common feature at the lower socio-economic levels. Cooking, tailoring or sewing can be taken up as a vocation by men. Thus, suitability of women for these tasks appears to be a myth.

Broad regional patterns which show that there is no uniformity in the type and quantum of work expected of women also point towards this. What a woman does in one society or region is often dubbed as non-feminine in another. Weaving is the monopoly of woman in the North Eastern Hill areas, whereas in the lower parts of Himachal Pradesh it is a male activity. In Maharashtra and parts of South India it is done by men and women together and the woman is an indispensable assistant. Phulkari work of the Punjab is a women's craft whereas embroidery in Kashmir is done only by men.

In agricultural activities there are significant regional differences in the parts played by men and women. It is generally stated that men are supposed to do the heavier work. This is a supposition or belief which is not borne out by facts or by a cross regional survey of India. Men's tasks are not necessarily more arduous. What is more important is that men do work which is considered more prestigious. Ploughing and sowing in many parts and all the work of transportation by bullock-cart and large-scale marketing of produce are the domain of men. In the hills, women's contribution to the economy is distinctly higher than that of men, in addition to household work which is very burdensome, for example, bringing water from far-off places, keeping a vigil throughout the night to scare the wild animals away. "In Bashahr, Chamba and Mandi, women help their mates in wood-chopping. While men fell the trees women slice the timber. They carry the timber on their backs from the place where it is sawed to the place from where it is to be floated down the riven. They have been seen carrying logs weighing anywhere between 200 to 300 pounds with perfect ease and equanimity". These are the unpaid family workers of rural India.

In the middle-class (which constitutes an extremely amorphous category) the spheres of men and women are more sharply defined. Ordinarily, all the work that women do is viewed collectively as being an important component of feminine roles and it is not forgotten, that they are being performed by those, who have a certain identity in the context of the family, i.e. as mother, as wife, as sister, and so on. Since women are mostly confined to the domestic sphere, their work falls into entirely different sectors. Where the family business consists of grocery, knitwear, embroidery, snacks, and other things which can be made at home, women are the main workers behind the scene. These are the unpaid family workers who may not be returned in the census under the category of workers. Most of the work that women do in the domestic set up is semi-skilled. There is a clear differentiation between work done for one's own household and that done for others, so the question of doing this category of work for others does not arise. It is only in unfortunate circumstances that women of middle-classes, who have no other qualifications and skills, may be forced to do these jobs as a means of earning a livelihood; crafts like knitting, tailoring and embroidery are in some cases adopted by women to make small personal earnings, sometimes without the knowledge of husbands. Ideas of personal and family prestige are strong at this level; people take pride in the fact that their women do not go out of homes to work for others.

This traditional concept of women's role is gradually changing as girls have started taking up white collar jobs. In some families, the earnings of the girl are set aside for providing her dowry and marriage expenses, but gradually, the inhibition of the parents to be supported by the earnings of a daughter are also breaking down. There are extreme cases of parents not wanting the daughter to get married, as it would deprive them of her earnings.

Amongst the well-to-do also the spheres of men and women are well-defined and separate. Even though with domestic help, the burden of drudgery does not fall on the woman, but she is still expected to run the home and bring up the children. Her precise activities would depend upon a rural or urban setting, level of education norms of segregation and seclusion, notions of purity and pollution. Homemaking is raised to a fine art and trifling details assume exaggerated importance, but even here there is insistence on a role differentiation, according to conventions.

On the question intended to evoke responses on the pattern of division of labour by sex in the family, 84.1 per cent respondents said that cooking is entirely a woman's job; only 3.84 per cent said that it is shared equally. As for sweeping and cleaning the house only 3.94 per cent said that the work is equally shared and only 2.14 per cent said that the work of cleaning the utensils is equally shared. These two activities were undertaken only or mainly by men in less than 1 per cent cases. Washing of clothes is shared by men to some extent. In comparison to this, only 50.74 per cent respondents said that care of children was in the hands of women, either entirely or mainly; 28.90 per cent said it was shared equally, and 10.05 per cent said that men did it entirely. Sharing in decision making about the household expenditure reveals a different pattern. Only in 28.18 per cent cases, expenditure on food was decided entirely by women. Decision making seems to have been largely shared (48.48 per cent) by men and women. In 33.96 per cent cases decision about expenditure on education is entirely in the hands of men, as compared to 9.66 per cent cases in which it is mainly in the hands of women. Responses clearly indicate a pattern in which, besides equal sharing in decision making, more women take decisions about the kitchen, other domestic matters and matters concerning the future of the daughters. Men, rather than the women, more often exercise their judgement regarding choice of school, type of education and job the son should take. As is to be expected, various sociological and anthropological studies of village and of urban localities and communities clearly point towards male and female spheres of activity. For example, in Gore's sample of Aggarwal families in and around Delhi, women were expected to remain at home and look after the kitchen. 80 per cent of the women were busy exclusively with household work. They did not handle the money. Desai's findings based on the replies given by 369 married women students tell us that a majority of men did not share the household work. A study of 500 college students of Jhansi in UP brings out a sharp contrast between the daily routine of boys and girls, between the restrictions on girls and relative freedom of movement for boys and between the range of exposure to the outside world and to their travel.

Notions of distinctiveness between the spheres of men and women, patterns of division of labour, and expectations of differential behaviour between the sexes have a direct bearing on the process of socialization, on opportunities provided for the education and training of girls, on the kinds of ideals projected before them, on the kinds of expectations they come to have, from life, and on the way they conduct their lives.

In the process of preparation for adult roles the spheres are distinct. However, amongst the enlightened sections this distinction may not be emphasized, but even here feminine tasks and over all abilities are assumed to be different. A girl has to be prepared for feminine roles as conceived by the stratum to which she belongs. Parents also have to take note of the attitude of the world outside the home, and special protection is needed for girls.

In the middle-classes, distinction between femininity and masculinity gets crystallized for the children in the pattern of domestic responsibilities, distribution of financial resources, and planning for the future. Domestic work is the domain of women and in very few families are the boys asked to share it. They may be asked to lend a helping hand in making purchases and running errands, bringing medicine, and escorting sisters, but household chores are beneath their dignity. Boys interested in cooking, knitting, or embroidery hardly ever get any encouragement from the family members, instead they are often ridiculed and discouraged.

Girls are sent to school but they are not sufficiently motivated to achieve excellence; neglect of studies and lack of interest is easily condoned. Very few parents visualize a career for daughters. Their main interest lies in finding a good match for them. Still many parents view education as security for unforeseen eventualities. Even where school or college performance is praised, lack of interest in household work is not condoned. Girls have to live a constricted life. In allocation of scarce resources, a daughter's education is often the first casualty. Parents are not inclined to undergo the inconvenience and strains involved in giving proper facilities to the daughter for better performance. At this level also girls may have to drop out because of family circumstances such as mother's illness or death. Attending functions like weddings and other ceremonies are considered more important than a daughter's education.

In the middle-class families there is a premium on boys' education for it is essential to enable him to get a job. Parents are ready to make all kind of sacrifices for the education of boys. Despite all the misgivings of modern times, they still hope that their efforts will bring them comfort in old age. Various sociological studies clearly bring out the fact that if the family does not have enough resources, even if the girl is brighter her brother will be sent for higher education and she will be told that ultimately she has to mind the kitchen. In fact, what is not always stated in so many words is the culturally determined attitude, that conservative parents cannot and should not depend upon a daughter for support.

It is necessary to note the effects of this emphasis of feminine roles on the development of personality and identity formation for girls. Girls receive informal education for roles which they are expected to perform in adult life. Many give up their ambition to take up career as these are regarded as incompatible with smooth and peaceful family life. They learn early in life that society expects greater flexibility of mind, capacity to adjust, and submissiveness from a woman. In respect of ideologies and values, girls feel that it is no use their committing themselves to any particular ideology because they may not be allowed to adhere to it after getting married.

Thus the constraints, visible as well as invisible, that are placed on girls have an effect on their personalities. Some of these girls join the workforce of the country as white collar workers, in professions and even take up challenging careers like politics. This is either before marriage or after marriage. When married women work outside the home they encounter problems of harmonizing their two roles. They have to evolve a pattern in which they can perform the two roles satisfactorily.

At the relatively lower economic level, both in the rural and urban sections, girls start their contribution to the running of household much earlier than boys. They take care of the younger siblings, help the mother in various domestic chores, and also participate in work of production which falls in the feminine sphere, or activities which fetch some extra income.

Both as preparation for adult roles and as a contribution to the work of the household, the girls' share is important. It is depressing to find that a fairly large proportion of girls are still out of school. In the rural areas there is a lurking fear that education makes girls less useful for adult feminine roles. If they get a little education they develop a distaste for the kind of work expected of them in the village and aspire to get married in towns. In fact, this problem is very real for the cultivators and artisans. It was voiced before the committee in very strong words in Himachal Pradesh and Andhra Pradesh. Education does alienate its recipients from their environment and creates a distaste for manual work.

Home and Work

In a discussion of the dual role of women we may first take note of the quantum of labour, both domestic and extra domestic. In the rural areas, even those who are confined in the home, because of purdah or other norms of respectability, contribute hard labour in activities such as running a dairy processing and storage of grains and other foodstuffs, spinning, coir-making, preparation of cow dung manure, and so forth. It has been seen that a woman's direct contribution to the family economy and her actual control over many of the products gives her considerable power and initiative. Their economic value to the family and their own capacity to earn a living frees them particularly from rigid family controls, and bestows on them a certain measure of autonomy. In contrast the lower middle-class women of urban areas, who have little education and no independent source of income, are in a less advantageous position because of stricter norms of behaviour and almost total dependence on men.

In the social context, due to the low status attached to manual labour in our society and the cultural value associated with women's confinement to home, the work of rural and urban women as wage labourers, unskilled factory workers and menials is not conducive to a better status.

The average woman in rural areas can give little attention to the bringing up of her children. With dual roles and without any mechanical aids for housework, she is definitely overworked. So also are the women engaged in unskilled or semiskilled work in organised and unorganised sectors in urban areas. Overwork and more than a culturally acquired attitude of unconcern about public affairs, is responsible for the limited participation of women in activities like those of the trade unions or political parties. They may become vocal and assertive only when non-availability of essential commodities, or escalating prices threaten to upset their household budget and routine.

It is necessary to assess the status of housewives of the middle and upper economic strata belonging to the urban areas, and also the urbanized rural families. Closely allied to this is the appraisal of the gains achieved in terms of status, by the women who have joined the workforce in white collar professions. The reform movements for the education of women in the late nineteenth and early twentieth century, along with the realization of the need for a measure of economic independence towards the late twenties and thirties of this century, helped to improve the position of women of this class to a large extent. The passing of Hindu Women's Right to Property Acts of 1929 and 1937 was an important measure to give widows some economic independence. Later, organised efforts were made to provide remunerative work to such women. As the number of helpless women with education upto higher secondary or graduation is increasing, need for work which suit their earlier status and which they can take up only after a brief training is also increasing. Desertion and widowhood in this class often result in a sharp fall in the composite social status of the woman.

Initially society accepted a widow's gainful employment and gradually a young unmarried girl's employment till she got married received approval. Post 1940, the Second World War gave an impetus to women's employment and even married women came forward to take up gainful employment. In the post-Independence period, the structure of opportunities expanded, education qualified more and more women for a variety of jobs, and economic compulsions increased.

The socio-cultural environment of India has changed rapidly in the last five decades, especially in the quarter century after the attainment of India's independence. Forces of modernization continue to make a powerful impact and the society has to respond to the new needs and urges of the people. Mahatma Gandhi and other leaders who combined in them the roles of social reformers and political leaders projected the vision of a new society; the humble and the oppressed were to get a new deal and the women were to secure a measure of emancipation in the society visualized by them. It is true that their philosophy and action did not bring about an instant transformation in social attitudes towards the women but it did nevertheless have a powerful effect, and over the decades legitimized many of the new roles contemplated for women. A series of powerful forces are in operation today to bring about perceptible changes in the social milieu. Education, with all its inadequacies, has made a definite impact. It opens up an arena in which women can compete freely with men and prove themselves equally worthy. It also creates for them new avenues in the competitive employment market. The mass media, especially the film and radio, despite their faulty conceptualization and constricted reach have contributed towards refashioning social images and goals. The most significant impetus to change has been provided, however, by demographic pressures and economic compulsions. These have been responsible for women seeking to take advantage of the new structure of economic opportunities. Politicization and articulation of new ideologies has acquired a new meaning and a heightened significance in the changing economic context. In consequence, the legitimacy of the new roles for women is increasingly becoming a social reality. At least on the overt level, the attitude to women has undergone significant modifications, although on the covert level the alteration in the basic attitude structure does not keep pace with the more explicit changes. Thus we find that there is considerable role enhancement, or at any rate a role expansion for women. Beyond their traditional roles they are called upon to assume several new roles also. This is particularly true for the upper stratum of the lower class and for the middle strata of the entire society in which education has been taken up as a mark of social respectability and also as an instrument of economic gain.

The persistence of traditional norms in regard to women's essentially domestic roles and the addition of new work roles in the wider society has created problems of adjustment for them. It has added to their burdens. Everyday domestic chores plus full time employment imply a workload that cannot be managed easily by them. On the domestic front there is little help; they cannot neglect their responsibilities in this sphere. The in-laws and even the husband and the children do not extend to them the measure of sympathy and support they need. Added to this are the latest prejudices and built-in rivalries that are constantly at work in the home atmosphere. These contribute considerably to the psychological stress that a working woman has to undergo. The lot of the working woman, unless she has a really well-paid job and a set of educated family members who are attuned to her psychological needs and physical capabilities is still deplorable. She has in fact to carry on two full time jobs leaving her little time for rest and leisure or for self improvement. The pattern for social interaction demanded by her out-of-home job cannot be smoothly worked out: the demands of the home and the built-in prejudices create impediments that cannot be managed easily.

New lifestyles of women are now visible. In pre-independence days some women had voluntarily decided against marriage in order to devote their life to the national cause or social service. Today in the professions; services, and in the field of social work, we have a number of successful unmarried women who enjoy high status. Along with married women, who are primarily housewives, there are women who combine housework and job, and there are also those who may return to their work or take up a job after their children have grown up.

The pace of change in attitude to women working outside the home or participating in public life has been slow and uneven. These attitudes are related to conceptions about women's inherent attitudes and capacities, her proper sphere of work, and man-woman relationships. Thus, education as a field of employment is more popular because the hours of work are more or less fixed, work at home and outside can be satisfactorily combined, and the work involves less contact with men. Even in mixed schools and institutions of higher education, contact with male colleagues does not have to be close. Work in the field of education does not conflict with traditional norms of femininity.

Although nursing does not conflict with the feminine ideal of service, the job involves contact with impure objects, contact with male patients, doctors and paramedical personnel, and odd hours of work, during night and day. It is only in recent years that nursing is becoming a more respectable and therefore acceptable calling in some regions.

Entry of women in films or the professional theatre had been frowned upon by almost all sections of the community. In many regions participation in domestic performances was associated with particular castes and communities whose women were professional dancers and singers. Now the situation has improved, though the prejudice still persists. In the past, dancing and singing were associated with courtesans only, but gradually with the cultural renaissance, they are becoming more acceptable to society. Giving a remunerative performance before an audience may be accepted in large cities, but it would still be considered unbecoming for the wife or daughter-in-law in small towns. The All India Radio had greatly helped in weakening this prejudice. Teaching music or dancing or organising music programmes is now acceptable. However, living by music or dance performances alone is laden with problems which a woman finds difficult to manage as a career.

In small towns and villages, young women, more so unmarried girls, find it very difficult to work because of the attitude of the people. A touring job is even more difficult. If a girl has been brought up on a traditional home she is likely to be handicapped by her own personality, and if she has been brought up in a modern atmosphere she is likely to create more misunderstanding.

In recent years women have done well in administrative jobs. But in this field the difficulties are of a somewhat different nature. At the utmost, men are prepared to accept a woman as an equal, but men still do not relish working under a woman superior. The traditional conception of women's limitations and her proper place were responsible for the well-known episode in Uttar Pradesh when the former chief minister Charan Singh stated that women officers should not be entrusted with administrative responsibility. He thought that women were unfit for administrative jobs. The Press said that the chief minister was of the opinion that women were too 'delicate' to be entrusted with executive jobs. He also refused to meet a delegation of women officers wanting to convey their protest. Earlier, he had abolished the Mahila Yojana. According to press reports he exhorted the women to go back to their kitchens and look after their children.

This may be an extreme case but it does indicate a certain mind-set of thinking. There are many who share this view and relate the stories about the stupidity and failures of women in high positions, but who adopt a progressive posture in public. The view that women do not possess the essential attributes of an officer to function in high executive ranks cannot be attributed to male chauvinism or a conservative attitude alone. Even some women appear to assume it tacitly. For example, Shivani, a popular woman writer in Hindi, has portrayed a fictitious woman officer of the Indian Administrative Service in a manner that highlights the frailty of woman. Her novelette on this theme was serialized in a popular weekly and later issued in book form. The book leaves an unmistakable impression in the minds of the common reader that women do not quite measure up to positions of higher authority.

The problems connected with dual roles of women may be viewed as those of burden of work, interpersonal relations within the family, and of role conflict. Gainful employment of wives is often viewed with a degree of ambivalence by men. It is approved because it lessens the financial burden and raises the standard of living. However, it can be a source of disruption in the smooth running of the household. The other aspect is the economic independence of women, which is resented by many husbands. It is difficult to say how many women are in a position to take decisions regarding their own earnings. According to a study the freedom of association and movement which outdoor work involves, is not approved of in many homes and puts a stigma on working women. Even in those regions and communities which have had a long tradition of women working outside the home, husbands still do not tolerate women coming home late from office.

Most men do not want to give up their traditionally superior position in the family and do not offer any assistance to their wives in domestic chores. In middle-class families where they cannot afford domestic help and the husband does not share any work, the burden on the wife can become unbearable. A change in older attitudes and values is essential for achieving rationalization of the load of the work. During our tours, we were repeatedly told that men while living in the West helped their wives with domestic chores but when they returned to India, they stopped giving this practice.

Often women themselves do not like the idea of their husbands doing domestic chores as they consider that to be a feminine role. The attitude of relatives and neighbours is also unfavourable. They criticize working women as bad mothers and inefficient housewives. A study focussed largely on middle-class working women of Patna reveals that husbands of 131 respondents thought that it was the wife's duty to carry out household jobs and to look after children. Sixty six were of the opinion that since both were working, it was the duty of the husband to share some responsibility. Many women have to leave their jobs in order to be able to do their household duties satisfactorily. This, however, depends on the financial condition of the family.

Although the in-laws still tend to expect the same amount of attention from a working woman as they would from a non-working woman, there are positive indications that the situation is changing. When the woman's earning is an absolute necessity for the family or if the woman has a well-paid and high status job, she does get consideration.

It is often remarked that if the woman has to spend most of her income on servants and conveyance her employment is of no consequence. But it is seldom understood that a career in itself has its rewards and satisfaction.

The situation of women alternating between work and home leads to a role conflict. Some of them develop a feeling of guilt that they are unable to look after the children and home properly. Working women tend to pamper their children because they want to make up for what they consider to be lack of proper attention on their part. This is because of their role perception rooted in their socialization and the expectations of other members of the family. It is not realized that a child does not need the continued presence of its mother for its proper growth, nor is it realized that the other parent is as important for the healthy growth of the child. Role conflict makes working women tire themselves out giving personal service to the husband and attending to various tasks which are often beyond their physical capacity and endurance.

Besides the strains of shouldering the burden of dual roles and of facing a role conflict, there is often another kind of strain arising from a lack of adjustment between a woman's position at home and in the place of work. She may be better educated and lesser paid than the husband but he claims absolute superiority over her at home. According to Promilla Kapur (1970): "The husband's denial of the right of the wife over her own earned money or her privileges to relax or to move about freely.. was found to be related to his patriarchal attitude towards wife's privileges and obligations."

But the problem of status inconsistency is deeper than this. Unfortunately our society is extremely status conscious and status bound. If the wife enjoys a higher status in her work place, her circle of associates are also of higher status, and however the wife may try not to bring in her office status at home, the husband's adjustment with her becomes difficult. He tends to consider it a reversal of roles. Such a husband tends to become more domineering. Sometimes the wife is also to be blamed, for she too is a part of the status conscious society.

The situation in which the husband is employed in an inferior position in the same office or directly under the wife is perhaps the worst. Many wives are known to have deliberately refused promotions, in order to maintain peace in the family. Thus, when the position of the husband as not the principal breadwinner, as not superior to the wife, or his authority in the family being challenged is when serious problems can arise.

Another aspect of status inconsistency emerges in situations in which a wife has a relatively low status job with limited earnings. For example, nurses marrying doctors are found to leave their occupation mainly of reasons of status. Women working in low paid/status jobs generally leave their jobs after marrying businessmen or executives and thus waste their training, aptitude, and experience. It has been found that sometimes these earnings of the wife may be necessary for the household, and because of the presence of relatives or servants in the house, the wife may not be occupied fully at home, but still her working in low status jobs is not allowed, for it brings down the status of the husband. An idle wife attuned to the life pattern of the husband is more appreciated. It is seen that a woman is not allowed to work in low status positions even in an honorary capacity. By leaving their jobs women are forced to withdraw the support that they were giving to their needy parents or siblings prior to marriage.

It should be a woman's right to play a dual role. A woman should not be penalized for her important contribution as mother in the perpetuation of society. Childbearing is treated as purely a matter concerning women and hence the attitude that a woman must either give up her job or her right to bear children. A distinction between man's work and woman's work in respect of household jobs will have to be removed. If what are called woman's jobs come to be respected by society, men will cease to hesitate doing these jobs. This attitude needs to be built into the socialization process of children, both in the home and in the school.

It is necessary to make adequate provisions to give women opportunity to do both their jobs efficiently and satisfactorily. To this end, it is necessary to provide for creches, nurseries, and labour saving devices. Since all families cannot afford to buy gadgets it will be necessary to provide gadgets to do washing, vegetable chopping, preparing chapati and such other things which make household work a drudgery.

In the absence of many social and physical amenities like labour saving devices, easy transport, creches, inexpensive processed foods, as also conditions of service, such as transfers many women will have to remain principally mothers and housewives. Some may have to confine themselves to the role of a housewife while the children are young. If family is important, home-making is so too.

The inputs of household work and the mothers' role in rearing of children need to be recognized by the family and the society at large.

The housewife certainly contributes, even though it may be indirectly, towards a stable national economy by consolidating the economic structure of her own home. Her efficient management of her home alone ensures the saving potentiality of her earning husband. Recognition of her work for the purposes of 'national accounting' would certainly enhance the status of woman and acknowledge the debt of society to her.

Some Special Problems

In a rapidly changing and culturally differentiated society, a slow process of adjustment in its social value system and rigidity of its institutions, results in various forms of incongruous behaviour. The changing social patterns without restructuring or redefining social values and norms always cause deviant behaviour. Structural changes in the socio-economic system are needed for a smooth process of adjustment.

The problems of women discussed in this section cannot be tackled by legal methods of penalization and prevention alone but by providing 'institutional infrastructure' for their reform and rehabilitation. The gap in the perception of their needs and available opportunities, are conducive to exploitation of the weaker section of society and cannot be offset by development programmes alone but by adequate understanding of the magnitude and intricacies of the problem and providing supportive institutional framework.

Prostitution

Prostitution is the worst form of exploitation of women and as an institution it speaks of man's tolerance of this exploitation on an organised level in society. Women are viewed solely as a sex object and as an outlet for man's baser instincts. The condemnation of the woman and not the man is the continuance of the standards of dual morality which prevail in most countries with regard to men and women. Some societies have continued to regard prostitution as a necessary evil and have tolerated it as such.

The social anthropologists' explanation of prostitution is that it has been in existence in some form or the other as long as society has attempted to regulate and control sex relationships through the institutions of marriage and family. Promiscuity or sexual communism preceded marriage and family, and sex was shared by all without any taboo or control. With the institutionalization of sex behaviour through marriage and particularly in society which lays great emphasis on the chastity of its women, prostitutes became an evil of necessity. In a way, they helped to retain the chastity and purity of women in society and hence performed a social function. Even now among certain tribal communities entrance of women into commercialized prostitution is a recent phenomenon and has only started with the advent of outsiders into the tribal community. In tribal communities which always, enjoyed a certain degree of sexual freedom, the institution of prostitution did not exist. According to Rao and Rao in Prostitutes of Hyderabad: "In India, the emphasis on chastity value prior to marriage compelled women of deflowered innocence to court prostitution. Dowry among the upper castes has been a constraint in marriage and some frustrated women were forced to become prostitutes." Rao and Rao further say: In parts of Andhra Pradesh, college girls, and young women practise prostitution and save their earnings. Some even have passbooks in which they indicate their savings which they say will form their dowry to enable them to make a decent marriage. "Child marriages and social discouragement of re-marriage of young widows have greatly helped in the recruitment of prostitutes from village in India. Caste inequality and sex exploitation by the economically well off castes are other factors."

In the 19th century, certain social customs were responsible for many women resorting to this profession, who were otherwise outside the hereditary and customary groups of prostitutes. The spread of child marriages, early widowhood, social taboos on widow remarriages, caste rigidity, dowry system and the practice of polygamy and polyandry among certain communities, the decay in the joint family system, and the generally low status accorded to women in society contributed to women being driven to prostitution as the only occupation for livelihood. At the same time, the beginning of industrialization and consequent urbanization in the latter part of the 19th and early 20th century, drew in large number of women other than hereditary prostitutes into this profession. One reason was the wide sex disparity in the big cities when the migrant worker who had to leave his family behind in the village for mainly economic reasons, became a customer for the prostitute.

Briefly, the following social and religious customs which may have contributed directly or indirectly to prostitution are enumerated as follows according to H.R. Trivedi from a survey on "Exploitation of SC Women" undertaken by the Harijan Sevak Sangh.

The Devdasi system which was so widespread in pre-Independence India that it necessitated legal measures such as the Madras Devdasi Prevention and Dedication Act of 1947 and the Bombay Devdasi Protection Act of 1954 is a system that continues today in parts of Tamil Nadu, Mysore, Andhra Pradesh and Orissa, practised particularly by the lower castes. A study conducted in Bombay in the mid sixties reported that as many as 30 per cent of the Bombay prostitutes were of Devdasi origin. In a study of the Bijapur district, girls are still dedicated to the temples amongst certain sections of the lower castes and enter the occupation with the consent of the parents. No social stigma is attached to this. The reason is mainly economic. These girls are also taken out of the town or village by an agent and a large part of the earnings of the Devdasis goes to the family members and agents.

Prostitution has been the traditional occupation among certain castes, for instance, the Naiks from the hilly regions of Uttar Pradesh where the woman is traditionally the breadwinner and the men have to marry from another caste, as their own womenfolk take to prostitution. The Uttar Pradesh Naik Girls' Protection Act was passed as early as 1929, but the practice continues even today and

Punekar and Rao's study indicated that 43 per cent of the prostitutes were drawn from the Naiks of Uttar Pradesh.

Certain castes practise historical and traditional prostitution. A survey conducted in the Raipur and Raigarh districts for the Committee on the Status of Women found that very loose marriage ties in which adultery is scarcely regarded as an offence, encourage prostitution. "A woman may go and live openly with other men and her husband will take her back or two men each will place their spouse at each other's disposal". Women of the lower castes earn money and support themselves through prostitution which is carried on at the weekly bazaars or fairs. The women have historically been exploited by the higher castes, and are often handed over or mortgaged temporarily to creditors on return of loan. The men of such communities indulged in drinking and gambling and encourage their woman to earn money for them and also the emergence of the new industrial towns has encouraged commercialization of prostitution. The survey also found that agents and intermediaries come from outside the community and parents, in-laws and husbands take the initiative in getting women into prostitution for commercial gain. A large part of the income is sent back to the families. Prostitution is the only way open to women to earn a livelihood for the family. No stigma is attached to the woman if she brings wealth or income from prostitution to her natal or conjugal home.

A recent study of the immoral trafficking in women from the Purola Block of Uttarkashi district (UP) reveals that a large number of girls from the lower socio-economic communities go in for prostitution. In 1969, 45 women had entered and remained in this profession for three years. It was estimated that about approximately 500 families were dependent on this profession on account of extreme poverty. 60 per cent of girls from Rawain area were operating in Delhi and 77 agents were engaged in procuring women for prostitution. The causes for prostitution were the high bride-price and consequent indebtedness of the couple who were forced to work as bonded labour. The girl was then compelled to earn money to free the family from this debt through prostitution. In other cases, a man from a higher caste may pay bride-price and contract a marriage with one or more girls of a poor family and take her to Delhi and sell her into the trade. In other cases, Delhi brothel-keepers used girls from Purola to entice other girls or their cousins, etc., by showing them the easy life they could enjoy in the brothels. According to one report the history of this traffic in the Rawain area is about 60 years old, but it has increased recently, with the entrance of officials and traders.

Among the Bajgi caste in Purola region its occupation in service of the temple may be closely connected with the large number of women who go into the trade. Though the Devdasi system as such does not exist much now, certain castes closely connected with work of the temple are more prone to prostitution. Families of majority of these prostitutes are landless and up to 75 per cent bonded for life to upper caste money lenders. Many of these communities belonging to lower socio-economic groups practise polyandry due to high bride-price. This may be sociological cause for the ease with which the women descend into prostitution. Women generally occupy a very low social position and labour incessantly in homes and in the field once they are bought or sold. Trafficking is on the increase in these regions and sometimes higher castes or powerful men in the village act as agents and are in liaison with procurers and brothel-keepers for taking young girls into prostitution.

According to a sociological analysis of prostitution in India, there are about 10,000 dancing and singing girls in India usually known as "Nautch girls". This community practises the occupation on an hereditary basis in different regions. The majority of 'Nautch girls' in Delhi are Muslims. The study also mentions a recent addition to the poor and customary army of prostitutes from the middle-class. These women practise prostitution often with the connivance of their parents or husbands in order to secure huge sums of money to keep up an appearance of affluence. Educated and outwardly respectable, these women are prompted to take to prostitution because of the undue emphasis on values of affluence.

Middle-class prostitution can ultimately be traded to the economic factor, though it is the cult of consumption which encourages this pattern of prostitution. Large number of prostitutes also come from a group of women who have been deserted or abandoned by husbands and have no other source of income or employment open for them. According to a former commissioner of police, Calcutta, a large number of middle-class families are surviving on income from prostitution in the absence of alternative avenues of income. A number of these women are educated and quite a few are even graduates.

The causes of prostitution may broadly be classified into the following six groups:

(a) natural events such as death of father/mother/ guardian/ husband or relatives;

(b) economic causes such as ill-treatment or neglect by parents, husband, or relatives;

(c) domestic causes such as ill-treatment or neglect by parents, husband, or relatives;

(d) social causes such as kidnapping, seduction, deception, bad influence;

(e) causes of physiological significance such as sexual urge, illegitimate pregnancy, etc.;

(f) causes related to mental disposition of attitudes such as ignorance, desire for easy life and normal moral values.

Types of Prostitutes

The present practitioners of this trade can broadly be divided into two groups — hereditary class, where prostitution is the ancestral profession and the non-hereditary class who are driven to prostitution or introduced to prostitution due to number of reasons such as economic distress, desertion, destitution, lack of protection, family problems or pathological reasons, desire for easy life, etc.

The report of the Committee on Moral and Social Hygiene of the Central Social Welfare Board in 1958 divided the prostitutes into four groups, namely: (1) hereditary (community, customs and social patterns), (2) religious or traditional, (3) victims of social and sociological conditions and (4) highly sexed, pathological cases.

Prostitution must be viewed not from the traditional or historical aspect, but as a form of exploitation of women and girls. According to Mahatma Gandhi, "Man is primarily responsible for the existence of these unfortunate members of society". Prostitution has now been commercialized and a number of intermediaries, the brothel-keeper, the pimps and touts for whom the profit motive has become the guiding principle, has increased the exploitation of women and girls.

Taking into consideration the three elements of prostitution, payment, promiscuity and emotional disturbances there can be two broad categories — professional and non-professional (clandestine). Professional or the public prostitute derives her sole and only livelihood from this profession in a brothel or in red light districts in big towns. The higher type in this profession are street walkers and 'call girls' who find their clients in hotel lobbies, bars and luxurious establishments. Non-professionals are those who conduct their business in a clandestine manner.

Prostitution represents the exploitation of the poor by the rich and of women by men. If women have really to reach the level of equality with men, society should be in a position to ensure economic, social and psychological security for the traditionally exploited womenfolk. Prostitution is the worst form of women's exploitation and inequality.

What must be emphasized is the growing commercialization in the exploitation of women and girls. While the urbanization process and industrialization with its accompanying evils, particularly socio-economic insecurity, poor living conditions, etc., are important forces for the increase of Prostitution in recent years, this profession like any other, operates on a commercial basis according to the law of demand and supply. The growing incidence of prostitution in metropolitan cities and urban areas is an indication of the growing demand on the one hand and poverty on the other. Some sociologists have emphasized the role of economic factors over and above the traditional and customary factors, such as poverty, low wages, lack of gainful employment, partial or complete unemployment which are contributory factors that constrain helpless women to embrace prostitution.

The increasing commercial aspect is represented in the host of intermediaries and allied trades which gather around prostitution. The most important ones are the procurers, pimps, landlords, musical instrument players, intoxicant sellers, panwallahs, hotel-keepers, flower-sellers and the rough elements whose help is sought for protection. Some intermediaries work on a commission basis, like pimps. Procurers are engaged in the purchase and sale of women. The survey of exploitation of Scheduled Caste women has also emphasized that commercial prostitution has gained preponderance over the sacred or traditional prostitution, which used to be practised in the Bijapur region. An agent usually contacts a family and buys a girl or a fake marriage is declared and she is taken out of the town or village to practise this trade.

Once these girls have been lured or enticed, and in some cases forced into this profession, they are taken to a brothel. If the girls are unwilling, they are mercilessly beaten and punished and even locked up if they do not conform to the brothel-keeper or *gharwali*. Their status is that of an employee and their income is divided between the brothel keeper and as commission for the pimps and procurers. The rest is taken up for rent, lodging and food, while the remaining income is so small that the prostitute has hardly any savings or security for old age. They are fully exploited by the brothel keeper who enters into a bargain with customers and the prostitute has no choice, but to follow his or her orders. They are kept strictly under control and surveillance of the brothel keeper and his hired men. The prostitute is not permitted or encouraged to save or keep any valuables which are usually stolen. As she grows older.

a prostitute desires to set herself up as a brothel keeper, if possible, or amongst some of the traditional communities like the Barias, the Bednies and Takyaies, they admit their daughters into the profession when they are grown up. She herself initiates her into the profession so that she may continue to support herself through the daughter's earnings. Amongst Deredar girls' they are given training in music and dance by their mothers from girlhood so that their mehfils and *muftas*, get large number of customers. In some cases, after a woman has been in the profession for 10 to 15 years, and is not able to attract customers, she is thrown out on the streets by brothel-keepers, and is reduced to beggary.

In certain tribal regions, particularly where new projects for construction, industry or mines, etc., have been established, contractors, traders and petty officials have seduced and then abandoned tribal girls. These girls have been forced into prostitution because they have been alienated and thrown out of their own tribal society. In Baladila (MP), for example, a serious situation was created, but the management forced the men to marry these tribal girls and thus saved them from drifting into prostitution. Generally such strong measures are not resorted to and the fact remains that a very large number of tribal girls are being lured into prostitution by unscrupulous men who have made this a very lucrative business for themselves.

The Suppression of Immoral Traffic in Women and Girls Act, 1956 repealed all previous enactments passed by the State and brought uniformity in the law. According to Beotra (1970): "The Act aimed at the suppression of commercialized vice and not at the penalisation of the individual prostitute, or of prostitution itself." In one case, the individual prostitute can be penalised if she carries on prostitution "within a distance of 200 yards of any place of public, religious worship, educational institution, hostel, hospital, nursing home".

According to M.L. Sahney (1974), a senior police official, this section has severely restricted their powers for suppression of this traffic. He opines that:

> "This restriction needs immediate amendment as the vice of prostitution has gone to posh colonies where the pimps have hired modern houses to run this profession. In the absence of these premises situated within 200 yards from the places as envisaged above, it is not possible to prosecute such women or girls soliciting their bodies for immoral purposes".

Police officers have pointed out that this proves to be extremely difficult particularly in the case of a woman witness. Considering the social conditions existing today in our country, no respectable man/woman would like to help the police in the prosecution of sex offences. If anybody turns up for such help, he has to face harassment and even repent for his action, as the persons prosecuted are themselves criminals or are supported by them. At first these witnesses are lured with money, wine and women. If these tactics fail they are threatened with dire consequences with immediate danger to their lives and properties. Efforts were made to procure witnesses through welfare associations and agencies but all in vain. A letter was written to the Association for Moral and Social Hygiene in India for furnishing some names of social workers including lady social workers so that they could be contacted at the time of raids on brothels and places of disrepute. They have replied that although the members of the association were very sincere workers they were not certain whether any of them would be prepared to come forward during raids and face cross-examination in courts.

Social workers and police officers have repeatedly brought to our notice that the punishment imposed under the Act is inadequate to deter people from this crime particularly in view of the enormous income that can be earned from this traffic.

It has been realized that the Act was itself not sufficient to control this commercial exploitation and traffic in women. In fact the number of prosecutions under this Act have been very small in comparison to the volume of the traffic. A report of the Central Bureau of Correctional Services indicates that while the number of prosecutions under the Act has increased from 6428 in 1965 to 7573 in 1969, i.e. by 17.8 per cent, the rate of prosecution for the same period has gone down by about 10 per cent. About 58 per cent of these persons were only fined, 14 per cent acquitted and 8 per cent were released on admonition. Only 11 per cent were sentenced to imprisonment with a fine which is nominal (Rs. 200) and 4 per cent without fine. 78 per cent were charged under the Act for seducing for purposes of prostitution (Section 8 of the Suppression of Immoral Traffic Act). During the same period the number of such women rescued declined sharply. Only 7.2 per cent were charged under Section 4, which prosecutes persons over the age of 18 years for living on the earnings of prostitutes but exceptions are made in favour of mother, son, daughter and sister or other persons unable to support themselves on account of age or mental and physical incapacity.

The Department of Social Welfare set up an expert committee in 1968 to consider various proposals and suggestions for enlarging the scope of the Act with a view to make it more comprehensive; various amendments are under consideration.

It is important that certain changes be made in the Act to help eradicate this social evil. It is essential to prevent the women caught under this Act from returning to the profession by adequate rehabilitation arrangements. The persons who pay for their bail are invariably the procurers or brothel-keepers. Instead of sending the women and girls to jails, it is necessary to send them to protective homes. The age limit should also be lowered from 21 year to 18 years. Adequate arrangements should be made to give protection to girls and women in moral and social danger particularly destitute women, unmarried mothers and helpless young widows. At an orientation camp of the Association for Social Health in India held in March, 1974, one of the participants suggested improving the existing institutionalized services providing proper protection for abandoned and illegitimate children, especially girls, as a method that may help control prostitution. As far as the rehabilitative aspect is concerned, the Rama Rao Committee, 1954, had said that the after care homes are not adequate and they should be associated with some programme to help prostitutes earn a decent living. Those who are detained under the Act require long-term treatment for rehabilitation. Special counselling service towards better understanding of the problems of prostitutes is important. The children of prostitutes should be prevented from entering the profession, especially the girls. They should be segregated from their mothers and institutionalized, but not in special homes which would put a social stigma on them. Women and girls, who do not wish to continue in this profession, but are compelled to do so for economic reasons should be rescued and engaged in remunerative work. There is, therefore, greater need for understanding the cause underlying prostitution and to make efforts to prevent more women from entering this profession as well as to rehabilitate those who are already victims of the trade.

These women need to be rehabilitated and their emotional and psychological problems are to be tackled with understanding. The most significant aspect is preventive. This applies particularly to women and girls in moral danger. An important segment of this group are women who are victims of family discord. Counselling services could help them and prevent their taking recourse to this profession. Counselling centres should also have homes for such women.

Women in Prisons

According to an estimate, women members constitute about 4.3 per cent of the convicts and 3.2 per cent of the under trial prisoners, 73 per cent of female convicts and 54 per cent of undertrials are from Andhra, Maharashtra and Tamil Nadu. Since they constitute numerically a small segment of the total convict population, the condition of women prisoners has not received adequate attention. 72 per cent of the female convicts are between 21-40 years of age, and around 10 per cent are between 16-20. 12 per cent of women convicts are illiterates, 73 per cent of them are married, 15 per cent unmarried and 12 per cent are widowed. This means that a large section have children, who are either deprived of maternal care or in the case of very young children, are living with their mothers in prisons.

It has been found that more women serve short sentences as compared to men. Habitual proneness to crime is found to be less among them. This also means that a large majority of women prisoners are 'freshers' and are exposed to the influence of prison life for the first time. We would like to draw attention to the fact that the Law Commission has recommended that convicts on short-term sentences should not be sent to prison, where they are exposed to the unhealthy influence of hardened criminals.

Separate living quarters or wards with female wardens or matrons are provided for women as a rule. In rare cases child care services or creches for mothers in prisons are available in a few States. Training in skills such as niwar and dari making, tailoring, spinning, weaving, bidi-making, embroidery, etc., are not necessarily in tune with market labour requirements or conducive to self-employment.

The background of women prisoners studied by one or two experts reveals that their crime comes mainly from poverty or social helplessness. Most common are pickpocketing, attempted suicide, family feuds and domestic quarrels, questions pertaining to the custody of children, infanticide, destitution or vagrancy and murder of a lover.

The generally low level of literacy among women convicts, except for Kerala, where 45 per cent of women convicts were illiterate, reflects the lack of effort by prison authorities to educate them. In general, the women sections of the jails have practically no positive education or work programmes, presumably due to few prisoners; they cannot participate in the general routine of work due to strict segregation. Sometimes the women prisoners have dependent children with them for want of any family arrangement outside. Life for these young ones can be equally futile. Efforts to set up creches for children of women prisoners did not succeed due to very small number of children. Discrimination against women is prevalent, since they hardly share any of the privileges available to men convicts such as wage system, canteen, outdoor work, PT drill, library or prayer meetings or general recreation, or holidays. This is explained by the problems of segregation and inadequate staff to organise such activities for women.

It has been reported to us by senior officials of the police force that in some prisons, lunatics, both criminals and noncriminals, are housed along with other women prisoners. This appears to us to be not only unhealthy, but a dangerous practice. We fail to understand how any reform or rehabilitation of these convicts or the treatment of these lunatics is at all possible under these circumstances. Another problem that has been brought to our notice is that women prisoners are often sent to places away from their normal residence. This makes it impossible for their family, particularly children, to visit them. This isolation increases the difficulties of rehabilitation and readjustment to family life on their release.

The committee feels that the problems of women prisoners deserve special attention, particularly with regard to the care of the children if any, their rehabilitation and education. Since most of the women prisoners cannot return to their families or do not have families to return to after they are released, suitable arrangements for their rehabilitation needs to be considered along with after care programmes. While in prison, these women must be taught some activity or imparted training in a skill which would enable them to earn their livelihood on release. A suggestion made to us is to involve women's voluntary organisations for arranging useful educational, recreational and work programmes for women in prisons. Successful results have been seen in Maharashtra and Gujarat State where long-term women prisoners are released to the care of recognized women's institutions run by social welfare agencies.

Suicide

Suicide is a social problem affecting both men and women. However, a study of the causes and factors for committing suicide provide an indication of the status of women. Suicide is a reaction to problems that apparently cannot be solved in any other way a final response which a human-being makes to inner emotional distress. Cultural patterns, socio-economic conditions, and group activities influence the extent of suicides and act as inhibiting or encouraging factors. In India, the medieval Hindu institution of 'Sati', which was finally stopped due to vigorous efforts of social reformers like Raja Ram Mohun Roy in the 19th century, was the earliest institutionalized form of suicide for women. Though it was thought to have had religious sanction, it arose out of a social system which had degraded and dehumanized the widows. Regardless of age, a number of those widows had to mount on the funeral pyre of their husbands forced by relatives and others. The prohibition of widow remarriage, the austerity imposed upon a widow and the cruel treatment meted out to her must have persuaded some of them to end their lives on the pyre in preference to leading a miserable existence. According to the vital statistics deaths by causes and sub-causes prepared by the Registrar General's Census (Sample Registration System), suicides were reported to be the highest for women in the age-group 15-34, both in 1966 and 1969. The overall incidence of suicide for women was reported to be higher than males in 1966 and 1969, but it declined in 1967 and 1968.

In 1970 on an 'average 41.4 per cent of the persons who committed suicide were women. Among causes for suicide, the following were listed: (1) despair over dreadful disease 14.1 per cent (2) quarrels with parents-in-law 8.6 per cent and (3) quarrels with married partners 6.3 per cent as the major factors. An analysis of the percentage distribution of total deaths by the cause and subcause for women indicates that the maximum percentage of suicides occurred in the age group 15-34, the second largest being in the 35-54 age group.

In Status of Women and Suicide by Dr. Jyotsna Shah, it may be assumed that in this age group, "suicides committed by females were mainly due to quarrel with parents-in-laws and quarrels with married partners. The joint family system still prevails in India, therefore, the suicides by females may be taken to reflect the extent of oppression of the daughter-in-law in the joint family at the hands of the in-laws".

Though no national survey or in-depth study on a national scale on the causes of suicides have been done so far, the report of the Suicide Enquiry Committee in Gujarat studied the problem of suicides between 1960-64 in the State. The study found that the number of women committing suicide for physical factors, mental factors and social and domestic factors, were larger than men, being respectively 514 males, per 516 females, 431 males per 513 females, and 562 males per 1,192 females. As far as the economic factors were concerned, 256 men committed suicide as compared to 196 females.

A further analysis of the social factors indicates that out of 1,784 persons, 1,192 women committed suicide, and out of these the largest number were due to failure to adjust in matrimony, domestic unhappiness or ill-treatment at the hands of relatives. These were further cross-analysed with levels of education and a definite negative correlation between the educational level of women and the number of suicides was observed. The percentage of illiterate females constituted 61.9 per cent of the total cases of female suicides. As the educational level increased, the number of suicides decreased. Among the number of persons who committed suicide due to unhappy human life and other factors, the largest were from the illiterate group, next being literates below primary level followed by primary, middle and higher categories. Significantly 1,058 married people against 95 single people commit suicide due to domestic unhappiness and out of these 836 were females which corroborates the statement about suppression of women in married life particularly by in-laws. The study established that more women in the 15-34 age group commit suicides due to domestic unhappiness.

This report pointed out the 'cultural lag' in our social institutions which have not kept pace with educational and technological advance as the basic cause behind the suicides. It listed as reasons, the lack of freedom in the choice of the marriage partner, changes in the family units and especially joint family relationships, child marriage.

dowry and lack of education about sex and married life among others.

The report recommended homes for women to which they can resort in times of extreme hardship or family estrangement. Some voluntary homes have been established in Gujarat.

An earlier survey of suicides in Bombay State in 1954-57, indicated that the existence of suicide per population is 3.4 males and 3.9 females in Ahmedabad range, 4.1 males and 8.9 females in Rajkot range per one lakh of the population. The highest number of suicides was in the rural areas. 2,006 females who commit suicide out of 5,173 were in the 15-24 age group. The highest number of suicides was by women due to domestic quarrel. 75.8 per cent of females were from the literate group. The Suicide Enquiry Committee of Saurashtra in 1952-55 also bore out the fact that twice as many women commit suicide as men.

Though apart from Maharashtra and Gujarat, data on suicide and causes are lacking from other states, suicide remains a widespread social problem. There are various items appearing in the daily Press from time to time giving news of women who die to injuries received from bums, etc. Some of the reported accidental deaths due to bums, etc., may very well be self-inflicted. The majority of these women are housewives in the susceptible age group mentioned above. The causes have to be searched for in our social structure, enjoining upon women an inferior status and position, socially, economically and culturally.

Another cause that in our opinion also pushes many women to end their lives is breakdown of family economy. In recent years there have been reports of women committing suicide along with their children. The burden of economic insecurity and grim poverty presses more heavily on women's minds particularly when she has children to feed. This increasing strain causes complete breakdown in many cases. The absence of social security or adequate employment opportunities leave a woman utterly helpless, in the absence of a breadwinner in the family. Rather than see her children starve, it is not unnatural for, her to prefer ending her life. Suicides thus represent a serious malaise in social organisations, which will increase as life becomes harsher with increasing poverty and destitution.

Unmarried Mothers

Data on unmarried mothers is not available as there has been no attempt to examine the prevalence of this problem by any agency. Nevertheless it remains a social problem. Some indication is available in the Report of the Suicide Enquiry Committee which studied suicides in Gujarat between 1960-64. One of the causes of high rate of suicide among women was due to illegitimate pregnancies. Some time back, a leading gynaecologist had observed that there was an increase in the number of abortions asked for by unmarried girls after passing of the Medical Termination of Pregnancy Act. Social workers have long been aware of the problem of illegitimate pregnancies and unmarried mothers. Before the liberalizing of the Abortion Act these women and girls had either to resort to quacks for abortions and in the process a number of women may have lost their lives. The other alternative was to abandon such children in the destitute homes. Very often these unmarried mothers joined the ranks of the destitute women and were exposed to moral and social danger. Some of the women in the brothels may have initially joined the profession because of this stigma. While for some these illegitimate pregnancies may be due to rape, others were due to unhappy or maladjusted family life, broken homes, sexual maladjustment or even ignorance. A large number of women who were pushed into prostitution or into committing suicide did so because society does not accept an unmarried mother.

At an orientation camp held by the Association of Social Health in March 1974, some experts have advocated sex education since a great deal of confused thinking prevails with regard to sex. A medical expert citing case histories and research findings said, "there is either complete ignorance or complete misunderstanding about the role of sex and this results in social and sexual maladjustments. This calls for evolving an intelligent and comprehensive programme for sex education."

A medical expert at the same seminar cautioned against the alarming rise in venereal infliction among teenagers, due to profound socio-economic changes in society over the past few decades. They advocated sex education, health education to control this. Apparently prostitution accounted for only 20 per cent in the spread of venereal diseases.

The committee in the course of its tours met a few such cases in women's homes. Some of them had conceived as a result of rape, but the refusal of the family to accept them or assist them in any manner had wrecked their lives completely. In one instance, in Andhra, the father wanted to kill his daughter, but the mother; with the assistance of a school teacher, got her admitted into a women's home for safe keeping. The number of such homes are most inadequate and very little is known about them, particularly in the villages.

The problem of unmarried mothers is a result of rapid socioeconomic change. The value system is changing and the struggle for existence brings out tensions leading to deviant behaviour. In Western countries it was found that the existence of this problem rapidly increased with increasing urbanization, growing affluence and the cult of materialism. The resultant breakdown of the moral order systems leads to the disintegration of traditional social values. Indian society even now practises segregation of the sexes and tremendous emphasis is placed on the chastity of women. Under such circumstances the tensions are often aggravated and problems become manifest.

We feel that this problem requires much greater attention than it has received so far from both official agencies and voluntary welfare organisations, particularly as the indications of its increasing incidence are already manifest. It is important to provide adequate assistance to these women for their rehabilitation and care for their children. Counselling services are essential to persuade families to take a more humane view of this problem.

Aged Women

Traditional Indian society had through the joint family system provided for the care of aged persons. Even in the absence of the joint family, traditional norms of behaviour required the children to take adequate care of their aged parents and grandparents. The pressure of socioeconomic changes, the breakdown of the joint family and of traditional values have increased the significance of the problem of care of aged persons. It is easier for old men to live on their own but it is much more difficult for women. Most of them are economically helpless; even the minority, who may have some source of income are not in a position to look after themselves or protect themselves. This problem was brought to our notice by the Ramakrishna Mission in Varanasi which is running a home for old women.

The committee also visited an old-age home in Pune where all the inmates were from well-to-do families. Their relatives were paying Rs. 125 per month for food and lodging and some of them were paying for extra services like milk, etc. These women had been sent to the homes because they could not get along with their daughters-in-law. We also heard of cases where old women were living in destitute homes, not because they were destitutes but because there were no other homes available for them and the only way they could enter these homes was by declaring themselves destitutes. It was also brought to our notice that these women, even if they had any family, are seldom visited by the latter.

A number of State Governments are operating schemes for old age pensions and the annual expenditure on such schemes is now about Rs. 10 crores. The reports received by us in most of the States indicate, however, that the amounts are very meagre, and the number of pensioners falls far short of applications or even recommended cases. We were also informed that because of their helplessness these pensioners have to give a share to the intermediaries, who assist them in obtaining the pension. This becomes a continuous process, because the women are threatened that without the commission the government will be informed of their death so that the pension will cease. We were also told that payments are not always regular causing great hardship.

In the changing social milieu the problem of aged women who are regarded as encumbrances by their families is going to increase. Greater attention to their assistance and care is necessary from the State and voluntary agencies.

Destitute Women

The number of destitute women has been increasing in recent years. According to one report, a large number of such women were found scrounging for small fish in the nullahs along highways leading out of Calcutta. A majority of them are elderly women. In a village in Birbhum, we met a group of Santhal women who had been reduced to complete destitution because their ill health and age prevented them from obtaining any employment. They were agricultural labourers whom the landowners would no longer employ.

A large group of destitute women were widows and deserted women who have no means of support for themselves or their children. They swell the ranks of beggars and are exploited for immoral traffic. The Department of Social Welfare has estimated that about 1 lakh women, in the age group of 20 to 44, join the ranks of destitutes every year. We believe this to be very short of reality. Institutionalized services now available for them are highly inadequate, both in numbers and in the type of services provided for rehabilitation. Services for this group have only touched the fringe of the problem. It is imperative to obtain more reliable data to assess the magnitude of the problem and organise adequate services for their rehabilitation.

The reviews of the disabilities and constraints on women, which stem from socio-cultural institutions, indicates that the majority of women are still very far from enjoying the rights and opportunities guaranteed to them by the Constitution. Society has not yet succeeded in framing the required norms or institutions to enable women to fulfil the multiple roles that they are expected to play in India today. On the other hand, the increasing incidence of practices like dowry, indicate a further lowering of the status of women. They also indicate a process of regression from some of the norms developed during the freedom movement.

We have been perturbed by the findings of the content analysis of periodicals in the regional languages, that concern for women and their problems, which received an impetus during the freedom movement, has suffered a decline in the last two decades. The social laws that sought to mitigate the problems of women in their family life have remained unknown to a large mass of women in this country, who are as ignorant of their rights today as they were before independence.

The changes in social attitudes and institutions cannot be brought about very rapidly. It is, however, necessary to accelerate this process of change by deliberate and planned efforts. Responsibility for this acceleration has to be shared by the State and the community, particularly that section of the community which believes in the equality of women. We, therefore, urge that community organisations, particularly women's organisations, should mobilise public opinion and strengthen social efforts against oppressive institutions like polygamy, dowry, ostentatious expenditure on weddings and child marriage, and mount a campaign for the dissemination of information about the legal rights of women to increase their awareness. This is a joint responsibility, which has to be shared by community organisations, legislators, and the government.

Nine

In Authority

In an authoritative role, women's participation in decision-making process is vital for the betterment of their human right conditions. If real democracy has to be sustained, the women, comprising about half of the world's population have to be incorporated at different levels and different processes of decision-making. This fact was realised at the UN convention on the political rights of women in 1952. All congresses worldwide emphasised the need for political participation of women. They discussed and planned strategies to achieve this objective. Significant deliberations on women's empowerment were made in: (a) World Plan of Action in 1975, in Meidco, (b) The Copenhagen Programme of Action 1980; (c) World Conference on the UN Decade of Women in Nairobi (1985); and, (d) the World Congress of Women in Beijing (1995). Women's involvement in decision-making processes at different levels was necessary for them to acquire confidence.

When analysing the woman factor in decision-making, the foremost consideration would be to find out whether women have taken key decisions or just helped in taking a decision. The next step would be to identify the internal and external situations in which they could take key political decisions, and third, the interaction processes followed by such decision makers. Moreover, the analysis should throw light on the formal as well as non-formal structures in decision-making system on central, state and local levels, wherein women performed their roles as key or non-key decision-makers.

Thus decision-making positions acquired by women would give a general idea of the vertical as well as horizontal mobility of women to power position. The study by its very nature generally becomes a study of elite women in decision-making positions. In this study, the key decision-makers are actors- who could convert decisions into political action or one, who possessed efficacy or who had impact upon the political system in some way or the other.

It is true that women in top power positions in politics were no Indicators regarding the social, economic or political status of the women masses. But they indicated the span of mobility in recruitment process and gender toleration in a political system. This kind of study would help in understanding the elite structure in a society which in its turn would depend upon the political culture prevailing at that time.

Scope

The universe in this study is within the Indian context and limited to those women only, who were or are key or non-key political actors in the decision-making process, and whose efficacy could be assessed on the basis of the results of their performance. As Indira Gandhi was one of the strongest political leader in the world, this paper intends to start with her and then proceed to few other women who joined the political arena after her. These had been either chief ministers or held key party posts. Nevertheless, all of them have affected political scene in their respective states or at the national level. When this study was being completed, BJP led coalition had already taken over power at the Centre. The women's reservation bill could not be introduced in Parliament because some members in the opposition had scuttled it.

Actor in Planetary System

Indira Gandhi's environmental interest revealed her as one of the first true planetary leaders. Maurice F Strong, executive coordinator, United Nations Office for Emergency Operation in Africa, wrote about her: "She was the first leader of any great nation to appreciate that the concerns for environment which has been so dramatically manifested in the late 1960s and early 1970s in industrialised societies had a profound relevance to developing countries. At that time, most of the developing world regarded the emergence of the environmental issue as a preoccupation of the rich, which threatened to divert attention and resources from the development needs of the poor, but Indira Gandhi saw the indispensable need to force an alliance between environmental and development concerns in meeting these needs.'"

Maurice F. Strong held that Indira Gandhi's ideas were the single key to the sources of Stockholm conference on environment in June 1972.

As Key Actor in Indian Political System

Indira Gandhi's impact on India's political system was such that it became unrecognisable and totally different from the Nehru period. Under Jawaharlal Nehru's style of politics, there was a system of checks and balances between conflicting regional interests and powerful party bosses. The dominant political leaders were accommodated by the federal structure of the Indian Constitution. This gave strength to India to weather the turbulent formative years. The Shastri government also followed the Nehruvian line.

The Indian political system was confronted with most serious internal crisis during the latter period of Indira Gandhi's regime. Well accepted peaceful procedures and peaceful means for resolving internal conflict were shattered. Fragmented political culture and battered accommodative attitude became the features of the Indian political system. The systemic and structural failures became obvious. She had personalised and centralised Indian politics. Indira Gandhi was intolerant of political personalities who showed signs of entering into competition with her. She dismissed non-congress ministries in the different states and imposed her confidents as chief ministers in the Congress ruled states.

The structure of the Congress party changed qualitatively. There was enormous centralisation of power in the office of the Prime Minister's secretariat. The personalisation and centralisation of political authority made a dent in the capacity of the system to accommodate regional demands.

The political system was affected by Indira Gandhi's decisions in such a way that the system went on working under its inertia. Terrorism raised its head in Punjab and Kashmir. Democracy declined. The institutions of party parliament and judiciary were twisted to make her more secure in her decision-making position. The style became authoritarian and the Indian political culture broke off its moral moorings. In 1969, when the Congress was split, the political culture scenario changed basically. All political parties in India were affected by Indira Gandhi's decision to divide the historic Congress Party reducing it to a collection of subservient sycophants.

Indira Gandhi went on with her populist image, by propagating the concepts of a committed bureaucracy and a committed judiciary. She showed scant respect to the Constitution of India. Inspite of the fact that the Shah Commission report denied any threat to law and order in the country, Indira Gandhi declared Emergency in 1975. She claimed that Emergency was a necessity for preserving law and order in the nation. The probity of the civil service was impaired and press came under attack. The electronic media was misused and suppersession of an army general was considered necessary.

There was no place for Nehru's style of consensus during Indira Gandhi's regime. She stressed on cohesion. The syndicate in Congress was delegitionised by her tirade against it. The breaking of consensus resulted into opposition agitational politics and the government had to become repressive.

Populism came to be established as an important element of politics. It meant direct appeal to the masses. Consequently the intermediate structure and the elites were ignored. With the Sanjay Gandhi factor, musclemen and local mafia came to form the new infrastructure of politics.

Rajni Kothari had observed that "now, it is clear that almost the entire Institutional order (not just the Congress system) has very nearly broken down. The system had under gone a series of changes." The new model of politics had been as follows:-

(i) Displacement of a cabinet system of government.

(ii) The abrogation of parliamentary system by first permitting a brute use of party majority by the executive wing, and then under mining the simpler mechanics, let alone the spirit of election mandates by frequent recourse to defections and toppling of duly constituted governments.

(iii) The erosion of the federal framework by recourse to similar practices engineered from the very apex of the system.

(iv) The undermining of judicial independence and probity by executive manipulation of the concept of parliamentary supremacy.

(v) The uncalled for use of presidential powers.

Indira Gandhi had few equals in recent history in the art of power wielding. Her rapport with common people was extraordinary. After Mahatma Gandhi and Nehru, she had been the most charismatic leader in India. She could bypass all the stalwarts of her party as well as the most fiery leaders in the opposition. Even when she was out of power the she enjoyed the same popularity among the masses. Her dynamism was unmatched and she was the only woman Prime Minister to be assassinated. The Congress syndicate was totally disillusioned with its scheme about her, that is, to use her as a sophisticated totem for the Congress.

Indira Gandhi was a bold key decision-maker and her decisions resulting into Important actions, had great impact on the Indian political system, with its processes and its culture.. As mentioned before, she personalised and centralised politics in India. By her decisions she eroded the federal system in India.

Indira Gandhi went on with her concept of 'committed judiciary'. It was during her regime that India witnessed Emergency for the first time. She displaced the cabinet system and abrogated the parliamentary system. During her regime, the constitutional system of India became Prime Ministerial system. Many important constitutional amendments were passed by Parliament without any debates.

Some other Actors in Decision-making

After Indira Gandhi, some women leaders in states had made their strong impacts on state politics as well as on national politics. Keeping in mind the time frame for this chapter, after studying Indira Gandhi's role in decision-making process as key actor, I have taken current examples like Sonia Gandhi, Mamta Banerji, Jayalalitha, Mayawati and Rabri Devi. The former two were leaders of a national party. The others belong to regional parties and have adorned the chair of chief ministers in their respective states. Except Rabri Devi all the others have been dynamic and active in politics. Their decisions and styles have left impacts on national parties, state politics and party politics.

The Late, 1980s and 1990s have witnessed the emergence of women political leaders who have influenced political decision-making at the national and state level. Jayalalitha emerged as a powerful Chief Minister of Tamil Nadu after the death of M G Ramchandra. The, 1990s saw the emergence of Mamta Banerji in Bengal representing initially the Congress (I). She has steadily consolidated her position and could not be contained within the fold of the Congress Party. In 1998, she broke away and founded the Trinamul Congress. The year 1998 also witnessed the emergence of Sonia Gandhi as the prime decision-maker of the Congress party. She also exerted pressure on the government at the Centre. Mayawati made her presence felt in the politics of Uttar Pradesh with her Bahujan Samaj Party. Aggressive, and to some extent very articulated in her speeches and actions, she has emerged as a very strong leader of the Dalits.

The Sonia-Mamta-Jayalalitha trio is affecting the course of political events. They affected structure of their respective parties and influenced them. The trio also challenged the Vajpayee government on several occasions. Mayawati, who was the Chief Minister of Uttar Pradesh twice, showed her persistence in the state politics and also as a leader of the Dalits. Rabri Devi is a puppet installed as Chief Minister of Bihar, the second-most populated state of India. Her installation developed certain serious constitutional and political trends in the politics of Bihar.

After a Pause

After a long silence, Sonia Gandhi decided to campaign for Congress (I). She started her first four campaign meetings in south India on January 16, 1998, and created an excitement among the Congress workers. She made a dramatic entry on the central stage at the Netaji Indoor Stadium, on August 9, 1998, where the Congress plenary session was being held. A virtual riot broke out as scrambled the members by to take a glimpse of her. She sat down on the floor, the place for All India Congress Committee (AICC) delegates. When Congress president Sitaram Keshri rose to speak, he was hooted down. He came down to Sonia, dropped his Gandhi cap at her feet and beseeched her to join the leaders on the dais. In 1993, P V Narasiniha Rao, also had to face similar treatment and he had to invite her to the dais. At that time she had refused. The message was clear that the Nehru-Gandhi family and Sonia herself had greater appeal among the party workers. Ultimately, she displaced Sitaram Kesri from presidentship of the Congress.

Another occasion when the sycophancy regarding Nehru-Gandhi family had become more obvious was during the golden Jubilee celebrations of Indian Independence on August 15, 1997. Sonia was given place of pride in the Central Hall, in the front row with Congress president Sitaram Kesri and the BJP president L K Advani. Other members of the Nehru-Gandhi family, Priyanka Gandhi and her husband Robert Vadhera were seated in the row just behind her. No other Congress leader has been able to pull as large a crowd as Sonia because of the Gandhi family factor.

Some old Congress men who joined other parties were of the opinion that Sonia Gandhi entered politics essentially to keep a hold on the Congress (1) as a political vehicle for her children.

The way the dynastic principle worked in Sonia's own estimation, could be assessed by her own prologue in Rajiv by Sonia Gandhi. She wrote: "We had both observed the world of politics from a distance. We had come to understand the critical line that distinguishes ambition from a sense of purpose." She remained non-political for a long time. But when Sanjay Gandhi met a violent death, Indira Gandhi turned to her elder son so that the dynastic. principle could go on working. Sonia claimed that she "fought like a tigress" against this decision, but she respected her mother-in-law. "I understood Rajiv's duty to her. At the same time, I was angry and resentful towards a system which, as I saw it, demanded him as a sacrificial lamb. It would crush him and destroy him - of that I was absolutely certain." After Rajiv Gandhi was killed, she said at Sriperunibudur that she put aside her Inclination to remain as a "private person." and stepped forward in the sanctified family tradition of duty before personal considerations.

Congress had been a party as well as a process because it was the principal carrier of India nationalism. More over, "the dynamics of electoral competition at the local level created a broad convergence of political interest between particular sections. This under wrote the consolidation of an electorate between social classes, which dominated the realm of representative politics... The key to the Congress success was its ability to remain awake to local political situations... But the social factions deserted the party. One of the reason was dynastic political succession which ensures the survival of neither commitment nor vision. The Congress organisation, which was the key to its ability to recruit loyalties at the local level, is today in shambles. The decline began in Rajiv Gandhi's regime. Organisational elections were never conducted for about more than seven years. There was lack of local leader, who could create durable alliance. The electoral appeal of the Congress depended solely on the charms of the Nehru-Gandhi family. When Sonia became president of the Congress (I), she emphasised on reorganising party. On July 28, 1998, she led a Congress rally and marched to Rashtrapati Bhawan against "price rise and the all round failure of the BJP government." It seemed that she was taking pro-active steps to succeed in competitive politics. She marshalled support for the candidature of P M Sayeed for the post of deputy speaker of the Lok Sabha. These actions showed that after emphasising on strengthening organisational machinery, she appeared to have switched suddenly to a policy of bold initiatives. BJP deferred the decision on the election of deputy speaker and withdrew its candidate Rita Verma. BJP virtually admitted defeat. After playing this game, Sonia announced the prospect of assuming responsibilities of power. It was a dramatic change in the position of the Congress (I) president. Sonia earlier virtually rejected a call by Chandra Shekhar to bring down EWP. The reason behind the aggressive policy could be to retain her popularity among the party workers. Before scandal had tainted the name of her family, Sonia has been calling for transparency in the Bofors crisis so that the Nehru-Gandhi family's name was steer-cleared. But the CBI affidavit before the Delhi High Court candidly declared that "investigation had shown that the families of the then Prime Minister of India (Rajiv Gandhi) and Ottavio Quottrocchi were on very intimate terms with each other and they used to meet frequently. Quattrocchi and his family had free access to the Prime Minister's house." A E Services of Ottario Quottrocchi entered into negotiations to cheat "because the two parties to the agreement conspired to deceive the Government of India, and dishonestly induced it to part with money to the tune of US$ 7.34 million," says the CBI affidavit.

Sonia could not chart out a political strategy at Panchmarhi Congress (1) session to revive the party and even clarify its ideological positions on many questions.

There is no doubt that Sonia has rejuvenated the dying Congress party, to a certain extent. She is gaining popularity, and this became evident when the Central Election Committee (CEC) of Congress decided to complete the selection of candidates by January 11, 1998. There were disputes between various groups and for the final list all sought Sonia Gandhi's guidance in the matter. Sonia war, not the president of the Congress at that time. She was waiting to take over the organisation, which she did later. Her entry into active politics helped the Congress (1) in its electoral battle against other political parties. But it exacerbated factional conflict within the Congress party itself.

Though belated, Sonia decided to come to the aid of a dispirited party, which was rapidly declining. She made difference to the outcome of the contest, and was able to produce another hung Parliament. The effect of her entry into electoral politics for the 12th Lok Sabha, lifted spirits within the Congress party, and attracted a noticeable degree of curious mass voters. BJP alone could not get majority and with "friends" it had to form another shaky coalition government at the Centre. Sonia controlled the drift away from Congress.

However, Sonia Gandhi has steadily consolidated her position not only as the head of the party, but also as a formidable player in the decision-making process at the national level. On January 12, 1999, at a function at the Ramkrishna Mission in Delhi she spoke strongly against conversion of Hindus, while just a week ago she visited Gujarat to express her solidarity with the Christians there.

The Congress party had been earlier in support of the reservation bill for women, and Sonia Gandhi had also announced her decision to implement 33 per cent reservation for women in her own party hierarchy. She had inducted four women - Mohsina Kidwai, Yanga Patai, Ambika Soni and Laxmi Devi - in the party working committee in as reported to have been effected in the last week of January in the Hindustan Times of January 29, 1999. Simultaneously, she also made a statement maintaining that the bill advocating for 33 per cent reservation would ensure only the entry of affluent women in the Lok Sabha and Rajya Sabha. On February 8, she lambasted the BJP government at the Centre for Misgovernance, while there was trouble brewing in the Congress led Orissa government, after the killing of an Australian Christian missionary along with his two young sons. After much discussion Sonia Gandhi took the decision that Chief Minister J B Patnaik be replaced. By taking this tough stand she sent out a loud message to the BJP government and Congress itself. She did what the BJP could not do in Gujarat after her clear enunciation that the BJP and its front organisation have no monopoly over the Hindus or Hinduism. After visiting Tirupati, she chose Haridwar as her next venue to address partymen in Uttar Pradesh. By urging Congressmen to fight against communal and castist forces she has taken the battle not only to the territory of its principal enemy - the BJP but also to the other two strong parties in Uttar Pradesh the BSP and the samajwadi Party.

After the massacre of Dalits in Narayanpur, Bihar, on February 10, 1999, she expressed "deep shock and abhorrence." At another massacre of Dalits in Bihar within a fortnight while stating that "any government which is helpless in presenting such henious acts forfeits its moral authority to govern." She reenacted the visit of her mother -in-law in Belchi in 1978, by going to Narayanpur on February 13, 1999. It seemed to ring bells of warning for the Rabri government. However, the Congress party remained non-committal on President's rule in Bihar. Now Sonia Gandhi has very clearly stated that the Congress will oppose the ratification of President's rule motion in the Lok Sabha and Rajya Sabha. The Bihar Pradesh Congress Committee reacted sharply to the party high-command's decision, and requested Sonia Gandhi to reconsider her decision. Many senior leaders of the Bihar Congress Committee resigned in protest.

The months of March and April of 1999 have been hectic for political turnovers. Sonia Gandhi has changed her attitude several times. The dismissal of navy admiral Vishnoo Bhagwat triggered off a controversy with the opposition parties rapping the government for reinstatement of the admiral. Personal insults were hurled at George Fernandes by all opposition parties, Congress and AIADMK leading the process. Towards the middle and end of March 1999, Sonia Gandhi categorically rejected the Left offer on alternative government at a meeting in Calcutta. She maintained that the BJP led ruling coalition will collapse on its own. She promptly remarked to newsmen that the question of forming a govenment with the help of the Left parties does not arise. She also remarked that there was no need to talk to Mamta Banerji but for Jayalalitta, she remarked. "why not, we can talk to her'.

Sonia Gandhi still denies the plot to dislodge Atal government on April 10, 1999. Speaking at a huge meeting in Karimnagar, she maintained that the Vajpayee government was itself digging its grave. The Congress was ready to shoulder constitutional responsibility of forming government at the Centre if and when situation arises. She also rapped the government for its reluctance to set up a joint Parliamentary committee (JPC) to probe into the corruption charges against people in high government position. She recalled that the same party had earlier demanded setting up of a JPC to probe into the Bofors gun deal based on a report broadcast by a foreign radio station. Earlier on April 7th she denied that she was having talks with Jayalalitha.

The Vajpayee government, fell on April 17, 1999, by the lowest margin of just one vote as the BSP leader Mayawati cast her vote while one day earlier she had given indications that BSP will abstain from voting in the Lok Sabha. Immediately efforts were made for the formation of an alternative government. The Congress being the second largest party claimed to form the government. Sonia Gandhi met President Narayanan on April 20. The spokesperson of Congress party Arjun Singh remarked, "we will have letters of support from all parties that voted against the Vajpayee government." He also maintained that the Congress will establish its majority and an alternate government will be formed by Sonia Gandhi. Sonia had meeting with other opposition party leaders including Jayalalitha, RJM leaders and Laloo Prasad Yadav. Mulayam Singh Yadav dealt a severe blow to the plans of Sonia Gandhi when he refused to support the government led by her. Despite hectic efforts Sonia Gandhi was unable to produce the list of 272. Mrs. Sonia rejected the requests for sharing of power with other parties. Earlier, she had told the President that the Congress will form minority government with outside support. Samajwadi Party, RSP and Forward Block categorically opposed the plan for a Congress minority government. Sonia Gandhi was able to produce a list of only 239 MPs. As a result, the President had to dissolve the Lok Sabha. Fresh elections was declared by the Election Commissioner.

Sonia Gandhi after much speculation met Jayalalitha at a tea party, organised by Subramanium Swamy. The coming together of these two leaders was termed as a 'political earthquake.' Thereafter, they met several times. But ultimately the plans misfired and Jayalalitha finally packed her bags and left for Chennai on April 27, 1999.

Sonia Gandhi played the key role in toppling the Vajpayee government and the next general elections will be a testing ground for her acumen, charisma and manipulations. She has been able to rejuvenate the Congress party.

The Bengal Factor

Like Sonia Gandhi, Mamta Banerji was also instrumental in pulling down Sitaram Kesari from the presidentship. Mamta Banerji is a firebrand leader. She protested against alleged rigging in the election of delegates who were to elect the Congress president. election to the post of the Congress president was being held for the first time after 47 years. Mamta split vertically the Congress (I) in West Bengal on August 9, 1997. She declared the formation of a new state wing of the party and christened it the Trinamul (grassroots) Congress. Mamta boycotted the AICC plenary session held in Calcutta. She addressed a huge rally of the Trinamul Congress at the same time, and said that the new wing was needed "to save the party from fake leadership, and launch an uncompromising fight against the niling CPI(M)."

She claimed that she still belonged to the Congress. Her Trinamul Congress was the real Congress. She would use the same flag, the tricolour. She also claimed that it was she who represented the real Congress in West Bengal. She bitterly criticised the Congress president Sitaram Keshari, and alleged that he had reduced Congress (1) into a signboard organisation. She formalised the infrastructure of the Trinamul Congress, three days after the plenary session of the Congress (1) in Calcutta. Mainta announced the names of conveners of parallel district committee, heads of organisation and 116 - member steering committee. Mamta also formed 'Save Bengal Front'. She urged like mined parties to be its constituents. She left her post as the West Bengal Congress president, for one of her loyalists. Many thought that Mamta would face disciplinary action for the formation of Trinamul Congress, holding a rally parallel to the Congress (I) plenary session by boycotting it. But nothing happened. Central leaders were unable to make her desist from holding the parallel rally. The party high command decided to ignore her and isolate her. Mamta set up a parallel party office and announced that her supporters would not be accountable to the AICC or the Pradesh Congress - Committee. She said, "we looked towards Delhi for far too long. From now on we will fight our own battle".

The advent of the Trinamul Congress was seen to end the politics of polarisation between the Left Front and the Congress (I). One of the senior state Congress (1) leaders conceded that the presence of the Trinamul Congress had changed political equations. Congress (I) feared that Mamta's party would eat into its traditional support base in West Bengal. It received jolt when former Union Minister Ajit Panja and Krishna Bose joined the Trinamul Congress.

Mamta did approve of the BJP candidate Rita Verma for deputy speakership. Though her Trinamul Congress gave its support to the BJP led collition, she joined the opposition on the opening day of the monsoon session of Parliament. She alongwith her partymen, accused the government of failure to control prices. She demanded that to check price rise, the government should ensure better delivery of essentials through the public distribution system to check prices. She also expressed disappointment with the government because it failed to introduce the bill for women's reservation in Parliament.

Mamta had entered the coordination committee of BJP and its allies with some reluctance. On the issue of rising prices of essential commodities, she resigned from the coordination committee. After much persuasion, she accepted Vajpayee's offer to join the Cabinet at the Centre, but she again put up a bargain - she wanted the railways portfolio for her party MP. Talks broke down on this issue. In a dramatic development after the visit of George Fernandes and Pramod Mahajan, a joint rally was held in Calcutta on February 10,

1999, where a mellowed Mamta did welcome and felicitate Fernandes and Mahajan after they had assured Mamta that most of the demands in the package for Bengal will be considered and fulfilled by the Centre.

Mamta was very critical of the communal killings and attacks on Christians in January and demanded the resignation of Home Minister LK Advani on January 28, 1999. She also trained her guns on Murli Manohar Joshi, another BJP hardliner. She reacted against the inclusion of Joshi in the three-member cabinet team on a fact-finding mission on the murder of an Australian missionary and his sons in Keonjhar, Orissa. Earlier Mamta had joined hands with the Congress demanding ban on Bajrang Dal. She had taken a mellow stand towards the Vajpayee government throughout the months of March and April 1999. She was impassioned in the Sabha during the no-trust motion against the government. She pledged her party's support to Atalji's government. But the Vajpayee government was edged out by just one vote. After hectic consultations between both the government and the opposition, Mamta agreed to a joint election, alliance in the new elections, but also reiterated that Trinamul Congress will have its own symbol and manifest.

The Southern Factor

The famous actor of Tamil cinema, the founder of AIADMK party and its symbol of two leaves was M G Ram Chandran. He was also the Chief Minister of Tamil Nadu.

Jayalalitha was also the Chief Minister of Tamil Nadu. But she faced an electoral route in 1996. A revolt broke out in her party, AIADMK. She was secretary of her party. Many top leaders left her faction. As a result, she was defeated. The deputy general secretary Thirunavukkarasu led a faction against her. Jayalalitha expelled him from the party and the latter expelled her from his faction.

Jayalalitha was a former film actress and a follower of M G Ramchandran. When she assumed chief ministership of Tamil Nadu, it was alleged that during that period three of her associates acquired assets worth more than Rs 66.65 crore, according to the chargesheet filed by officers of the Directorate of Vigilance and Anti-corruption (DNAC) in a case relating to Jayalalitha!s wealth. It was alleged to be disproportionate to her known sources of wealth.

The chargesheet ment on June 4, 1997 before the special court-III judge P Anbazhagan named Jayalalitha as the first accused. Other accused were her 'surrogate sister' Sasikala Natrajan and Sasikala's sister-in-law J I Thirunavukkarasu Lavarsi. Jayalalitha had publicly renounced her relationship with Sasikala and with her foster son Sudhakan.

Besides the crisis created by corruption charges, Tamil magazine Dine Manu and a Tamil biweekly Junior Vikatan published a colour photograph of Jayalalitha with a group of people, which they claimed included 'Dhanu' the human bomb, who assassinated Prime Minister Rajiv Gandhi alongwith Sivarajan, the leader of the LTrE assassination squad. Since it was photograph of other persons totally unconnected with the murder of Rajiv Gandhi, the sensation flopped. It was a case of sheer media irresponsibility. But Jaylalitha had to go through humiliating experience.

Jaylalitha's party became the principal ally of the BJP led government in 1998. She kept on harping on her demand for the dismissal of the Karunanidhi government in Tamil Nadu on the grounds of failure of governance. On Cauvery issue, the AIADMK warned Prime Minister Vajpayee of "disastrous consequences" if his government did not notify immediately the scheme on Cauvery water in the official gazette and table it in parliament. According to her, there was no possibility of a compromise between Tamil Nadu and Karnataka.

The AIADMK chose to celebrate the 90th birth-anniversary of Armadurai. She was isolated from other Tamil parties, and also from BJP in these celebrations. Her speech was carefully worded and was contered around three themes. First, was her justification for her repeated threats of reviewing support to the BJP led government. Second, was meant to be a warning to her allies at the Centre and in the state against treating ALADMK unfairly. And the third, was condemning the "anarchic DMK rule" in Tamil Nadu. She indicated to EVP that in a mixed vegetable dish, no single vegetable was important. The ALADMK was as important as the vessel in which the dish could be prepared." Jayalalitha tried to grab BJP attentions by alleging Karunanidhi's indifference towards maintenance of temples in the state, for which she had launched schemes when she was the Chief Minister in Tamil Nadu. Despite all these she was eager to retain her links with BJP.

Jayalalltha consciously put pressure on BJP led government at the Centre. Despite, all allegations of corruption, she is still a very popular political figure. Vajpayee had to tread carefully where Jaylalitha was concerned. No wonder, Jaswant Singh had to rush to Chennai quite often to pacify Jayalalitha and restore her good humour. At the meeting of the coordination committee of BJP and the allies, a common statement was released stating that the allies should not criticise the government in public, Jaylalitha had her reservations and refused to sign the statement. George Fernandes rushed to Chennai to appease Jayalalitha on February 2, 1999, but the 45 minutes talk could not bear any fruit. It has been evident that Jaylalitha had openly criticised the Vajpayee government on several occasions, and threatened to withdraw support of her party. She had maintained a belligerant stand towards the Vajpayee government. She pushed the government to the wall by demanding that George Fernandes be sacked from the Union government. She wanted to know why the defence minister was being shielded the Prime Minister when serious charges had been made against him by a naval chief. As a prelude to putting out of the BJP led coalition, Jayalalitha withdrew her two ministers from the government after the Union Cabinet rejected outrightly all her three demands on the Vishnu Bhagwat issue. She also held talks with other political leaders to explore the "formation of a government that livers rather than promises and does not discriminate on grounds of religion, caste or region." The government on April 7, 1999, signalled that its ties with AIADMK have been apart and attacked Jayalalitha that she could enter to a deal with the Congress to dismiss the Karunanidhi ministry and seek withdrawal of corruption cases against her. Ultimately, on April 9. 1999. AIADMK withdrew from the coordination panel. By April 12, Jayalalitha was all set to withdraw support from the Vajpayee government. She declared that withdrawal of support to the Vajpayee government was inevitable as there was "no room for any repprochement". She also admitted that it was a wrong decision to support the government, and that one year had been wasted. Later, she met Congress president Sonia Gandhi. To a querry by a newsperson that whether she was Prime Ministerial candidate, the AIADMK leader remarked, "I am not ruling out anything."

Earlier, in the last week of March Jayalalitha announced the reservation of 33 per cent party post's for women, and she promptly packed her party's hierarchy with 48 women joint district secretaries.

It was termed as a "political earthquake" when Jayalalitha and Sonia Gandhi met over a tea party arranged by Subramanian Swamy. They ultimately unseated the government. A very uncharitable comment became the headline of major newspapers, which was 'two women send Atal packing'.

The Dalit Factor

Mayawati is one of the most dynamic Dalit leaders. She was earlier the general secretary of the Bahujan Samajvadi Party. She donned the chair of Chief Minister of Uttar Pradesh twice. First time she was the Chief Minister in 1995 with the outside support of BJP. Second time she became the Chief Minister in 1997, when BJP was a constituent of the her government. She is also presently the Chief Minister of Uttar Pradesh.

Mayawati is shrewd and assertive. Ideologically, she proclaims that she was against Manuwad. At a rally of the United Front government and its constituent partners in Lucknow against Mayawati, the erstwhile Prime Minister Deve Gawda supported the Samajwadi party's stand against Mayawati. They had alleged that the Schedule Castes and Schedule Tribes Acts were being misused. It had alleged oppression of Samajwadi Party workers. Mayawati Issued counter waring to the UF at the centre, to hold back attempts to topple her government. Against the allegation of this act being misused, Mayawati justified her "casteist" action for enlarging her support base.

During her first Chief Ministership in 1995, Mayawati found that BJP was not unhappy with the government. It supported from outside and created no hurdles. She retorted to the remarks of Mulayam Singh that BSP was communal because it had formed alliance with BJP for her second Chief Ministership. She, however ignored Samajwadi Party's remarks, accusing that Mulayarn Singh or indulge in communalism only when it suited his purpose. When the daughter of a Dalit was helped by BJP to come to the position of Chief Minister Mulayam, finds communal forces behind. He had no problems about joining BJP in 1989 to become Chief Minister himself.

Mayawati has been an opportunist like other politicians. Before forming the coalition with BJP, she had agreed to this "grand alliance" arrangement. But even then she had insisted to take up her chance first. Her condition for agreeing to remain in coalition with BJP was that they would have to agree to her being the Chief Minister first. The volatile Mayawati is perhaps the only woman Chief Minister, who confronted physical assault allegedly by "Samajwadi goons" at the state guest house in June, 1995.

As regards her style of functioning, one of the Samajwadi Party leaders, leaders, Beni Prasad Verma, in his speech addressed to a ray, compared Mayawati with Hitler. Soon after the elections in 1997, Bahujan Party had made it clear that it would join hands with any force that would make Mayawati, Chief Minister. BSP secured not only the Chief Ministership but also half the ministerial positions although it had only 66 MLAs compared to 173 MIAs of BJP. BSP was sure that power position would help it to grow. In the issue of the expansion of the ministry on March 27, 1997, Mayawati asserted that there was no need for it and left out many senior leaders of BJP. The allocation of portfolio also met with rough weather. Mayawati kept home, finance, health and planning. The CPM politbureau member Prakash Karat said that everybody knew Mayawati's style. Transfers and postings on a large-scale started even before the government had begun functioning. He remarked that the real problems of the people would be neglected. Farmers would face difficulties, many public sector undertaking could be shut down, workers would be deprived of their jobs and growing crime would be the major problem in the state. However, BJP complained that It was not consulted in majority of transfers and postings. It also alleged that Mayawati had been misusing the SC/ST Prevention of Atrocities Act against the upper castes.

According to a report of Venketesh Ram Krishna, Mayawati held that "the job of identifying and appointing loyal officers in key posts is of utmost importance for the government and it is being carried out smoothly."

Mayawati government's handling of law and order did not seem sound - there were communal, caste and sectional clashes. There were allegations and counter allegations, too. The Samajwadi Party alleged that the government arrests their workers under the Scheduled Castes and Scheduled Tribes (Prevention of Atrocities) Act and Goonda and Gangsters Act. These two acts had became the bone of contention among the coalition partners.

When the BJP government was formed under Kalyan Singh, it instituted a vigilance inquiry against bureaucrats considered close to Mayawati and reinstated officers suspended by Mayawati. Kalyan Singh transferred 184 senior bureaucrats in the first 15 days of his government.

BSP demanded a mechanism for regular consultation at the state level, like the one at the national level. Mayawati also complained that Kalyan Singh's measures were against Scheduled Castes and Scheduled Tribes and an anti-Dalit mood was created in the state.

In the last week of May 1997, the Union Home Minister Indrajeet Gupta and Chief Minister Mayawati exchanged letters over law and order situation in Uttar Pradesh. Mayawati, however, denied any deterioration of law and order situation in the state. She personally directed administrative actions to be taken against senior officials, particularly in the police department. Senior bureaucrats described these actions as "self defeating frenzy". The Union home minister disapproved these so called "corrective" steps. It was alleged that the "punishment transfers" were made against those who had expressed views before the media against the state administration. According to Mayawati, these actions violated discipline of the police and brought disrepute to the administration.

One of the BSP ministers, whose women welfare department was taken away from him and was given the portfolio of culture and youth affairs, revolted and resigned. He also accused Mayawati of taking bribe during her regime.

Mayawati won the Lok Sabha elections of 1998. She is still very vocal and critical of the Vajpayee government. At the state level, she continuously rapped at the BJP led Kalyan Singh government. She is undoubtedly a force to reckon with in the politics of Uttar Pradesh. She still is the undisputed leader of the Dalits and if strategies are planned with some care, and her harsh tongue is checked a little, she can form a strong political front of Dalits.

Mayawati did it again. After promising to abstain from voting in the Lok Sabha on no-confidence motion against the Vajpayee government. she cast her vote in favour of the motion and thus, her one vote toppled the government on April 26, 1999.

The Bihar Factor

A great writer has said that some are born great, and upon some greatness is thrust, In a similar strain it could be said that (in Bihar) some are born leaders, and upon some leadership is thrust. It could be appropriately applied to Rabri Devi - the Chief Minister of Bihar. Her Chief Ministership is an example of family principle of succession. It was adopted for keeping Bihar under the freedom of the Rashtriya Janata Dal (RJD) supremo Laloo Prasad. The dynastic principle had been applied earlier also with Indira Gandhi and Rajiv Gandhi, and now on Sonia Gandhi by the sycophancy of the congressmen to maintain the influence of Nehru-Gandhi dynasty. Sonia came out of nonpolitical "private life," and as suggested in her own writings, she jumped to national politics for family's sake. But she waited for the appropriate moment. Her intention seems to preserve her hold on the Congress party as a vehicle for her son and daughter. In Bihar Rabri was suddenly made Chief Minister. In her case, it seemed to be Laloo's intention to keep RJD as a vehicle for his next generation. He did every thing hurriedly. He made a travesty of the principles of doctrine of responsibility in the cabinet system of the government, by appointing his wife Rabri Devi as the Bihar Chief Minister. He had resigned because he was facing corruption charges before a CBI-designated court. He surrendered on July 30, 1997. Laloo Prasad also violated the principle of probity and accountability in public life by appointing his wife as Chief Minister. As he was alleged to be a "trained" Chief Minister, the person who had to replace him should have been a person distant or independent of him, but this did not happen. The requirements of accountability and responsibility were put on the shelf.

In the appointment of Rabri Devi as Chief Minister, a high voltage drama in a very short period was played. Laloo Prasad, RJD legislators and Rajyapal Kidwai played the main roles in this drama. The people of Bihar were unable to believe the news that Rabri Devi was appointed the Chief Minister and sworn in within hours after the resignation of her husband from the post. On July 30, Laloo Prasad was remanded to judicial custody after he surrendered before the CBI designated court. He resigned as Chief Minister on July 25, 1997 after the court issued an arrest warrant against him. He proposed the name of his wife as his successor at a hurriedly convened meeting of RJD legislative party.

The Rabri episode ensured proxy rule by Laloo who had said in jail, "being in jail does not mean I am a rotten egg. Several leaders had called on me and others will come." It was alleged that many Bihar officials met him regularly and received orders from when he came out of jail, he accompanied Rabri Devi everywhere and acted as an extra constitutional authority on behalf of her. It was alleged that Sitaram Kesri and I K Gujral had approved of Laloo's decision regarding installing his wife as Chief Minister.

Rabri Devi has no formal education and no interest or experience in active politics. When she became the Chief Minister of Bihar, she was neither a member of the Legislative Assembly nor the Legislative Council. She perhaps had never thought of such a windfall. Laloo had said that when his party legislators had unanimously elected her as a new leader, she was not ready to accept the new assignment. "It was only after a great deal of persuasion, that I prepared her for the changed situation."

The Governor of Bihar, Shree Sunder Singh Bhandari, gave Rabri Devi 15 days time to prove her majority in the Assembly. Before surrendering to the court, Laloo ensured and made his wife's position secured. He arranged for his wife to seek vote of confidence on July 28. She won the vote by a huge margin. She won confidence by winning 194 votes against 110.

To consolidate Rabri's position, Laloo made her to appoint a jumbo ministry of 32 cabinet ministers and 44 minister of state. She became a target of controversy and butt of jokes by many. The CPI(M) leader Harkishan Singh Surjeet emphasised Laloo's decision as an insult to those who elected him. BJP and Samta Party were furious, but Kesri ordered his party's Bihar MLAs to ensure Rabri's accession to office. Rabri could not make speeches. The television focussed upon her everywhere, but barring very few occasions, no one could hear her voice. In the first week of October 1997. She had to face a tricky situation created by the non-gazetted secretariat employees. Ministers and senior government servants were not permitted by the employees to attend their offices. It is said that she shut down the secretariat for four days and then the employees agreed to negotiate with her.

In month of September 1998, the Rabri regime was threatened by the Centre's recommendation to the President of India for the promulgation of Article 356 in Bihar for non-governance and detracting law and order. Every one knows that she is a puppet because she had not been trained in the art of politics. But gradually, she seemed to be maturing in carrying herself with confidence in public functions. The Rabri government was saved in 1998 as the President disagreed to promulgate Act 356. The Shankarbegha carnage at Narayanpur on the eve of Republic Day also threatened the Rabri government; it came under severe attack from all comers. The cabinet advised the President, to dismiss the Bihar government and promulgate Presidents rule. Ultimately, the Rabri government was dismissed on February 12, 1999, and President's rule was promulgated in Bihar for the seventh time in a sudden development, the governor of Bihar, Shree Sunder Singh Bhandari was recalled to Delhi. Laloo Yadav continued attacking the BJP government. He received support from the Left parties. Sonia Gandhi did not comment on the justification or otherwise of President's Rule. Meanwhile, the pressures on BJP government mounted and the President's rule in Bihar was ended on March 8, 1999. The RJD government under Rabri came back to power again. A radiant Rabri Devi once again took oath as Chief Minister on March 9, 1999 and submitted a list of 164 members to the governor. Bhandari was sent to Gujarat as governor on March 13, 1999, and Chief Justice B M Lal was made the acting governor of Bihar on March 16. The RJD hailed his appointment but very soon there started a rift between the governor and the Rabri government.

Women as Legislative Actors

At the legislative levels of the Centre and the states, women have not been given much importance as political actors.

Though there has been a substantial increase in voting participation by women, have not fared as contestants in national elections or state elections. They could never occupy more than 8 per cent seats in Parliament, and more than 10 per cent in state assemblies. In the Council of Ministers, the highest percentage of women had been 12.96 per cent in 1962.

With regard to the efficacy of women legislators in decision-making, there have been some studies in India as well as in Bihar. In R K Verma's study on rural political leadership, the writer held that women legislators had been contributing to the new models in 'developing national politics' of India. A Ph.D. thesis by Prabhawati, presented to the Magadh University in 1994 came to the conclusion that the representation of women in Lok Sabha was never substantial. In one of his studies, S M Sayeed was of the view that in near future because of social, cultural and practical reasons, female representation in legislatures would not increase.

The suggestions made in one of Dahelrup Drude's studies (1986) with regard to 'critical mass' theory becomes relevant here. In the context of study of women in the Scandinavian countries, she held that, when two factors combined in any political system women became 'critical mass' that is, politically strong. This happened (i) when women got at least 25 to 30 per cent seats in the legislatures, and, (ii) when support to women legislators from outside was given by strong women movement.

In the Indian political system, women in legislatures could not become a 'critical mass' because they were only 8 per cent in Lok Sabha and 10 per cent in state assemblies, and there were not sufficiently strong political women movements in India to support them.

In the legislative process, women legislators do not seem to have much impact. Recently, on the 81st constitution Amendment Bill seeking reservations of one-third seats in Parliament and state legislatures for women, they could not be effective. Though women MPs had been united inspite of their diverse political allegience and ideologies, the bill could not be passed.

Though they differed ideologicaliy, women from different parties had come together to support the bill. There were some prominent women among them like Ratanmala, Savanoor an Uma Bharati, who had supported the stand taken by Sharad Yadav and the Muslim league, MPs that there should be sub-quota within the quota for the women of the backward castes and the minority communities.

The former Prime Minister I K Gujaral had inducted in his cabinet the most vocal women like Renuka Chowdhury, Jayanti Natrajan, and Kamla Sinha. Different impressions were created by this act of the Prime Minister. One view was that Prime Minister Gujral wished to correct the impression created by Sharad Yadav that Janata Dal did not intend to give space to women. The other view was that Gujral took this step to put a constraint upon them in raising a hue and cry over the women's reservation bill. Gita Mukherjee (CPI) refused any cabinet post because she wished to remain outside so that she could fight for the reservation bill for women. Thus, he had included five women in his cabinet; all of them were placed in the second rank.

There were some controversy from the very beginning among the women MPs on the formation of the committee on empowerment of women to be chaired by Gita Mukherjee of CPI. It held its first meeting on the May 6. 1997. Margret Alva (Congress) was apprehensive that this committee would put hurdles in passing the 81st Constitution Amendment Bill 1996. According to Alva, there was no need for it because the joint committee had already discussed the bill in detail. The new empowerment of women committee would now review the bill and It would be scuttled.

The quota system became a goal in itself and created its own momentum. The original purpose was lost. Now sub-quota within quota would bring disaster upon the society. Quota for women in the Panchayats would, let us hope, gradually brings more and more women into the political field.

Madhu Kishwar in her two articles 'Not a gender war' and 'a Flawed measure' in The Hindustan Times, Patna, had discussed about the provisions of the reservation bill along with other related matters. She had pointed out that the lottery system of gender-based reservations proposed in the 81st amendment bill meant that fresh set of constituencies would be earmarked for women at every elections. It would mean that the women would not be able to develop stable relationship with their constituences. That would be true for men also who would not like this scheme. Secondly, when once the bill was passed, the men would not like that women should be allowed to contest general constituencies. Third, in the Scheduled Castes and Scheduled Tribes constituencies, which were permanent, the male would not give space to women. Quota system would ensure that women would contest only women and never men. This would mean "a sure way to perpetually ghettoies women's politics". To add to all these harmful effects of the reservation bill, in another, it would be impossible for a woman to get elected twice to the legislatures in Centre or in states, because the same constituencies would not be likely to be reserved twice in succession.

The suggestion for multiseat constituencies should be considered seriously. These constituencies could be clustered together to make one. These would be represented by three people, one of whom must be a woman. The first two seats would go to the two candidates who polled the highest number of votes - man or woman. The third seat would to the woman who polled highest number of votes among the rest of the women candidates not elected on either of the two general seats in the constituencies.

After the fall of the Gujarat government and the installation of Vajpayee government in March 1998, preparations were on for introduction of women's reservation bill in the Lok Sabha. All major parties had included the issue of women's reservation in their election manifestoes. However, there was so much rumpus in the Lok Sabha that the bill could not even he placed on the table. Copies of the bill were destroyed by Laloo Yadav and Mulayarn Singh Yadav, Sarad Yadav was also against the introduction of the bill. He maintained that the bill would be beneficial only to educated elite women.

The attitude adopted by most of the male MPs cutting across party lines was an expression of their fear and anxiety over the loss of more than 180 seats in the Lok Sabha, if 33 per cent seats were reserved for women.

At the grass root level institutions, the 73rd Amendment to the Constitution did provide 33 per cent reservation for women in Panchayati Raj institutions (PRIs). It has produced very good results in Bengal, Maharashtra and Karnataka, but in Bihar, elections to PRIs have not been held even once in the last six years, since the passage of the amendment.

Some organisations like the People's Union for Civil liberties, Rashtriya Lok Samiti, Nav Bharat Jagriti Kendra and Jan Jagaran Kendra, Prayas, Catholic Centre and Xavier's Institute of Social Service came into existence for mobilising women, besides other programmes. Except Prayas, all these groups were part of wider national movement.

Apart from these organisations and action groups in which women are involved politically, socially, and economically, Bihar had witnessed the rise and growth of several woman organisation during the pre-Independence days. One such organisation was the Mahila Charkha Samiti, known as Mahila Charkha Class in its initial days. Several great personalities like Gandhiji, Rajendra Babu, Jay Prakash Narain and Prabhawati Ji were associated with it and were involved in its activities.

Another important women's agency was the All India Women's Conference, already mentioned before, which in its earlier days was known as Women's India Association. At the Centre in Delhi, Margret E Cousins, the secretary of Women's India Association, made concerted efforts to establish the present All India Women's Conference. Its branches were gradually established in different states.

Another old and important women's organisation in Bihar had been the Bihar Council of Women. Working women had also organised themselves under the leadership of Lakshmi Menon. The Centre for Women Development studies (CWDS) was started a few decades ago in Bihar by the encouragement and initiative of Veena Mazumdar. This organisation is quite active in the tribal belt with its social and economic programmes. There are some other NGOs like Aditi, which are also involved in women's field.

Political Parties' Role

Maciver defined political party as "an association organised in support of some principle or the policy, which by constitutional means endeavours to make the determinant of the government" This definition focussed attention on the associated and the organised aspects of a political party, while brining about the rationale for its existence in terms of some guiding principle or policy and linking the same to political power as exercised by the government. Political parties are the closely connected with government, and thus, in decision-making position. The parties furnish the government with personnel.

In order to socialise the masses effectively, every political party must have competent leadership. Party workers or cadres must establish contacts with the people on a regular basis so as to aggregate and articulate their interests, educate them politically, and thereby, secure their support for the party. The party officers and workers aim at imbibing the ordinary members with the party spirit, imparting party ideologies and motivating them to be active in implementation of party programmes.

Since recruitment by political parties encourage circulation of elites, it infuses new blood to keep the party vibrant. Their neglect of women would not augur well either for the parties or the women, who formed half of the body politics.

Political parties in India have shown neglect of women in recruiting them for party posts like presidents, secretaries, treasures, spokesperson or whips at the Centre, state or local levels. The Congress party, as compared with any other party, has been most liberal towards women in their recruitment policies. But even then women members never exceeded 10 per cent limit. Even the Left parties did not find women very much fit for their tickets in elections of posts. It was only EVP who found in Sushama Swaraj party spokesperson. Though the number of women in politics has increased, their appearance into the ranks the politically active or key decision-makers or non-key decision-makers is still very low, if not nil.

There might be several reasons for acquiring less decision-making positions in a political party by women. Besides their socialisation or political culture in the society, one very important reason was that the party system in India itself is in shambles. They have no proper organisations or proper offices or definable ideologies or identifiable issues and long-term programmes. They seem to be interested only in seeking chairs for the sake of collecting benefits and privileges accruing from different positions. In such chaotic situation, even if women entered decision-making apparatuses of the party, they would have bleak future. They would affect very little - either the party system or the political system as a whole.

The role of, specially the mainstream political parties is very important. They have to be sensitise to provide space to women in their decision-making forum. Merely reservation of seats for women might not be much successful in creating a 'critical mass' in the legislature.

Women in politics have not been held in esteem and with respect by political parties as has been disclosed in a study Bhog by well known Journalist Vikas Kumar Jha. The writer has narrated the sad story of many women party workers, who were lured into the organisation by politicians as "workers". He alleged that "women political workers" had been exploited by the male politicians for satisfying their lust. The writer of Bhog includes fake characters also in his study of Indian politics in order to establish his point. Vikas, in his earlier work, had thrown light on corruption in politics and a brief history of the country. In Bhog, Vikas has probed and made efforts to determine women's status in politics.

Political parties have gradually recognised the importance of including women's issue in their election manifestoes as witnessed during '91, '96 and '98 general elections. But neither in '96 nor in

'98 the parties gave enough tickets to women. It has not gone beyond 10 per cent by any party. Women were given decision-making positions of the secondary level except Kanti Singh in Deve Gowda Ministry, some good vocal members in Gujaral Ministry like Renuka Chowdhury.

Indira Gandhi has been the lone example of a potent political decision-maker. At the planetary level, she was the first to strongly formulate a guideline for the prevention and presentation of environment. At the national level, she was a powerful and effective Prime Minister. She left her father Nehru way back in the game of real politics. She almost replaced the parliamentary form of government by a Prime Ministerial form of government. It is often remarked that she was the only 'male' is her Cabinet. She ruled her party and government as an autocrat never witnessed before.

After Indira Gandhi, several other women politicians have emerged exerting considerable influence on the formulation of national and state level politics. Mamta Banerji exerted pressure on Congress party, even broke away from the party to formulate a new party which to her was the 'real' Congress party in West Bengal. She dictated terms to Vajpayee government regularly. The year 1998 saw the emergence of Sonia Gandhi as a leader with ample influence and political clout. To certain extent she has revived the Congress party. Then there is Jayalalitha, a very strong and popular leader of Tamil Nadu. Then there is Mayawati, the undisputed Dalit leader and an important decision-make in Uttar Pradesh politics.

The years 1998-99 witnessed the crucial role played by women leaders of the likes of Sonia Gandhi, Jayalalitha, Mamta Banerji and Mayawati. While Sonia Gandhi succeeded to a certain exact in pumping new blood in the otherwise anaemic Congress party, Jayalalitha and Mamta Banerji put pressures on the Vajpayee government from its very inception. Jayalalitha continued threatening the government that she would withdraw. When the Vishnu Bhagwat issue flew up, Jayalalitha ultimately decided to withdraw the support of her 18 MPs on the issue of formation of JPC. The final act was performed by Mayawati when she voted against the government. These four women leaders brought down the Vajpayee government. Obviously in 1998 and early 1999, Indian political scenario had been virtually dominated by these women leaders.

Part -IV

Empowerment

Ten

Political Participation

The subject of discussion is the definition of the term 'political participation' from the vantage point of women's studies, its various manifestations and components, significance in terms of its effectiveness and limitations.

The concept of political participation is closely involved with the concept of power. Since politics is a study of an exercise in power, any political participation should mean a participation in this exercise of power, the power to effectively influence decision-making processes and policies, to reverse the existing situation wherever they are disadvantageous and to bring about the necessary social changes. Hence, political participation Is much more than a physical participation in formal Institutions and structures, though physical participation in formal political institutions is very much necessary for itself and as a means for influencing decisions. Direct and visible participation helps to enlarge freedom of the social group and accelerate the pace of its advancement, but this is not enough. Even an enlarged participation by way of numbers may not lead to the advancement of the cause of that social group. It is, hence, untenable to argue that a substantial increase in the representation of women will automatically lead to greater promotion of women's interests. Further, it is one thing for more women to hold political positions and it is another thing for them to use such positions and power for women's aids. This would also imply that it is lack of sufficient representation of women in various positions at present, which is responsible for their low status or share in the development. It is very much the reverse. A sexual division of labour, the exclusion of women from certain positions and levels of power and their poor representation at decision-making machineries are themselves the result of their poor status.

There are further instances of women when put in positions of power have been the first ones to cut off policies and schemes specially helpful for women. One also finds there is no correlation between extent of participation in formal institutions and the extent of development of women in society. There have been instances where the socially backward regions in India have sent more women into Assemblies, where women have gone in greater numbers to vote (as in Utter Pradesh). In fact, the first woman Chief Minister as well as the first woman Prime Minister in India belonged to this state, even though from the point of view of all development indicators for women, Utter Pradesh is one of the lowest.

It is thus necessary to ask the question as to whose benefit is this participation directed and what impact has this participation made on the policies and the system over a period. For effecting this impact, it is equally necessary to assess as to the levels at which this participation is taking place. Mere number is not enough; it has to be situated at levels which are significant and effective for exercising power. Massive mobilisation and numerically impressive participation in political processes, formal or informal, are not goals in themselves. They are a means and a strategy for achieving something more, which the group can do, only when its participation touches at the structure of politics itself. One has to therefore identify the broader processes of the political structure and the way power is arranged in a particular society. The ideology of the state, the interrelationship between the important components in its structure, like class, caste and gender, and its basic development goals are essential in understanding the repercussions of participation. Often, a vastly expanded participation and wide mobilisation of a socially weak community - in this context women has led to the strengthening of the present pattern of development rather than directing this pattern to their own development. Even values like equality (constitutional, political and economic), rights (property, access to resources) etc.

may be meaningful only when women possess and exercise them for bringing about a change in their own position as well as of the society; otherwise they will merely add up to strengthening and reinforcing the existing social system by operating within the framework of patriarchy. Values like equality and rights, and concepts like participation and mobilisation need to constantly keep before them the objective of the client group. Above all, it should be related to and tested against another equally important value justice.

Any assessment of the political participation of women in India, then, has to start by asking questions like: Whether such participation has led to bringing about or moving towards improving the quality of life for them or simply making it more liveable for women? Whether such participation, by women, either as individuals or as group, has meant developing alternate strategies for development as well as structures of power? Whether political interventions, which women seek to make, start with women as points of departure or merely help women to infiltrate systematically in the existing hierarchies of power, thereby lending themselves to becoming women performers or even worse, careerists? If increasing political participation has to have any meaning for women, such participation should be based on a widespread and well orchestrated mobilisation of women on the central Issue of women's oppression and subordinate status in society and family.

Any analysis of political participation of women in India, hence, would have to combine a few components like (a) the extent, level and nature of women's participation in the political processes of India, by way of both formal and informal institutions; (b) the impact and significance of such participation for women's rights and living conditions, and, (c) types of feminist issues that were raised in the course of this participation.

With the above three criteria in view, one can assess the nature and extent of women's participation in some of the significant formal and informal processes of Indian politics. The Freedom Struggle, peasant and trade union movements, electoral and legislative institutions, the local self government (Panchayat Raj system) and administrative and judicial functioning are some of these formal processes wherein participation of women can be evaluated. There are also institutions like political parties; interest and lobby groups; and, regional, linguistic, religious and casteist, movements where women are participating increasingly. Finally, it is the women's movement, with various women's groups and organisations.

This chapter cannot aim to examine all of these. To illustrate the main argument of this chapter on how to assess participation of women, Let's take up a few examples.

Contribution to Freedom Struggle

The Freedom Struggle in India is one of the few liberation movements in the world, where women had participated in great number. Ever since the formation of the Indian National Congress In 1885, the participation of women in its activities grew steadily, but slowly. The years of social reforms for women from the second quarter of the 19th century, had helped to make them come forward and participate in many ways, both directly and indirectly, formally and informally, with support and backup or many which are now been unrecognised. The huge increase in women's participation following the clarion call of Mahatma Gandhi is, however well documented.

What was the impact of such participation on society, family and on women themselves? The mobilisation of women in large numbers weakened the bondage of traditions and helped them to develop a perspective on wider sociopolitical problems. Their close link with the national movement helped them acquire the right to political participation, to franchise and to other constitutional rights. There developed a tacit acceptance of women occupying various positions, both in the political and professional spheres. It gave them the space, as well as the power to claim rights and question its noncompliance. It thus, helped in bringing about significant changes in the way of thinking and attitude to life of women. Women were initiated in politicisation, and the effect of it could be seen in the gradual but a definite change in the bringing up of the next generation of girls.

The Impact

The net gain in the process was a heightened political awareness, and a much greater social consciousness among women. There were, of course, very few instances of women having defied the family to join in the nationalist movement, or of having given up her traditional values and roles. But the fact that many women, of all classes and walks of life, even housewives and the uneducated joined picketing, moved from house to house collecting clothes and donations, courted arrest and were imprisoned in distant jails, showed that there was nothing which could really prevent them from moving beyond traditional roles. The prevailing political environment and values, seem to have accepted and even positively encouraged such activities on the part of women. The Freedom Movement and Indian women's widespread participation in it, thus, brought out a conducive climate for perceptible changes in many areas. Women's education and participation in work outside home and in the income generation, were some of the changes which come about. The nationalist movement under Gandhi stressed on the simple ways of living, giving up of ostentation in daily lives as well as marriages, in eating habits as well as in women's relief from daily chores so as to give time to picketing, spinning, etc. These broader changes, undoubtedly, led to a changed attitude towards life and women's position. Marriages became simple; dowry system got weakened; education of girls went up; potentialities of girls were identified, tapped and encouraged; widow remarriages and singleness of girls definitely showed an upward trend. More and more women gave up purdah.

The impact of women's participation was immediate and visible on the Congress leadership. Gandhi and Nehru recognised the women's valuable contribution to the nationalist movement, and felt the need for improving their situation. Gandhi said, "I am uncompromising in the matter of woman's rights ...she should labour under no legal disability not suffered by man"

The liberal egalitarian legacy of the Indian National Movement, in turn, had led to the Constitution of free India granting a position of equality to women by way of political rights. The provision of Fundamental Rights to women as equal citizens of India, it was believed then, would automatically provide a status of equality in actual political life. It was assumed that such a constitutional provision would take care of the various issues that had been bedevilling women for centuries and pave the way for their development much in the same way as it was viewed earlier that women's upliftment would come once freedom was achieved.

However from the point of view of women's studies, it would be interesting to see the impact of women's participation and contribution on (a) cultural institutions in society, whether it could break some of the shackles on women and mitigate the social oppression by way of illiteracy, economic dependency, social movement, etc; (b) on the family and its patriarchal structure and values. Did women's role and contribution increase their status in the family to one of equality? Did the nationalist movement then, and the policies and programmes of independent India reflect the recognition of women's contribution and potentialities? While Gandhi's clarion call to women helped them to come out of the four walls, of their houses and join the ranks of soldiers for freedom, he could not deliver much to women by way of rights or policies. His economic policies for women by way of charkha or spinning wheel, did not find a place in the future economic plans. It is only of late that such questions are being pursued. Studies on women in the Freedom Struggle are gradually moving away from women in history to one of women's history.

There is also the question as to how far has this promoted a feminist consciousness in them - whether the women were able to perceive and analyse their own position and work to promote their own rights, within or outside the context of India s freedom. The struggle against a common enemy (the British rule) seemed to have diverted the women by and large, from their own specific oppression. The questions of women's rights within the family, protest against their traditional roles as wives and mothers, against the traditional power relations within the family or to the male defined values etc., did not seem to have figured in a big way. Freedom Movement was born, the movement did not seem to feel concerned with the women's rights issues so as to face them squarely.

This also leaves us with another nagging doubt - 'did this (if so, how far) massive participation of women make any impact on the Indian nationalist movement itself"? Did it affect the stances of the leaders, as well as bring forth any type of policy decisions or programmes for women? Obviously, the concern for women's rights and social position did not pervade the whole of national movement nor did it have any impact on their policies and perspectives. Those like Gandhi and Nehru who recognised women's valuable contribution to the nationalist movement, believed in the need for improving their small proportion.

Nothing really happened or was undertaken for emancipating the women from their various disabilities. There was never any such well articulated organised campaign for women's emancipation, in the same way as there was for Harijan reforms or communal equality. Not that much success could be achieved in those areas either but at least it led to much social awareness. This was evident from the fact that when (soon after Independence) the resurrected report of the BN Rau Committee on the Draft of Hindu Code called the Hindu Law Bill was placed before the Constituent Assembly, it was opposed by many traditionalists in the assembly Apparently, the Fundamental Rights and the equality that Congress had talked about, related only to the political spheres - not to the private and familial spheres. It took more than seven years before the Parliament could finally adopt one small portion of the original draft, viz. with regard to marriage, divorce and maintenance. One had to be happy with the mere inclusion of the Uniform Civil Code in Article 44 of the Directive Principles of State Policy of the Constitution. Obviously, the voice of women was not loud enough to shake the leadership nor their participation in the decision-making was strong enough to demand their rights effectively.

Participation in the Democratic Process

In any modern political system, elections occupy the most central place. The nature, periodicity and rate of participation by the masses in elections, is viewed as the touchstone for the representative character of democracy, and hence, democracy itself. Almost all nations in the world have adopted universal adult suffrage, wherein every adult, without any additional qualification or conditions, has the right to vote in general elections held periodically. How regular are these elections? What is the percentage of participation in voting by the people? How organised or peaceful the polls are? These, in turn, indicate the health and strength of democracy.

Elections being a forum for and method in self-government and democracy, occupy a significant place in drawing the attention of the nation to the problems and needs of the disadvantaged sectors. The party manifestoes, campaigns, individual candidate's promises, track records and future course of action, are indicative of the national concerns, as well as, mandates for action. As the instrument that brings into being the national Parliament and state Assemblies, the outcome of elections in terms of parties and individuals are significant for the adaptation of policies and measures for women's development.

Democracy does not, and cannot operate by proxy. Every citizen, conscious of his and the national movement's development, and aware of the value and utility of the vote to fetch the same, needs to correlate this right with development. This, he can do only by exercising this right (or by participating) in elections. The participatory theory of democracy believes that direct participation in decision making would be the ideal of citizens ruling themselves in a modern state whose size and population are large, whose problems are complex, and the art of governing almost a managerial technique, the next best would be a representative democracy. It is then that a psephologist worries about the voting percentage of the population in general, and of the depressed sections in particular. The proper selection of a correct party/candidate in an election is vital, if this representative democracy has to function in the interest of a majority of the population, which are depressed and disadvantaged.

Many studies believed that women are not independent voters; (ii) that a majority of them are illiterate; (iii) that a majority of them make their choice on the basis of suggestions given by male members of the family husband and sons; (iv) that women lack information and political awareness; and (v) women were not politically conscious. However, these studies defined the words political participation very narrowly. Despite these limitations, one way make a general analysis of the voting pattern of women. A quick glance at their participation in elections over the past four decades will confirm the initial hopes placed by the founders of the Constitution. The extent, nature and level of Indian women's participation is much greater than in many other countries developed or developing, except possibly in the countries that were going through radical revolutionary wars. A certain cultural background as well as the freedom struggle could be the main reasons for this. This participation has been more or less expanding steadily over the years, through the various elections-by way of voting, as candidates and participation in campaigning etc. The gap in the turnout between men and women is getting more and more narrowed. The number of women getting elected to the representative bodies is slowly increasing.

This increase in the turnout of women voters, particularly of the lower class and castes, may be attributed, to a high degree of mobilisation rather than of one's own political consciousness. In India, one can talk in general of high level of awareness of the value to vote which is possessed and cast eagerly by the poor and the Scheduled Castes at times very pragmatically and rationally. They are politically sensitive, well aware of their interests and even the political issues. But this awareness, in order to be translated into a political exercise like voting needs tremendous mobilisation. This is all the more in the case of women as poverty and daily work, household chores and care, patriarchal and family norms, act as great disincentives. Distance of booths, possibility of violence, health and other factors further discourage them. The linkage between the 'personal' and 'public' is missing; and women do not feel automatically impelled.

Recognising the significance of the women voters many political parties have, of late, been exerting themselves to devise various methods. Mobilisation in the past have been mainly at the time of decisions in the form of adhoc promises made on populistic and opportunistic short-term basis, rather than on long-term goals of a social change for women.

To the extent there was any correlation between the campaign promises and voting support, it also reflected on the low impact that the women's movement had made in educating their lot, as well as in making a dent on the patriarchal politicians. The Congress Party too, was not far behind. In 1984, much of the victory of Congress (1) could be attributed to a sympathy vote by women for the young Prime Minister and against the slaying of the women Prime Minister Indira Gandhi on a woman-to-woman basis.

The increase in the number of women voters since independence and their eager participation in voting, has made almost all political parties pay special attention to organising themselves, campaigning among themselves, and choosing them to contest elections. Definitely in the earlier years such campaigning among women and soliciting their votes were done rather casually. More recently, the parties have organised regular party forums, cells and front organisations, specially for women. These women's cells not only mobilise and campaign among women, and seek their support and membership for party issues during elections as well as normal period, but also quite often take up issues concerning women. Of late, parties are also taking stand on women's issues, organise rallies and demonstrations, pass resolutions, lobby with and pressurise the government for specific policies. Women are participating in them in great numbers and have even courted arrest on issues like sati, Muslim Women's Right to Maintenance, rape incidents, violence, police excesses on women etc.

Women in Party Positions

But in this context, there are many important questions to ask. In view of the extent of the recognition of the need for women's support, both for image building as well as electoral successes, how many women have been able to occupy important positions in the party? There have been many important political personalities among women at the helm of various parties. There have been a number of women who were members of the highest executive committees of their parties and have functioned as office bearers. The Congress Party, particularly, has taken care to give representation to women among its office-bearers. In fact, it has almost become axiomatic in India that the highest decision-making bodies of the various parties need to have definitely at least one or two women members. It is, however, necessary to ask the question whether it is a mere tokenism. Such representation by being very limited in number, as well as often occupied by weak and colourless personalities, does become more a symbolism rather than real power wielding. There are, of course, some exception to this.

Despite the increase, the number of women contesting the elections still constitute only one to 2 per cent. Even where seats are reserved as in the Panchayats, they do not come forward so easily. Out of these contestants, the ones who get elected constitute still smaller percentage. While those who belong to the major political parties stand a better chance of success, the non-party candidates and those who belong to minor political parties, are hardly successful. Despite this, many women contest as independents. This perhaps implies that political parties are, by and large reluctant to choose women as candidates, the maximum number of candidates being from the Congress Party. But even this party allotted only 3 per cent of seats in 1977 to women. Obviously, this is much more in the nature of a tokenism rather than an acceptance of women's equality or capability. Often women candidates are viewed as depriving men in their chances. Even the small number of women who contest, gain their candidates by their birth and close relationship with already established party leaders. Almost all the women who figure in electoral politics are invariably someone's wife, daughter, daughter-in-law or in other close relations. There are exceptions only among the Left parties, where a few of them can claim as having worked with the working class. Most of these women, thus, come from urban, middle class, with educated elite, background and cannot claim a stage-by-stage growth or participation in their political career. Apparently, there is no correlation between female population's voting percentage and their number in the elected assemblies. The subordinated position of the 'ordinary' women in families, their routine and normal duties of looking after the family, bringing up children, performing both the unpaid and paid work, do not allow them much scope to participate freely in public-political activities. To this must be added the economic factor. Elections in India as in all other modern democracies, has become very complicated, violent, dirty and expensive, inviting thereby very many legitimate and not so legitimate ways of finding and managing them. Women cannot obviously fit into this matrix of election. The participation costs in formal politics is at present too high for women. Political participation of women, by the conventional and formal yardstick, thus is low, and lower than men of even weaker sections. In the case of Scheduled Castes and Tribes, due to reservation of constituencies, the number of representatives is proportionate to the population. But it is ironic, if not cruel that only one of these seats had gone to woman. No study has yet been undertaken on an all India basis, on the nature and extent of women's participation in the legislative business. In the early years after Independence, the Parliament did witness many women like Renuka Ray participating vigorously in the Hindu Code Bill, etc. More recently, many women members of Parliament (MPs) belonging to different parties are drawing attention to issues like atrocities against women, women's rights, social crimes like sati, dowry, rape, etc. Still by and large, such participation is confined repeatedly to few women. A majority of them are silent on many issues, particularly on the general, political concerns. On the whole, it looks like those who are good and articulate and participate often. Others who are dormant, are invisible and silent on most of the issues. Political parties must exercise more care in choosing the correct type of women who are knowledgeable and can represent the majority of the poor and rural women. More presence of women in Parliament, even if of a greater number, will mean very little by way of women's development.

The above two processes have been taken up merely to point out some of the possible dangers involved in analysing the participation or pleading for increased participation of women in political developments and institutions. This is not attempted in order to discourage such pleas nor in a mood of cynicism nor negativism. The visible participation of more and more women in the public sphere, their greater representation at the decision-making and managerial level, are definitely important for more than one reason. Apart from their own possible contribution to women's development with a degree of empathy and understanding, they also would be able to project and sensitise fellow workers, politicians and executives on women's perspectives, and help adopt mid-term corrections in policies and their implementation. It acts further as role models for younger and other women with political and personal ambitions. May be it is too much to expect from every woman to have cultivated a perspective on "correct" women's studies on every issue, but one can hope at least some women to have images or acquire it in the course.

As women's studies are gaining deeper roots in India and as women's development is getting increasing attention, it is prudent that the women's studies scholars take stock of some of the developments and attempt conceptual clarification.

Eleven

In the Fray

Not only in India, but, almost in all countries, right from the developed to the developing ones, women's presence in the political process is marginal and low except a few countries (the Nordic countries). Women's movements for their rights started in the later half of the 19th century and continued till the first half of the 20th century, ultimately crystallising to a demand for the 'right to vote'. Women in many countries had to wage long and grim battle to get this right. In most countries, they got this from the second decade of the present century. Despite their struggle for a long period, women have, not yet been able to attain a rightful position in the arena of politics.

Radical feminists have gone beyond just the right to vote, maintaining that the demand for right to vote came from women of the elite class to find some room for themselves in the established power structure. There is now an emphasis on the right to participate in the political decision-making. And it is here that the crunch lies. The percentage of women as voters has increased considerably in most of the countries, but they have not been able to create a niche for themselves in the policy-formulating and decision-making bodies. Their political status remains secondary.

Barbare Nelson and Najma Choudhury, the editors of the book: Women and Politics Worldwide, maintain that a study has been carried out in 43 countries on women's political engagement, which reveals the fact that women everywhere have a secondary political status. They maintain that there have been women of substance in politics, holding on their own, but such women are exceptions and it's not the rule. They also imply that it does not mean that all women experience their subordinate political status in a similar way, or all groups of women are subordinate to all groups of men in a similar way. In most cultures there is a complex matrix of political power, composed of many social hierarchies, of which gender is only one component. Nevertheless, men of any group are more able to be active in politics than women of their group. They emphasise that the ubiquity of women's secondary political status demonstrates how politics is intertuned with other aspects of life. They see politics, economics, culture, religion and law as mutually constitutive, each creating itself and the other at the same time. The secondary position of women in each realm is reinforced by the total pattern of male privileges. But each sphere of society also creates unique elements of gender inequality and its own opportunities for resistance, innovations and transformation.

Women's political participation has to be discussed in the context of gender and patriarchy. Gender is defined as the social construction of relations between women and men and among various groups of women and men. Feminist scholarship places gender as the "sociocultural manifestation of being a man or women- at the focus of inquiry in research and study and arrived at a 'gendered' understanding of society. It has been a long battle to show that a woman is not a mere composite of female anatomy and physiology, sex and gender are not identical. Sex connotes a biological difference between the male and female. The difference between sex and gender is at once a liberator as well as an explorator, for if we are convicted that discrimination, oppression and exploitation that are ascribed to natural difference are false deduction, and that body differences do not warrant these differentiation, and they are socially produced, then we have a basis for action. Gender is the most potent, significant and enormously useful analytical concept that feminists have thrown up. It is a matter of social ascription, a socio-cultural construction and provided a deeper analysis of inequalities existing between male and female. The feminist scholars through the application of the concept of gender have challenged the structures-socio-economic political and cultural processes. Simon de Bearnvoir maintains, "one is not born but rather made a women". To quote her, "she is defined and differentiated with reference to men and not with reference to her; she is incidental and unessential as opposed to the essential. He is the subject, he is the absolute she is the other". Nancy Chodorow maintains that since women have always been assigned the responsibility of primary parenting and nurturing, they develop a psychology of being most suited to the task of nurturing and caring, and thus, themselves choose the role of the care-giver and 'confinement to the private'. Rosaldo supports the theory that in most societies, so far gender has been a socially constructed category rather than biologically determined. Unda Nicholsan maintains that the gender structure in a particular time and space is less affected by other contemporary structures such as political, economic etc. more by the previous history of gender.

The concept of gender, thus, explains the division of spheres of action into private and public. The private sphere belongs to women while the male is assigned the public spheres. Firestone argues against this separation of spheres of activity.

This public/private dichotomy has resulted in women being marginalised in all spheres of activity - social, economic and more specifically, political. Rationality, self-discipline, competition, universality to mention a few are the priced qualities of political parlance. These are inherent in male. On the contrary, irrationality, indiscipline particularly, submissiveness, impulsiveness are some of the qualities associated with female nature.

Patriarchy looms large in feminist debate. Patriarchy implies that power is imperative in gender relations. As a substantive, it usually refers to some form of systemic male dominance. Kata Millet in Sexual Political and Shulasmith in The Dialectic of Sex sees patriarchy as a broad system of power of men over women. This patriarchal character of society pervades ideology and culture.

Millet, Firestone, Mackennon and the whole movement behind them have drawn our attention to the pervasiveness of sexual domination and the role of force and male violence as a major social-historical reality.

The origins of the concept can be traced to the 19th century women's movement and in Marxism. Mark and Engels in their German Ideology had incorporated crucial insight about women. Engel's major contribution was to bequeath to the working class movement, a conceptualisation that women were not naturally the, second sex. They were in fact being exploited within an oppressive family structure. Though, he used the term 'father right, this was essentially a conceptualisation of patriarchy.

Contemporary feminist theories of patriarchy emerged primarily in reaction to and in confrontation with the mechanical materialistic form of Marxism that had developed. This was because in the Marxist tradition concepts 'patriarchy' was retained in, however, inadequate a form. It has avoided biologism and retrained the nation of a separate male-dominated family/reproduction system. Radical feminism has sought to replace economic class struggle with a nation of sexual class struggle.

Without going into the detailed analysis of the various theories of patriarchy and later its downfall, we can for our purpose of study infer that power is imperative in gender relations, in producing gender relations and in maintaining these in some way or other.

In actual practice, the rule of the patriarch over the household and family has been extended into the rule of the male over the female in wider society, economy and politics. Experiences in various political systems with very different hierarchy and cultural patterns proves the patriarchal mindset of the male over female in all spheres of life and its activities. The resistance of female participation in politics is also a direct result of this mindset. The resistance to female participation in politics is a direct result of this mindset, although other environmental factors cannot be ignored. Even the definition of politics for centuries has been the result of gender-patriarchy considerations. The feminist academics have questioned the traditional definition and constituents of politics, and charged it with gender bias. Before going into the details of efforts at a redefinition of politics from feminist perspective, we turn to the conventional definition and constituents of politics.

Politics has been defined in various ways, but there is a common thread running through all of them, that it is inevitable in any society. It is about representation, policy, position and power with government as its area. Miller maintains that it is the activity which aims at bringing government to bear in a particular direction, to secure particular results. Laswell maintained that political process is the shaping, sharing and exercise of power. Involvement in politics is directed towards influencing power channels and elites for protecting one's rights and self-interests and giving legitimacy to political elites and their decisions. Conventionally, politics deals with the formal political structures but it has now been wined by political theorists to include movements, protests and struggle as legitimate expressions of political behaviour. Political sphere, thus, includes the "spheres in social relations, where power relations are generated, institutionalised and used to encourage, control or move people's attitudes, beliefs in a specified direction to control and regulate the distribution of resources."

Feminist scholars have been very concerned about what constitutes politics, that it is basically male activity. They have challenged the dominant hypothesis that politics is confined to public sphere. They maintain that traditional Politics legitimises women's exclusion or absence from the power spheres and also devalues women's concerns.

Feminists also argue for a redefinition of politics. An important feature of their efforts have been to proclaim the Political nature of private life and the relation between sexes, which has brought traditional political science into question and has forced the authorities to take account of Problems hitherto regarded as belonging to private life. Political participation has to be discussed and understood in this light.

Active Participation

Political participation has been defined in various ways, but in nutshell it refers to the participation of individuals in the political process, and that it ensures that individuals are able to take part in deciding the common goals of the society and the best ways of achieving it.

Kazenstein Mary Fainshod conceptualises political participations as public membership of citizen 'sharing' justice and orienting their action towards a public or a common good. Political participation also connotes activities for protecting one's rights and duties and advancing interest through competition.

The concept of participation as an instrumental action for having a close link with power is postulated by Laswell and Parsons Verba. Nie states political participation as "the activities by private citizens that are more or less directly aimed at influencing the selection of governmental personnel and/or the action they take. Political participation as instrumental action is close to 'exchange theory'. Politics is depicted in the language of bargaining, exchange and efficiency. A rational citizen is considered to be a consumer of private benefits. Participation is thought of as cost incurred in the political market only when one's vital interests are at stake. The result is a cost-benefit account according to which rational citizens minimise costs and maximise benefits. Rayon terms such action as rational. It may be assumed that participation is rational in the sense that it consists of the examination of alternative actions and the selection of that alternative, which yield the greatest expected utility. Self-interest, thus, is the main base for choice of ones action.

These two concepts are two different ways of representing rationality of political participation.

Milbrath maintains, "every person participates atleast passively in the political system in which he lives.... There is no such thing as not behaving. Thus, apathy or passivity is a form of Political participation for some.

In liberal democratic political systems, it is regarded as essential that more and more people participate in the system. However various studies have revealed that only a very small percentage, even less than 10 per cent participate in the political process. Actually participation and its extent is related to various factors - the psychological make up of the person, his total personality and external environment the social, economic, cultural, individual response to such stimuli, but his political attitude is outcome of his social Personality and his Political options reflect the characteristic modes of his adjustments to life.

Milbrath holds that political participation differs in relation to four major factors: (i) the extent to which the individual receives political stimuli; (ii) the individual's personal characteristics; (iii) social characteristics: and (iv) the political environment in which the individual finds himself. Dahi is of the opinion that some people are indifferent to politics, others are more deeply involved. Even among those who are deeply involved, Only some actually seek power and among the power seekers, some gain power more than others.

Milbrath basing on the intensity of participation divides input Political activity mainly into three categories (i) active: (ii) passive or supportive; and (iii) apathetic. Active political activity is again categorised into conventional and unconventional. Participation in protest process, is regarded by Milbrath as unconventional.

Low Participation

Participation of women in the political process has been very low. Their presence in the legislative and decision-making bodies is scarcely above 10 per cent except some Nordic countries. It has been often stated that the personality traits of women (lack of self-esteem to be precise) and the socio-economic cultural environment and, on the other hand, the political environment is to a great extent responsible for women's Marginal participation in politics.

Preceding observations reveal that self-esteem, standing in the society, the culture which puts maximum premium on the male and the political environment of instability, criminalisation and absence of political ideology are factors which influence the extent of political participation.

Women fall mainly into the group of those who are apathetic to politics because of the group of those who are apathetic to politics because of their low status in society (ii) lesser exposure to education (iii) very low economic status (iv) the restraining, cultural norms and, (v) the unhealthy political environment, the nature of political structure, such as party structure, process of political succession, which supports or opposes the recruitment of women to political offices.

In nutshell the socio-political environment determines the participation and involvement of women in politics. Culture is a very dominant factor. It deprives women of the self-esteem necessary for political leadership. Jean J Kirkpatrick observes "in a culture which values the male more highly than the female, women may never acquire the confidence and autonomy required to seek power and wield it effectively." Culture decides role choices, "The transition from the roles of housewife and mother to the role of political decision-maker is riot easy, and has not been frequently attempted. The roles of housewife, mother, law-maker etc, do not have what Eulau and Spranger have called professional convergence". Kirkpatrick refutes the established relationship between power, politics, and maleness. According to her, the female psychology is no more a disqualification for politics. She maintained that in the ultimate analysis, "to many radical feminists culture, ideology and social structure are conspiracy. The enemies are male and female are the most oppressed political caste in history."

Levels and Areas

The most prevalent political action is voting in elections. Although the 'right to vote' was won after a grim battle in most of the Western liberal democracies, at present women constitute a reasonable percentage of total voters in almost all political systems with the exception of some Middle East Muslim states.

Although there has been a global awareness and realisation that political participation does not only mean the right to vote (right from the Mexico conference in 1975 through Copenhagen, Nairobi and Beijing), yet women's presence in legislative bodies is scarce despite the absence of legal constraints.

So women have been accepted as voters but not as policy formulators and decision-makers. Women's movement has for the last two or three decades been demanding more space for women in the representative bodies, but things have scarcely changed. Demands for affirmative action/reservation as an instrument for ensuring more space to women has been repeatedly turned down in many countries. The ERA never got passed in USA. In India, although 33 per cent reservation was provided for women at grass-root level and local institutions through the constitutional amendment in 1993, the bill providing for 33 per cent reservation to women in the Lok Sabha and the state assemblies was not passed in 1996. It was not allowed even to be tabled in the Lok Sabha in 1998. This speaks a lot about the rigid patriarchal approach of the male political leaders. They will not let any effort for giving more space to women in politics go waste.

Even though democracy has made great gains in the 1990s, women average only 11.6 per cent of the world legislatures (inter-parliamentary union, 1997). Women essentially are appointed by men leaders in at least 37 undemocratic countries or are entirely missing from the national legislatures. In an additional 49 nations - the new democracies or the partially developed ones - men parliamentarians dominate the legislature with 93 per cent membership. Only in the 27 long-established but unfinished democracies do women have the greatest opportunity for equality in representation. Yet, women members of these Parliaments average only 15 per cent.

Government of the people, by the people and for the people - Abraham Lincoln's concept of democracy - is an ideal which remains unachieved in the world specially in the context of half the population of any country, the women.

Democracy falls short when women of whatever colour or ethnic groups cannot vote or caste votes, and cannot expect success in electing representation of their choice, or being elected to the legislative bodies, and have little hope for enactment of laws they believe are critically needed.

The reasons - narrow gender roles, restrictive religious doctrines, unequal laws and education, discriminatory socio-economic conditions, male biased leaders or other political elites and women-unfriendly election system. The barriers, while varying among countries typically are interrelated and mutually reinforcing.

Anne Phillips in her The politics of presence maintains that the shift from direct to representation democracy has shifted the emphasis from who the politicians are to what they represent. She further maintains that men may consciously stand for women when what is at issue is the representation of agreed policies or programmes on ideals, but how can men legitimately stand in for women when what is at issue is the representation of women par se.

Phillips speaks about gender parity and accounts that a significant number of political parties have adopted the measures to raise the proportion of women elected. She recounts the experiences in South Africa and European countries like UK, Germany, the Nordic countries where, when one party adopted a gender quota other parties also followed suit. The green party in Germany contributed to the quota - the Christian Democratic Party was adopted in 1986. There is consensus among major political parties in UK, atleast at the central level, in favour of selecting more women candidates.

She maintains that changing the gender composition of elected assemblies is a major and necessary challenge to the social arrangements, which have systematically placed women in a subordinate position and whether we conceive of politics as the representation of interests or need (or both) a closer approximation to gender parity is one minimal condition for transforming the political agenda. But she also mentions that this change cannot guarantee anything. The case for gender parity among our political representatives inevitably operates in a framework of pobabilities; rather than certanities. She maintains that politics of presence points towards rather different policy recommendation depending on the nature of the excluded group. In relation to women, a straight-forward quota seems entirely appropriate. In comparison to racial or ethnic quotas, the introduction of minimum quota for women and men is less inherently problematic because there are self evidently two sexes.

Phillips is, thus, in favour of politics of presence. It can ensure that there is a possibility of gender parity, as politics of presence can provide separate recommendation for the excluded group.

In the Process

Women in India entered the political process in the early decades of the present century, through their massive participation in the national struggle for freedom under the leadership of Mahatma Gandhi. Gandhiji was able to reach out to women and draw them Into the vertex of the freedom movement. Though Gandhi could not fully abandon gender bias and in some way perpetuated the traditional image of the Indian women he did manage to appeal to women to join the movement. Women played a very important role in the Civil Disobedience Movement, the salt satyagraha and the Quit India Movement of 1942. Together with their Participation in movement against the colonial rule, the educated women were simultaneously struggling to get the right to vote and right to get elected. Generally, It is maintained that the women participating in the struggle especially, those who were in key positions were from the elite class. Not much has been written about thousands of Infamous women, who were poor and had rural background, but who In their own humble way had participated in the national freedom struggle.

Some women leaders were very articulate in their ideas and their awareness of the situation was prevalent. For example, in 1917, even before women in England got the right to vote. Sarojini Naidu had petitioned to the British Parliament the Indian women's demand for equal voting rights with men.

Gandhi had said as early as in 1929, "women must have the right to vote and equal legal status. But the problem does not end there. It only commences at the point where women begin to effect the political deliberations of the nation."

Gandhiji brought an absolutely new dimension into the debate on women's problem. He began from the basic issue that subjugation of and exploitation of women was the product of "men's teaching and women's acceptance of them, and thereby broke away from the reform tradition by preaching the philosophy not only of absolute equality of rights between the sexes, but the pragmatic necessity of enrolling women's support to transform the nationalist struggle for the transfer of power from the British to India through social revolution.

There is little doubt that it was the willing and spontaneous participation of women in the Civil Disobedience Movement rather than the radical ideas of sexual equality that finally tilted the balance in favour of political equality between the sexes within the Congress party and later in the Constituent Assembly.

The Constitution of free India saluted the massive participation of women in the freedom struggle by equal rights to enter into politics irrespective of gender and other factors.

It is now nearly 49 years since the Constitution was adopted in 1950. Despite the opportunity of equal access to the political process guaranteed by law, the presence of Indian women in politics is still scarce. Their representation has never gone beyond 9 per cent in Parliament, 10 per cent in state assemblies and 15 per cent in the Council of Ministers. Even though India had a Prime Minister like Indira Gandhi - the longest surviving women Prime Minister- women have not been able to find space in the representative and decision-making bodies.

Women's movements in India have been struggling for women's political for nearly five to six decades, yet women have only managed to get their demands for quota/reservation in Parliament and state legislatures included in election manifestoes of the political parties in 1991, 1996 and 1998 general elections.

The parties despite their promises have displayed their gender bias in giving tickets to women to fight elections. The Congress (I) has not been able even to put 15 per cent women candidates, although the party has the record of putting up comparatively the highest number of women candidates.

A major reason forwarded by all political parties is that the chances of women candidates winning are very thin compared to male candidates. However, the election reports display that the percentage of women winning in relation to their total candidates is much higher than male.

April 23, 1993 was a red letter day for Indian women, when the 73rd Constitutional Amendment gave statutory status to panchayats and provided 33 per cent reservation of seats to women at every tier of the grassroot political institutions. The elections have revealed that the number of women in gram panchayats is increasing steadily.

The granting of reservation to women at grass-root-level institution inspired women to make a similar demand with regard to Lok Sabha and state legislatures. Women activists and academics have been intensifying their demands in this regard, but it is being met with a constant protest by the males, as displayed in 1996 and 1998 by male members cutting across party lines.

Adequate representation in representative bodies is very important for women's empowerment in the political process, and reservation/ affirmative action is being seen as the most potent strategy. The negative aspects are being heatedly debated not only by men, but also by some women activities. The debate still continues.

An important shift is being noted in the last couple of years from representation to governance. The Centre for Women's Development Studies, New Delhi, organised a meeting on gender democracy and governance In September 1997, in which Rajni Kothari opined in his paper that from focus on representation to focus on governance was an important transition. Why this emerging interest in governance? Because representation without participation in governance will only underscore the existing order. All feminists agree that gender represents a system of power relation. In Indian history, however, it can only be defined as an instrument to maintain a hierarchical social order designed to perpetuate inequality and diversity of a multiethnic, multi-lingual and multi-cultural population, said Vina Majuradar.

Caste is an important factor in Indian politics. Social scientists have been grappling with the phenomenon of caste for a long time, but only few have appreciated that the major instrument for maintaining the hierarchy even more than diversity is the subordination of women. Srinivasan's theory of Sanskritisation with increasing subordination/control on women believed to be applicable only to upwardly mobile. The studies by the Centre for Women's Development Studies, New Delhi find it equally manifest among all other groups, including the tribals, generally believed to be more generous in recognising women's right.

Women by and large have demonstrated their stake in democracy, especially when they threw out Indira Gandhi's government which was the first major attack on democracy since Independence. With the resurgence of women's movement since the 1970s. it advocates that "transformational politics" have increasingly recognised the potential of the movement to deepen democracy in India. Most analysis however, continue to harness the fear that women's large scale entry into power structures will only result in cooperation instead of changing the undemocratic and corruptive elements in these structures.

Vina Majumdar suspects that these fears are based on the continued undemocratic view of power and a narrow understanding of politics.

Majumdar writes about 'social engineering' as democracy in India was a radical departure from the inherited social system. At present, social engineering has become politically incorrect and nation states are being asked to reduce their interventionist roles. In the kind of democracy India has this weakening and extremely negative impact on the quality of governance or the management of power.

The chapters of this book have tried to examine the role of women in the political process in India within the conceptual framework of gender and patriarchy. Women's role in the national freedom struggle has been analysed, and it has been found that gender equality was never the concern of our reformers in the late 19th century or our political leaders of the movement. They wanted a better place for women in the society, but for they never considered women's right as "individuals".

Similarly, the participation of women in formal political institutions and process has been severely restricted by gender considerations. The socio-cultural norms still restrict the movements and behaviour of women. Despite all the changes, women's behaviour is still restricted by the private female and public/male dichotomy. A very recent example is from Haryana where girls of 18 years are not allowed to cast their vote if they are unmarried. They can cast their votes only as married women if their husbands and family members permit and in the manner they want.

The opposition to women's reservation provided by the 81st Constitutional Amendment in 1996 by the male MPs and again in 1998 clearly mirrors the patriarchal attitude of our men in politics. It is very clear that they will not permit the loss of nearly 180 seats in Parliament to women, which will happen precisely if 33 per cent seats in Look Sabha are reserved for women.

The gender and patriarchal norms have perpetuated the subordination of women in the family and extended their subordination in the wider society, economy and polity. The environmental deterrents - social economic, cultural as well as political factors are in a close way related to these norms. India is characterised as a nation which is poor, has low level of education and awareness, is overridden by the feudal considerations. It is a multi-ethnic, multilingual and multi-religious society, and not all groups have equal access to the arena of politics. Yet, among all groups men have better enhances of access than women. The present Parliament in India consists of a majority of members from the backward castes and Dalits, but has the number of women of these groups or communities accordingly increased?

True, women need to be made conscious of their role in politics, the importance of their participation in parties and women's groups are continuously trying to train and mobilise them but centuries of subordination and passivity cannot be wished away in two decades. More than 50 years of Independence have not been able to ensure reasonable space for women in the representative bodies. It has not gone above 10 per cent. Therefore, there is a need for affirmative action in the form of quote/reservation for women. It is the prime need of the time.

Twelve

Democratic Process

In democratic system, the process of election is the main wheel in the excercise. With the prevalence of indirect democracy in almost all the democratic countries of the world, it assumes great importance as a mechanism for choosing representatives for elective offices by means of votes by the people. By voting, we constitute the government and choose our law-makers and law-executors. It is not only primarily a legitimising instrument for those in, authority and for their governance, it is a positive right of the people, through which they decide the destiny of their political system.

The total population of any country does not constitute a homogeneous group. Similarly, our society is plural and consists of various well-organised groups and communities with different interests and needs competing for a share in political power through the mechanism of elections. Not each group has equal access to power in a democratic polity despite the popular myth of equality for all. There are minorities identified on the basis of religion, race and ethnicity all over the globe. Women do not constitute a minority in numbers as they constitute nearly 50 per cent of the total population of any country, but practically have a minor position and only a marginal access to polity due to gender bias.

Feminists have thrown up gender as the most potent, significant and enormously useful analytical concept. The feminist scholarship places gender, the sociocultural manifestation of being a man or woman as the focus of study in research. Gender is defined as the social construction of relations between women and men and among various groups of women or men. Sex is defined as the biological similarities and differences between and among men, and women.

Gender and patriarchy combine together to push women to the periphery of politics. Politics is regarded strictly as a male preserve. Rationality, self-discipline, competition, aggression, orderliness, universality to mention a few, are the priced qualities in political parlance. On the contrary, irrationality, indiscipline, particularity, submissiveness impulsiveness are some of the qualities associated with feminine nature. The result is the distancing of women from everything political. Women are perceived as part of the social structure and not as part of the "power" phenomenon, which Seinon De Behaviour calls as "being rather than doing".This socio-cultural perspective in addition to mass-scale illiteracy and poverty of Indian women prevents them from a meaningful involvement in the political process.

Women's right to vote and to stand for elections has only been a legal reality for about 100 years globally. Although men vote was not extended initially to all classes and races, generally their universal enfranchisement preceeded women. It was first adopted by the European countries, the Americas and Australia. The end of World War II in 1945 brought former colonial countries in Asia and Africa to grant women's suffrage, and the trend has continued worldwide, with South Africa enfranchising black women and men as late as 1994.

Although the right to stand for elections, to be a candidate and to be elected follows in theory from the right to vote. Earlier several countries had granted suffrage only. Women's right to vote was restricted to male candidates only. Canada granted women the unrestricted right to vote in 1950, but not until 10 years later did they gain the right to be candidates. Conversely, some countries put women's right to be elected as their first political right. USA, Norway, the Netherlands, and Guyana, for example, allowed women to run for office and to be elected by an all male electorate. Kuwait disallows women both voting and candidates rights while extending them to men, and four others. Saudi Arabia. Qatar, Oman and Somalia - deny them to both genders. Since Finland adopted both these fundamental democratic rights in 1906, over 95 per cent of the countries of the world have followed suit by the end of the 20th century.

The Constitution of India from 1950, guarantees equal opportunity for participation in politics to both men and women. Women were given this right equally with men in recognition and as a 'token' of appreciation by the national leaders for the massive role played by them in the freedom struggle. The Preamble to the Constitution of India resolves to secure to all its citizens. Justice, social and economic and political; Liberty of thought, expression. belief, faith and worship; Equality of status and opportunity; and to promote among them all, fraternity, assuming the dignity of all individuals and the unity of the nation. Article 14 of the Constitution ensures 'equality before law" and Article 15 prohibits discrimination" interalia of sex among other things.

The gradual transfer of power from the British to Indian hands gave women experience in participation in democratic process. The Government of India Act of 1935 extended the franchise to more than 6 million women, a great improvement on the earlier figure of 3,15,000 under the act of 1919. But for this franchise right, women did have to wage a grim battle. Lord Lothian, the head of the franchise committee after meeting the women's delegation led by Sarojini Naidu, remarked that "they were very firm in their demand for equality as a basis of the new Indian Constitution". As early as 1930, a meeting of the representatives of women's organisations had demanded immediate acceptance of adult franchise without sex discrimination. Though rejected by the British government, the Karachi session of the Indian National Congress in 1931 accepted these demands and committed Itself to women's political equality regardless of their status and qualifications.

In 1937 elections, eight women were elected from general constituencies and 42 from reserved constituencies. The Constituent Assembly set up for the drafting of the Constitution of free India in

October 1946 had among its members, Sarojini Naidu, Durgabi Deshmukh, Renuka and Hansa Mehta among other notables.

Women as Voters

India has experienced 12 general elections to date. It has not been possible for election analysts to decide which particular way the women have voted, but their votes have undoubtedly been Included in this "on course" corrective voting for giving a fresh lease of power to the elected parliamentary form of government.

With the rising number of electorate, the percentage of women voters has also registered a steady rise constantly from 37; 1 per cent in 1952 to 69.70 per cent in 1971. However, in 1977 the difference was 9.7 per cent to increase further to 10.77 per cent in 1977 and 10.94 per cent in 1980. In 1984, women had polled a higher percentage of votes to fall again steadily in 1989. Since then, however, there has been a discernable fall from 69.70 per cent to 55.85 per cent in 1977 and 51.22 per cent in 1980. The year 1984 was a 'watershed' when the percentage of women voters went upto 68.17 per cent to fall again in 1989 to 43.90 per cent and 47.42 per cent in 1991. In the 1996 Lok Sabha, elections the total number of women voters in the country was 28,03,69,086, while that of male voters was 30,98,15,776.7 There was a slight improvement in 1998 elections.

As compared to the total voter turnout, the figures for female voters have always been less by approximately 6 per cent. Looking at the trends in female voting, similar fluctuations as in total voting are evident. In 1967, the percentage of female votes was 55.48 per cent marking a decrease of 6.33 per cent. This decrease is somewhat equal to the fall in total voting percentage, which shows that in comparative terms, women's voting did not depict a discouraging trend.

A better comparative assessment can be had by looking at the difference in the percentage of male and female voters. This difference has always been unfavourable to women. In, 1991, the percentage difference was 27 per cent but in 1996 it narrowed down to 5.14 per cent.

The general inferences are that women have shown a gradual increase in the exercise of their franchise, and this increase has been proportionate to the increase in total voter turnout. In 1971 elections, there was decrease in the percentage of voters in general. The difference between male and female voters was 11.85 per cent. The low turnout was due to various factors operating at that time. The split within the Congress Party; election being held one year earlier due to the dissolution of Lok Sabha, etc. Both these factors proved detrimental to the mobilisation of voters in the 1971 election. However, the fact that the difference between male and female voting did not widen with the total fall in mobilisation shows that the female voters were more mobilised than their male counterparts while the total voter turnout increased only by 0.50 per cent (54.76 per cent to 55.35 per cent), the increase in female voter turn out was 2.52 per cent (46.64 per cent to 49.15 per cent). In 1974 and 1980, there was no improvement, rather a decreasing trend was visible with tremendous increase in 1984, when women's vote percentage was 68.17 per cent nearly 5 per cent higher than the percentage of male votes. It fell drastically is 1989, 1991, 1996 and 1998.

Another interesting feature is that states have been more or less steadily maintaining a consistent record of either maximum or minimum mobilisation of women as voters. While the states of Kerala and Tamil Nadu have maintained their position as maximum mobilisers of women, Orissa and Madhya Pradesh have been equally persistent in leading the list of minimum mobilisers of women. The difference between the maximum and minimum mobilisation of women has always remained high. The states of Kerala, Tamil Nadu, Maharashtra, Andhra Pradesh and Gujarat in the southern and western regions have shown a relatively higher degree of electoral participation by women. The states in the northern region with exception of Punjab and Haryana in the west and West Bengal in the east have shown a persistent trend of low mobilisation. Orissa, Madhya Pradesh, Bihar, Uttar Pradesh, Rajasthan, Assam, Himachal

Pradesh, Jammu and Kashmir present a dismal picture of persistently low mobilisation in absolute terms, and particularly in relation to men with percentage difference actually increasing in Madhya Pradesh. Except for Bihar and Uttar Pradesh the states with low mobilisation have been those which were late in participating in the Independence struggle. Socially extensive and severe restrictions on women's activities outside the family have been prevalent in these states. Economically they are poor with comparatively less urbanisation and industrialisation. Female literacy also has been lowest in these states. These are some of the factors that account for low political consciousness and less enthusiasm for the exercise of franchise rights among women.

The states and Union territories showing greater mobilisation of women socially and politically, are not backward and economically they are not deficient. Most of them being coastal areas they were the first to be exposed to the Western culture of the Dutch, Portuguese and the British colonisers. Places such as Delhi and Chandigarh, though not falling into the above category, have a cosmopolitan cultural outlook, an industrial base and urban character. The social structures of these states and Union territories are not very rigid and male dominated. On the contrary, a state like Kerala has a maternal society, which ensures a relatively dominant place to women.

Inspite of regional imbalances, the mobilisation of women voters is not depressing. But it is also not a factor which should lull us into satisfaction as regards women's political participation. Way back in the 1970s the committee on the Status of Women in India in its report had commented, "women's participation in the political process has increased both in elections and in their readiness to express their views on issues directly concerning their day-to-day life, their ability to produce an impact on the political process has been negligible." It still holds true even after the passage of two decades.

The increase in the turnout of women voters, particularly of the lower castes and classes may be attributed to a high degree to mobilisation, rather than their own political consciousness. The Scheduled Castes and other poor and backward communities are aware of the importance of their vote, but this awareness about the Issues affecting them needs tremendous mobilisation in order to be translated into a political exercise like voting preferences with regard to women who have many disincentives such as poverty, daily work, violence, health and patriarchal family norms.

The parties have recognised the significance of women voters, and have been exerting themselves to devise various methods. Mostly adhoc promises are made to women during election campaigns. Moreover, there was any correlation between the camping promises and voting support. It also reflected on the low impact that the women's movement had helped in educating the women as well as in making a dent on the patriarchal politicians (92). In 1984, much of the victory of the Congress could be attributed to a sympathy vote by womenfolk against the slaying of Prime Minister Indira Gandhi on a woman-to-woman basis ('92).

Women as Contestants

The number of women candidates contesting for the Lok Sabha has been extremely discouraging. It has not been much above 5 per cent of the total number of male candidates. The number of women contestants in Lok Sabha, however, has increased since 1952 with the exception of 1957 when it came down to 45 from 51. There has been a steady increase in the number in 1991-1996 to fall again in 1998.

The fall in the number of women candidates is not surprising since in this election the total number of candidates was much smaller than in 1996, may be due to the changes made by the Election Commission, and also the unexpectedness of the general elections.

The difference between male and female contestants of the Lok Sabha seats has also shown a declining trend from 1977 onwards-94. 17 per cent in 1977 to 93.82 per cent in 1980 and 90.23

per cent in 1984. The differences had increased slightly in 1991 and 1996.

The actual number of seats contested by women has been less than the number of women contestants since some of the seats were contested by more than one women.

The number of seats in the first to five general elections were 6, 5, 5, 5, 9, respectively. The number and percentage of the successful women candidates increased in 1957 from 19 to 25 and from 37 per cent to 62 per cent. Since then there has been a steady decline. In 1971 only 21 were successful out of a total of 86. In 1971, a sudden spurt in the number of independent women candidates from 10 in 1967 to 31 in 1971- added to the total number. At the same time independent candidates performed very poorly-only one succeeded, and thus the overall percentage fell from 42.4 to 25.9. an all time low. The number of contestants rose steadily from 1980 onwards from 142 in 1980 to 599 in 1996 to fall again in 1998. In the 11th Lok Sabha elections about 2/3 of the total 599 female candidates were independents. Experience has shown that women have rarely been successful as independents. Party build up and support is necessary for women to win elections. In the 1991 elections, a relatively mobile candidate Rita Verma from Dhanbad in Bihar won due to the massive support of BJP. Not exactly similar, but such experiences have been often repeated. The election of Alka Nath (1976) from Chindwara in Madhya Pradesh is another such example.

Statewise: The number of women contesting for Lok Sābha in the states and Union territories has roughly been in accordance with, though not in proportion, to the total number allocated to them. The maximum number of women have entered the race in Uttar Pradesh except in 1951 and 1971 when Bihar, the next biggest state in terms of Lok Sabha seats, took the lead by one number. In the elections of 1996, Uttar Pradesh has returned 10 women to the Lok Sabha, the largest contingent from one state. Some of the Union territories such as Delhi, Goa, Daman and Due and Madhya Pradesh have put up greater percentage. Madhya Pradesh needs special mention, since it has shown a poor turnout of voters.

The number of women candidates in various states and Union Territories shows wide fluctuations from one election to another. It has fluctuated in Uttar Pradesh, but in Bihar and Madhya Pradesh, the number has gradually gone up. In Kerala, it remained constant at one for the first three elections, then marked a slight increase to three in 1967 and four in 1971. In Orissa, no woman contested in the first three elections, but in 1967 one and in 1971, two women contested. In the Union Territories along with Jammu & Kashmir, Haryana and Mysore may be clubbed into one category, as the number of women contestants in them for all five general elections was either nil or just one.

The number of successful candidates has naturally been greater in Uttar Pradesh, Bihar, Madhya Pradesh and Andhra Pradesh, where the number of contestants has also been greater. Orissa, Haryana, Goa, Daman and Due and Manipur are the states and Union territories where women contested but were not returned to Lok Sabha in the first five general elections. In 1996, Haryana returned one, but Manipur, Assam, Arunachal Pradesh, Mizoram, Nagaland, Sikkim, Tamil Nadu, Jammu and Kashmir Kerala, Maharashtra, Meghalaya, Himachal Pradesh did not return a single contestant to Lok Sabha.

The number of contesting or elected women candidates for Lok Sabha in a particular, state or Union territory does not appear to be decisively related with the literacy among women in that area. Laxmi N Menon, while analysing the first general elections, inferred that the number of women candidates was in inverse proportion to the percentage of literacy among them. The electoral history of different states over the years does not project a consistent pattern of correlation between female literacy and their candidature. Literacy is not a single variable in this respect, and it influences the number of contestants, but only in combination with other factors. The social ethos and taboos prevailing in the state or in a particular constituency visa-vis women's role in politics did influence the success or otherwise of its female contestants, but only in a small way. What mattered most were the personality of the contestants, including their family background and involvement in politics, local conditions, campaign strategy and the political party to which the candidates belong.

Political Parties and Female Contestants

The maximum number of female candidates have been fielded by the Congress Party from 25 in 1957 to 49 in 1996. However, it has remained much below its stipulated target of 15 per cent of the total candidates. CPI and erstwhile Praja Socialist Party have been fielding female candidates from the very beginning, but the number has been small. In the 1996 elections, CPI(M) put up five female candidates and CPI fielded four. Smaller, unrecognised parties have shown continuous fluctuations.

As in number, the Congress has also covered the maximum area. Congress women candidates have appeared in most of the states during Lok Sabha elections except in 1971 when they were confined to states and one Union territory. Madhya Pradesh has always secured maximum tickets for women except in 1971. The largest number of independent candidates has come from Uttar Pradesh, Bihar and Rajasthan. The rest of the parties have put up women candidates largely in their strongholds - BJP in Uttar Pradesh, CPM in Kerala and West Bengal and erstwhile SSP in Bihar and Uttar Pradesh. Madhya Pradesh has also been favoured by most of these parties in terms of putting up a women candidate. The average of women contestants to Lok Sabha per seat is 0.30 per cent. Average share among contestants is 3.2 per cent and the success ratio is 28.5 per cent.

Notwithstanding a few exceptions, tne women contestants have been found poorly in articulate, in overall perspective and the issues pertaining to the particular contests. They have heavily depended upon either the party machine or the hands of loyal men workers in conducting their respective election campaigns, and after taken recourse to emotional and sentimental appeals to establish rapport with the voters. In 1989, 29 women were elected to Lok Sabha while in 1991 the number was 33 and in 1996 it was 38. In 1998, it increased to 40.

Women Elected to Lok Sabha

From 1952 to 1967, the percentage of women who contested and won was much higher than the men - 45.09, 65.05, 52.30; and for males it was 25.50, 39.54 and 25.95. In 1971, there was a sharp fall to 24.41 per cent from 46.96, rose slightly to 27 per cent in 77 to fall again to 19.71 per cent in 1980. It improved slightly to 25.6 per cent in 1984. Since there has been a steady decline in the percentage, successful women candidates in relation to the number of female contestants ... 43.6 percent in 1989, 12.00 per cent in 1991 and 6.88 per cent in 1996. In 1998 it was 72 per cent.

The percentage of women in the Lok Sabha in relation to the total number of seats has been very low, from 4.4 per cent in 1952 it increased slightly in 1957 (5.4 per cent) in 1962 (6.7 per cent), 1967 (5.9 per cent) to fall again to 4.2 per cent in 1971, 3.4 per cent (the lowest) in 1977 to increase slightly to 8.1 per cent in 1984 to fall again to 5.2 per cent in 1989. There has been a slight improvement in 199 1, 1996 and 1998.

It is ironical that although the success rate of female contestant has invariably been higher in relation to males, they are still a very small percentage of the total number of contestants and so their presence in the Lok Sabha is small, not even 9 per cent. The difference between male and female contestants is very high, hence, the gap is very wide. Therefore, although the number of female contestants has increased over the years, it is still a very small percentage of the total, and thus, despite their high success rate their presence in the Lok Sabha is negligible.

Women in Rajya Sabha

The presence of women in the Rajya Sabha is much better. Till 1996, while women were only 6 per cent is Lok Sabha, on an average the percentage of women MPs in the RaJya Sabha has been 10.3 per cent. However, it has to be noted that women also of through nominations to the RaJya Sabha. Many of them have not fought electoral battles.

Many factors are responsible for this state of affairs, the ideology of the Gandhi-Nehru era has totally disappeared. Elections have become very costly and expensive and most of the female aspirants cannot muster enough funds for fighting elections. Added to these are the extreme criminalisation of politics, excessive use of muscle and money power. Politics is a dirty game and many women do not wish to enter it. The support of political parties could do wonders, but all major political parties are reluctant to put up female candidates despite the high rate of their success in elections. For example in the 1998 elections in Bihar, BJP had put -up two female candidates and both won.

It is true that women suffer from economic dependency, illiteracy and, a particular image of the self nurtured through the socialisation process, and these factor, also influence their entry into the election process. The gender bias of the political parties adds to it. With the backing of a strong party, a woman candidate can also win elections Rita Verma has won thrice since 1991 on EUP ticket from Bihar. Same was the case of Alka Nath from Madhya Pradesh.

The fact remains that unless in Dehlerup's word, they become a 'critical mass', that is, by having 30 per cent to 40 per cent seats in the House, things are not going to change.

Women in Legislative Assemblies

In the period from 1952-57, the percentage of women in states, Legislative Assemblies has certainly not Impressive. Delhi is an average of 5-9 per cent women representatives. Next comes Madhya Pradesh with an average of 5.1 per cent. The lowest average is found in Nagaland with 0.5 per cent. The average of women Contestants per seat is 0. 19 per cent. The 6 per cent of share among contestants is 2.8. The average success ratio of women contestants is 21.0 per cent. The statewise percentage of women contestants is given in.

Impact on Electoral Politics

Inspite of rnafia politics, money and muscle power, Indian women have come on the political agenda of the country through the technique of collective action cousciousness raising programmes, petitioning and lobbying. Many struggles in Karnataka did result in the implementation of a 30 per cent reservation for women at the local and state level in early and mid-80s. Thus, all is not lost. Glimmering of hope can be seen in the determined efforts made by women of progressive social organisations and movement to challenge vested interests (caste, class and gender) and make a determined bid for power

Women issues and demands have found a place in election manifestoes of almost all the parties in the 1990s.' The demand for 33 per cent reservation for women was taken account of in the 1991 election manifestoes, but not complied with in 1996 elections. The bill for 33 per cent reservation for women in the Lok Sabha and the state legislature was placed before the Lok Sabha as the 86th Amendment to the Constitution in September 1996, but could not be passed. Male members cutting across party lines joined hands in ridiculing the bill, despite intense lobbying by women MPs of all parties and their threat to boycott the Lok Sabha session until. The bill is passed, the Bill has yet to see the light of the day. In the 1998 elections, all Parties-from Congress to BJP to RJD pledged the implementation of 33 per cent reservation to women. There is a strong demand both from inside Lok Sabha and outside by women activists to implement the demand by passing the women's reservation bill immediately. As Pramila Dandvate had remarked in one of her interviews to the Hindustan Times in December 1996 that the male MPs are afraid of losing 1/3 seats in the Lok Sabha, and what it would do to their patriarchal authority and control over the Lok Sabha proceeding. The bill could not be even placed on the table in 1998 under the Vajpayee government. The RJD and the Samajwadi

Party chief Mulayarn Singh and Laloo Prasad Yadav displayed utter disregard for parliamentary decorum. Document was tom into shred this is how women are made to remain in the margin of politics. Due to their scarce representation in Lok Sabha, their voice can hardly be hard. They are often pushed to the wall and gradually become a silent minority.

Women's movement had till recently taken an indifferent interest in election process, but with the debate on reservation of seats for women in the legislative bodies, some interest has been created which is reflected in the mobilisation of women's group during election campaign, etc. Some groups in Pune made a united front that is the Stree Mukti Andolan Sampark Samiti. The Krantikari Mahila Sangathan (KMS) of Pune has been actively involved in electoral politics. It has put up candidates independently or jointly with political parties like the Republican Party of India, Janata Dal or with Social Action Group as in Mumbai. This organisation, which came into existence in the early 1980s, has grown considerably and has branches in other cities outside Pune. It is involved at two levels contesting elections at grassroot level, and participating in election campaign for raising consciousness.

There are many women's groups in Ahmedabad, Pune and Bangalore, which have prepared women's manifestoes. They conduct exposure programmes on 'Know the Candidate' and leaflets concerning women's issues such as exposing a candidate who has a criminal involvement in murder, rape or molestation cases.

In Bangalore, Vemochana, a women's group campaign against such candidates, who have committed violence against women, by organising street comer meetings, writing in newspapers and issuing leaflets, as a result of its campaign, many a candidate lost elections. The campaign against the gang rape of a Kasthakari Sangathana activist by CPI (M) Cadres resulted in the CPI(M) candidate losing his Lok Sabha election.

The Nari Samata Manch, another feminist group in Pune, though small in size, has also tried to address itself to the issue of electoral politics. Putting up candidates for elections is beyond their capacity, but they considered it important to mobilise and educate women voters.

Nevertheless, the issue is of grave concern for democratic politics all over the world. Worldwide the representation of women in single or lower national assemblies in 1997 including authoritarian and long standing democratic countries - was 11.6 per cent. The range was from 0 per cent in Comoras, Djbouti, Kiribati, Micronesia, Palan, Papua New Guinea and Tonga to 40.4 per cent in Sweden in 1997.

At the United Nations Fourth World Conference on women, a commitment to achieve women's equal representation in parliaments and other governmental bodies was made by unanimous vote on September 15, 1995. One hundred and eighty eight nations participated in the conference held at Beijing in China. The delegates not only pledged to seek equality in governmental decision making for women, but also specified in their plan of action how nations might achieve it. These included governmental review of electoral systems and adjustment or reforms of them and positive-affirmative action by political parties to nominate and elect women. Following up on the United Nation's Universal Declaration of Human Rights, which specifies that every citizen has the right to participate in the government, the Beijing Conference adopted this statement "Women's rights are human rights." Therefore, women are entitled as a matter of simple justice and democracy, the delegates stated, to all political rights now afforded to men.

At the Beijing Conference stress was laid on two factors-electoral reforms and positive/affirmative action by political parties.

Proportional Representation and Women's Elections

In long-standing democracies, proportional representation has been repeatedly documented as the most significant factor among contextual variables, explaining women's election to Parliament (Rule

1981, 1987, 1994 Norris 1985, 1997). Wilma Rule through her studies has derived the correlation between proportional representation (PR) and women's election to Parliament. Her study revealed that the party list proportional representation countries were generally higher regarding women's recruitment to legislatures of single member plurality/majority countries. She maintains of a 10 candidate constituency gives a women a greater chance for party nomination than does a lower magnitude of three or more. It allow the electorate to choose on an open party list. The preference vote has been used successfully in Finland and Denmark.

Rule gives her observations on updated percentage of women's parliamentary representation in long-standing democracies in 1993 and 1997, and remarks that there has been an upward swing. The three major explanations are: (i) Political party quotas or goals to nominate an increased percentage of women to Parliament in PR countries; (ii) Laws requiring that a proportion (quota) of women be placed on party list in PR countries; and, (iii) Electoral system change from single member plurality to proportional representation. The first measure was adopted just by Denmark, Finland, Norway and Sweden with great success in the 1980s. The same happened in Spain in 1996 elections and in Great Britain in 1997 elections. The second strategy was adopted in Italy after the 1992 elections. A new election law provided that 1/4 of Italian Parliament was to be elected from party list and the remainder from single member districts. In 1994 elections the success of women on party list was 33 per cent but it was only 9 per cent in the case of single member constituency election. The third approach resulted in New Zealand rank as the sixth highest nation in women's parliamentary representation among long-standing democracies by 1997.

There is an urgent need of electoral reforms in India. The above mentioned strategies, which yielded very good results in long-standing democracies, could be tested in this country too.

The proportional representation facilitates quicker change than a single member majority/plurality system. It is easier for a political party to add women to its list for 10 constituencies averaging ten contestants. Then it is to change 100 single member majority or plurality constituencies from male to female representatives.

The laws requiring a quota of women to be nominated on party list provide that women's name be positioned so that they could be elected if their party won sufficient votes in the election.

Election laws may be changed to provide for proportional representation in place of single member constituency.

Positive action in the form of laws to ensure proper representation of women in Parliaments have been proposed by nine developing countries, which have a majority/ plurality system. A bill for providing 33 per cent reservation to women in the Lok Sabha and state Legislative Assemblies in India was introduced in the Lok Sabha in September 1996 and 1998, but despite much publicity debates and discussions, It has still to see the light of the day.

Dehlerup Dirude (1986) has Suggested several measures which when adopted could assists in augmenting women's place in political life. This included changing electoral laws (for Instance, proportional election system tended to be more favourable to women than election system with single member constituencies) women's political parties (successful use In Iceland in 1983) and public campaigns to bring more women into Politics. Political Parties should evolve a system of Yevolving funds to finance women contestants.

The most important is to sensitise political parties towards gender issues. Laws should be made to make it obligatory for Political Parties to nominate a percentage of women in their list of contestants. If the 1996 and 1998 elections are any Pointer. Political Parties in India have failed miserably on this score despite their commitments as reflected in their Party manifestoes in 1991, 1996 and 1998 elections. The Opposition directed towards the 33 per cent reservation bill for women by almost any major political Parties reflects the male antagonism towards the entry of women in politics.

It becomes imperative for liberal democratic governments on the one hand to go ahead with electoral reforms and seriously provide for their implementation and on the other hand. it becomes a responsibility of women's organisations and movement to exert pressure for the same especially in the wake of the Beijing Conference of 1995. According to Bernis Lot "Power generates power and powerlessness generates powerlessness. Because the society is patriarchal where men hold power more power will always be given to men, and women will be made powerless incapable. on the margin. This is a reminder to the fact that women under representation in legislative bodies all over the globe with the possible exception of Nordic and Scandenevian countries is a matter of grave concern for the future of democracy.

Thirteen

The Experiment of Panchayati Raj

The formulation of policies and programmes for national and international goals, women barring a few, have seldom played an effective role. They have been marginals in politics and political decision making process. In 1988, the average percentage of women represented in national parliaments worldwide stood at 14.6 per cent. What is more, it is decreasing considerably per cent. True, women in almost all the countries have de jure right to participate in political decision-making, but in fact they continue to be, under represented and marginal in political decision-making bodies at all levels. How can there be, then, equality in political decision-making? The urgent need of the hour at this juncture is to find a way to increase the number of women in the politically representative bodies. In a democratic polity, it is expected that the processes and decisions reflect the will of the people and represent the interests of all the various groups and formations in the population of the country. It rarely happens. The decision, in fact, are made by the powerful in the society for furthering their self interests of various groups. Women form the largest minority group, almost 50 per cent of any country's population, but are hardly visible in the area of politics, They are so scarce, their voices can hardly be heard. They are the silent minority unheard and unseen. But democracy does not and cannot operate by proxy. Every citizen needs to take part in the political activities and perform the political duties. Women have to take processes to ensure the democratic nature of the policy and for this they have to be present in political bodies.

It is easier seen than done. Politics Is an exercise of power and, denotes the functioning of a whole array policies of public institutions and forms, which are involved in moulding the lives of people by way of decisions, which influence their interpersonal relationships. Thus, politics throughout the ages has been constructed and moulded on the basis of those norms which have been identified though loosely, as masculine. Rationality, self discipline, competition, aggression, orderliness, universality to mention a few, are the priced qualities in political parlance. On the contrary, irrationality, Indiscipline, particularity, submissiveness, impulsiveness are some of the qualities associated with the feminine nature. The result is the distancing of women from every thing political. Women are perceived as part of the social structure and not as part of power phenomenon. Simon de Behaviour calls as "being rather than doing". The male-public and female private dichotomy in social perception has been found to be the greatest hindrance in the way of women's access to power and political decision-making, even in highly developed countries like the Nordic ones. "Democracy was still unfinished, since women constituted a minority in politics (as Drude ' Dahlerup remarks in The Unfinished Democracy: Women in Nordic Politics). It is even more true in the countries where cultural norms and traditions still restrict women to the private sphere of action. Politics is not for them. It is strictly "public" and male dominated sphere of action.

In a Wider Perspective

It would be apt here to discuss and define politics in a slightly wider perspective. An important feature of the feminist efforts has been to proclaim the political nature of private life, and the relation between the sexes which has brought traditional politics into question and has forced the authorities to take account of problems hitherto regarded as belonging to private life. It is now a well recognised proposition in women's studies/movement viz. that all spheres of lives involving any relationship is political; that millions of women are silently (and not always very successfully) waging a struggle against the patriarchal and feudal forces that seek to confine and contain them. It is not lack of consciousness of her human and political rights, but the vicious circle into which she is placed from the very beginning of her life. This struggle against patriarchy in its myriad forms is a prolonged and complex one, and it needs effective participation in politics in a visible and appreciable number at effective levels and in meaningful positions.

This brings us to a theoretical discussion of what a sizeable number of women can do in the political bodies. Drude Dahlerup maintains that it makes a big difference whether women constitute a small minority or a large minority, although still a minority. She developed a theory of the 'critical mass' in which she maintains that if women's number rose to 25-30 or higher, these women reached a critical 'mass' which permitted them to intervene and benefit from the support of women colleagues in what was 'nevertheless' still a male-dominated body.8 She considers support from outside by a strong feminest movement as a necessary requirement towards effectiveness of women's participation in the decision-making representative bodies. She quoted the developments in her own country where women now constituted approximately 25 per cent of all elected members of parliament and local councils. It is the same with other Nordic countries.

Various strategies have been suggested for augmenting women's place in political bodies, such as changing the electoral laws (for instance proportional election systems tended to be more favourable to women than election systems with single member districts) women's political parties (the successful use of these in Iceland in 1983 was noted), and public campaigns, organisational structure of political life.

Another important method is fixing a quota for women at all levels of political decision-making bodies. This question of quota, in order to Increase women's presence in political life was being discussed in Denmark and was applied in Norway in public commissions.

Scene in India

With this theoretical backdrop, let us come to the Indian scene.

The Constitution of India guarantees gender equality in all spheres of life including political. Thus Indian women (at least in law) have equal rights of political participation along with men. They can vote in elections, can fight elections and get elected to legislative bodies right from the federal to the grassroots level. They can hold executive, and leadership Positions at various levels. So it is that India can boast of a very strong leadership. In the Primeministership of Indira Gandhi for more than one-and a-half decade, besides a number of powerful chief ministers and governors. However; nothing much has happened for the masses of Indian women in the last four decades. There has been some mobilisation of women voters in the last two decades, especially during the Women's Decade (1975-85). The political parties to some extent have started to recognise the potential of women as a Vote bank. As regards their candidature for elections, the number has risen constantly, but the percentage of women getting elected to Parliament has declined. A raincheck on the election data to Lok Sabha reveals that women's percentage in the lower house has never exceeded 8 per cent.

Why is it so? Mere is the argument about a particular style of socialisation process for women, their generally weak economic position, lack of education especially in developing countries like India, and above all the danger of violence hanging over women In all spheres of life, and especially in the areas of politics. The political culture which is predominantly masculine, determines the attitude of political parties towards women, tolerates a few weak women, but is very hostile towards the entry of women in a viable and strong position in politics.

Can we leave things as they are? The question of participation of women in politics and the political process has been debated in Parliament many times. There is the human rights argument that as 50 per cent of the population comprises women, it was unjust that women were under represented in Parliament. The existing conflict of interests between women and men was a determining reason for women's entry in politics. Men would simply be unwilling or less capable to represent women's interests in politics adequately.

Despite the guarantee of constitutional equality, women have not been able to get equal treatment or opportunity because they are not present in the institutions and process relevant for It. Hence the need to get into these processes and institutions, again and entry into the functioning of the status and share control over the apparatus of state. This alone would lead to preserve and promote equality and justice, and bring about the necessary policy changes and social restructuring so as to usher in a humane and suitable social order.

So, this brings us back to the question of strategy, and one important strategy would be to fix a quota for women in all political decision-making bodies, atleast for sometime to come. This might mean, at least for a while, a certain compromise on the quality of participation. Fixing of 'quotas' or 'reservation' of seats for women would open up a possible entry point for them in politics, and this is necessary because it cannot be denied that a handful of women in legislative bodies cannot make their voice strong enough to be heard. How do they, then, equally share in the decision making and policy formulations?

It is precisely at this point that the 73rd Amendment to the Constitution of India, known 'as Panchayati Raj Amendment Act 1992, could have very important implications for women's political participation. This Act, although related to only the grassroots level Institution 'nevertheless provides for 33 per cent reservation for women in local bodies, both at the deliberative and leadership positions.

A Long-drawn Debate

It has not happened suddenly, India has witnessed a long-drawn debate on reservation for the various minorities and backward communities such as the Scheduled Castes and Scheduled Tribes and women. Although, reservation for the first two categories was provided by the Constitution, reservation for women has been rough weather from the very beginning. Reservation for women in all the elected bodies from the Centre to the local level has been a fiercely debated issue, and it began in the Constituent Assembly itself. One section of the women's movement had at that time suggested continued reservation of seats on the line of Government of India Act 1935. Women members in the Constituent Assembly, however, rejected this as against the principle of social equality. Much later, the Committee on the Status of Women in India (CSWI) decided to maintain the same position, through two members submitted a dissent note. A group of the social scientists consulted by the committee strongly advocated reservation for women, especially at the panchayat (grassroots) level. The arguments given in favour of reservation for women in the legislative bodies at the state and central level are :

(i) That the declining trend in women's representation was the result of the reluctance of political parties to sponsor women candidates which, however, offers real obstacles in making the few legislators act as spokesperson for women's rights and opportunities.

(ii) That in a situation of political parties reflecting the established values of a mal -dominated society, certain structural changes in the sociopolitical set up were necessary to make room for desirable social change; otherwise losing faith in the political process to change their condition of life, women might 'opt out' of the political system and become either passive partners or rebels.

(iii) That a system of reservation of a proportion of seats for women in elected bodies would pave the path for a fairer deal to nearly half the population in the various units of government; and,

(iv) That, a system of reservation could increase the women legislators sense of responsibility and concern for women specific-problems, and this would lead to increasing mobilisation of women both in the electorates and within the political parties. Social scientists associated with the committee also hold the view that improvements in the political status of women constituted an integral aspect of the overall problem of socioeconomic change and broadening the 'political elite structure. It was pointed out very forcefully that a 30 per cent reservation of seats in the legislative bodies will alter the very character of our legislature and will compel the political parties to change their strategies and tactics and induce them to give women their due.

There was opposition on this issue from the side of the representatives of the political parties and most women legislators. The 'Towards Equality' committee rejected the suggestion for a system of reservation for women to state assemblies and parliament. However, it recommended "statutory women's panchayats at the village level to ensure greater participation by women in the political process as an integral part of the Panchayati Raj structures. The recommendation was passed on to state governments, received mostly negative response and was, therefore, buried within the government. Some states, however, began a gradual process of induction of more women in, the panchayats, as they began steps to entrust more powers and responsibilities to the panchayats. The most daring was the Karnataka zila parishads, taluk panchayat, mandal panchayats and Nyaya panchayat Act of 1983 which provided for 25 per cent seats being reserved for women.

The National Perspective Plan (1988) proposed 30 per cent reservation to all elective bodies to be filled, at least in the initial Years, by nomination or co-option. The debate organised by the nation women's organisations refused the proposal for reservation in the state assemblies or Parliament but recommended 30 per cent reservation for women in Panchayati Raj institutions "with due precautions to ensure representation of the weaker sections of women, especially Dalits and tribals. The women's organisations were, however, emphatic on the need for elections to ensure the emergence of a new leadership from gramroots."

The 64th Amendment Bill introduced by Rajiv Gandhi was a step further in this direction. The 22nd Amendment in 1990 proposed one-third reservation for women in the Panchayati bodies with an additional provision of one-third among the reserved categories of Scheduled Castes and Scheduled Tribes and among office-bearers. Ultimately, the 73rd Amendment was passed by the parliament on December 22, 1992 providing for 33 per cent reservation of seats for women in Panchayati bodies. It was ratified by half the states by April 1993. Undoubtedly, this Act is most significant for the reservation provided to women along with the Scheduled Castes and Scheduled Tribes. If fully utilised as many as 7.95 lakh women including those belonging to Schedule Castes and Tribes can become panches and sarpanches (member and chairperson) in the Panchayat. Following are the provisions of the Act :

1. Not less than one-third of the seats will be reserved for women (including the Schedule Castes and Tribes) and these may be allotted by rotation to different constituencies of the panchayat.

2. In the seats reserved for Schedule Castes and Scheduled Tribes not less than one-third of total number of such seats to be reserved for women.

3. Not less than one-third of the total number of seats for the offices of the chairperson at each level would be reserved for women. This would be rotated among different panchayats at each level.

In addition, there are certain general features which could be taken advantage of by women, such as direct elections for membership and sarpanch (president) posts, at the local as well as the intermediary (block) level.

The duration in the case of such panchayats in operation would be five years from the date of its first meeting. Elections would be direct and held compulsorily every five years. For women it is significant in doing away with the old practice of co-option and replacing it with direct election, assuring that it would not become a stronghold and prerogative of women of rich and influential families.

The reaction of the states as expected have been varied. While states like Orissa and West Bengal did not even wait for the 73rd Amendment and amended their acts in 1991 and 1992 and held elections in 1992-93 electing about 25,000 women in each state of these bodies, the state of Tamil Nadu taking advantage of some loopholes may not genuinely implement the provisions because the ruling party is not is favour. Punjab held elections promptly after the amendment. Going by the old practice of co-opting women and Schedule Castes, it has avoided a true election for another five years.

In Operation

The Panchayati Raj system has operated differently in various states of India. In the particular context of women's representation, a good number of states showed adequate regeratation as in Maharashtra, Kerala, Himachal Pradesh, Andhra Pradesh, but the proportion varied. Only in the first two states mentioned above where was the reservation up to 30 per cent. In Orissa it was 33 per cent. In West Bengal, the government has not been too keen on reservation. Elections every five years have been held since 1978. The latest elections were held in May 1993. This election was held on the basis of 1992 Act, which gave one-third membership to women, to be filled up by election. In 1993 elections, the total number reserved seats for women was 25,460, and many more, about 41,000 women got elected. In some other states elections have been long over due. For example, Bihar had its last elections in 1978, Uttar Pradesh in 1988. Orissa and West Bengal amended their acts before the Panchayati Raj Act was passed by the Parliament in 1992. Elections in Orissa in 1992 brought 22,000 women to Panchayat Raj institutions.

The recent Panchayati Raj Institutions (PRIE) Act does have the potential to Include women in a very good proportion to male at the grassroots level political institutions. Presence of 33 per cent women is likely to affect and influence the political processes of decision-making and policy formulations at this level. It will not only enable them to give a women's angle to the decision and policy formulation activity. It will also awaken them to the problems facing the community as whole. It will enable a journey from the private to the public sphere of activity. It will train cadre of women political activists for partaking in the affairs of state and federal politics. Total sharing and equality in decision making may not happen for years to come, but Panchayati Raj Institutions (PRIS) showed a path towards that goal. When women armed with physical presence of a sizeable proportion reach the position of a 'critical mass', their voices cannot be Ignored. They have to be heard. No longer can they be ignored. It could be a road to women's political empowerment. However, for a wider representation effective sharing in power process, this needs to be extended to representative bodies right up to the federal level. Wider representation will not ensure instant quality. It will take time and practice moreover many studies have already proved that democracy, even while being the best form of government need not be the best government, that men as much as women are guilty of devaluating its quality all over the world. The experience of Orissa and West Bengal testify that women are capable of efficient political performance given the chance.

However, a word of caution is necessary at this juncture. Women's effective participation at the grassroots through the panchayat system will not become a reality unless women are made aware of the realities and are properly trained for their new role. Reservation alone cannot deliver the goods. It will still be a weak need to rely on, in tackling attitudinal, social and structural barricades. Nevertheless, by getting this one gate opened, women's movement can (and must) flood the rural side with the potentialities and political contribution of women. This will need much intervention by way of action and other inputs.

Political Education

Political education is the first step. For political education there will have to be two types of target groups. Wherever women have already entered the Panchayati Raj institutions through election or otherwise, these women need to be politically educated and informed. Such education should not be confined only to creating awareness among women of their powers, rights and functions but also about Indian polity, the nature of its democracy and constitution, policies and programmes for women and other weaker sections. For the general women it would mean mobilising them for voting in the elections, standing for elections, and even campaigning and questioning the candidates, both male and female.

Political information: For education, information on issues such as current political developments and trends, legislations, policies and plans is the basic step, information should lead to mobilisation.

1. For election - Possibility of creating a special fund or efforts for raising resources to help women for fighting elections. Election being fought on party lines, are becoming more and more expensive, corrupt and violent even at the grassroots level. Could women's organisations help the women candidates to raise funds for fighting election?

2. Need for the formulation of one a few models of curriculum development, and of designing a syllabi that would include the different areas in constitutional, political, socioeconomic, social rights and issues, as well as governmental policies, programmes and procedures.

3. Some type of political literacy manual which in brief, precise, easy/readable and commonly understandable style explains the various provisions for (general and women specific) rights, governmental policies, judicial judgements, non-governmental social actions, etc.

4. For sustained political education there is need for an organisation working at site, if not every village atleast in a cluster of villages. Existing women's organisations in the villages and NGOs working in a particular area can be trained, to act as trainers provided they have the inclination, correct and strong approach to feminist issues and women's rights and are somewhat natural towards political parties.

5. Formation of resource- centres with full time social activists could help by emerging as forums for information, dissemination, discussions, reading materials and even counselling services. The social activists with the necessary skill in political understanding,

raising resources and networking may organise various activities like group discussions, awareness camps lectures, by visiting scholars/ social activists and politicians.

As elections are increasingly being fought on party lines, political parties need to be sensitised towards women's right of political action by giving them some priority in fighting elections.

The strategy of reservation or quota for women at all levels of political deliberation has immense possibilities but it alone cannot deliver the goods. It has to be backed by a strong women's movement from outside. Even more, the presence of women sensitised women's problems in deliberative and decision-making bodies, will give strength to their voice. With time and proper training, they will not only be, concerned with women's issue, but in all Issues and problems related to the whole society and polity. They will lead to women's angle to issues of war, militarisation, nuclear power widespread violence and what not.

It is true that having been trapped by sociocultural norms and traditions they have been out of the so-called 'public areas' of activities. But this sad tale is not and should not continue any more, politics is as much a women's concern as a man's because it equally affects her life conditions. What is needed is proper mobilisation, awareness generation through political education and training. For this task the government, NGOs, women's organisations, both academic and action oriented, need to join hands in their effort. For a healthy democracy all need to participate in the shaping and sharing of power. If gender prevents half the population from participation in politics, it cannot be a democratic politics. For Indian women, the 73rd Amendment to the Constitution, the Panchayati Raj Act 1992 opens up the door to many possibilities, They have been given a chance, if one goes by the experience of some states. In India, the signals are very positive. The commonly held view that women have to be found for contesting elections has been somewhat disproved in practices so far. In the Orissa elections of 1992, 2,200 won at three levels. This was more than one-third reservation. In 1988

Karnataka elections out of 30,000 women 14,000 won the elections. A state West Bengal saw 59.2 per cent seats going to women in 1993. Thus, besides the reserved seats, women secured seats also from the general quota. Maharashtra presently have nine all women panchayats.

What is needed is awareness generation in women, their mobilisation and training for their new political roles. They have to know about themselves, their rights, the nature of their political system, the myriad problems facing the country the political process through which decisions are made and policies formulated. A concerted effort is necessary by all institutions and individuals who care for women, and do not want them to remain political cripples forever, with proper training and guidance. Women could share effectively the political decision-making, at least at the grassroots level.

Fourteen

Influence on Mass Media

In the context of women's lib, the mass media plays a significant role. It can either reflect existing values and serve to, strengthen and reinforce traditional ideas and the status quo or they can be used positively as forceful motivators of social change. Throughout history communication media have been powerful agents of social influence. In the early days, the story teller, the songster, the actor and the puppeteer were all using their art to record and preserve their culture. Not only this, they also used it to define the norms of their culture and to inform people about their society's nature, its goals and its imperatives. Modern journalism, be it in the form of newspapers or magazines, is still their basic goals. But in the last few years new technologies have been introduced which have greatly magnified the communication media power and the importance of media in the mores of societies has increased in proportion.

The focus here, is on women who influence the mass media, women as depicted by the mass media and women as influenced by the mass media. The methods by which the mass media can be used to further the cause of women's development and consciousness would also be discussed in this study.

Traditional Forms

Traditional media in all societies have been the folk songs, stories, puppet shows and dramas. Women have played an important role in these traditional forms of entertainment. Some aspects of folk-lore have dealt exclusively with women and their problems. For example, in northern India there is a whole folk-lore based on women's longing for husbands who have gone away to earn money or the fears of a young bride leaving for her husband's village and so on. Traditional folk stories also contain a large number of portraits of women who have very strong personalities.

Traditional folk-lore generally reflects traditional attitudes to women. Traditional media portray women in the old framework of wife or mother or daughter which still continues to be the basis of media presentation of women today.

Women, who have gone against the "stereo" role are rarely remembered, for example, in Indian history, a truly valiant woman ruler, Razia Sultana of the Slave dynasty has been almost forgotten and has no place in folk-lore. Perhaps the only exception in the Indian context is Rani Laxmibai of Jhansi, but it is worth recording that her story was popularized by a female poet, Subhadra Kumari Chauhan.

Influencing Modern Mass Media

Women are playing a big role in mass media nowadays. They participate in it in diverse fields. These have been listed as follows:

Films : They are film directors, producers, writers, music directors, dance directors and lyricists.

Advertising Firms : Proprietors, executives and designers. Though no exact figures are available. Women have played, and are playing, a very limited role as shapers of mass media. The women employed by these organizations are mainly in low skill, low prestige jobs. Admittedly, there have been some reputed women in controlling position in the media, but on the whole it is a field dominated by men.

TV and Radio: Women directors, producers, writers, announcers and media executives.

Newspapers and Magazines : Proprietors, editors and journalists.

There is only one exception and, that is in the case of a women's magazines. These magazines, both in the west and in the Third World, tend to have woman editors and executives, if not proprietors. But the target group of these magazines has been the traditional house-bound housewife and the magazines are about the usual pot pourri of recipies, beauty hints tips on how to please the husband or boss, etc.

Depicted by Mass Media

Films: The commercial films produced in the Third World countries have had a tendency to portray woman in the stereotyped traditional roles of good wife, good mother and good daughter. As opposed to these 'virtuous' women, the stereotype of the 'bad' woman is offered. Interestingly enough this 'bad' woman is generally portrayed as westernized, liberated, scornful of tradition. There have been very few films which have portrayed women as individual personalities different from the normal stereotypes of society in which the film was made. A few films which portrayed women as strong individuals have always been careful to portray them within the traditional framework of mother, sister wife relationships. This is specially true of the big Indian film industry. There have been very few attempts to break away from this stereotype except in a few "new wave" films.

Advertising Industry : In the present urban context, perhaps it is the advertising industry which has the single biggest impact after films. The advertisements which we see either show the harassed housewife magically transformed by a new brand of tea, cleaner or gadget, or a worried mother being told how best to look after her children or an attractive young girl wondering how to hook or keep her men. These advertisements are aimed at selling products bought by women. There is another category of advertisements dealing with products being sold to men. These generally show pretty girls drooling over a particular man, because he is wearing brand 'X' suitings, shoes, tie, riding brand 'Y' cycle, scooter, car, smoking brand 'Z' cigarette ad infinitum and ad nauseum. The general strategy of these advertisements being to catch male attention by showing pretty girls, no matter whether the product being sold is in any way related to women or not. The sexual identity alone of a woman's personality is emphasized, thus distorting her image, role and status in society.

TV, Radio, Newspapers and Magazines : These media are apparently used normally as a means of communicating to men. There are special times or places, set apart to deal with women's problems, somewhat similar to the children's sections. The underlying assumptions seem to be that women are not interested in the general issues but would prefer to learn about beauty hints, recipies; or new knitting designs. These things are of course of interest to women, but to set these items apart as special enclaves as different from the interests of the general public denies the fact that 50 per cent of the 'general public' is female.

There is very little attempt to identify or discuss the immediate problems of women in our changing societies. Outrageous acts of brutality, for example, dowry deaths in Delhi or sale of women in Dholpur are exceptions but common problems like sexual molestation of women, wife beating and unequal pay for equal work, get very little attention. Sensationalism is the key to media approach to woman's problems.

The entertainment provided, i.e., serials, plays, features, short stories, etc., all generally portray women within the traditional framework and unquestioning acceptance of this is taken for granted. (The few new women's magazines started recently in India, e.g., Manushi, Vama are in honourable exception). The usual woman's magazines though vary different in quality or presentation, etc., show general acceptance of the status quo.

Cartoons and Comics : This part of the mass media has become increasingly popular so much so that no newspaper or magazine is complete today without its daily cartoon or weekly or daily comic strip. The foolish woman and the nagging wife, or mother in law are dominant themes while the male is normally shown in sympathetic light vis-a-vis the females.

Influenced by Mass Media

(i) The mass media is very much a part of the socializing

process, and in this role, the media is being used to reinforce the traditional stereotypes of women. More than that, the distorted image of woman as a sexual being alone is being emphasized out of all proportion.

(ii) The second point is a corollary of the first. The coverage of women as participants in economic activity as leaders and as general participants in the developing process of our changing societies has been wholly inadequate.

Thus an impression is given that women have no role to play economic life of the community. This impression thus conveyed is false in as much as the total work force of the country consists of at least 20 per cent females. This figure does not include the unpaid labour of housewives or of rural women's dairy and farming activities in their own homes. The media thus gives an erroneous impression of women as consumers and dependents (mostly through advertisements, cartoons, etc.) rather than producers.

(iii) The media is attuned mostly to a male audience and caters basically to this audience. Woman's viewpoint on general issues is normally not sufficiently represented.

Thus women tend to see things mostly from a male point of view and are thus conditioned to accept the male world view rather than to evolve one of their own.

Discussion

1. The mass media specially through the advertising medium is influencing women more and more towards a consumer society in which the latest and the best must be acquired immediately. Due to prevalence of mass poverty, these cannot be had by most women and thereby it causes frustration and social disharmony.

2. How can participation of women as decision makers in media be increased?

3. At present no organization exists which can monitor media

performance in regard to presenting woman's viewpoints on general issues. How could woman's organizations act as pressure groups to monitor media content and analyse and review media performance?

4. How to carry out dissemination of women's problems to the media?

5. How can traditional media be used to change traditional, stereotypes of women?

Influence of Mass Media

We have seen that religious tradition as well as some features inherent in the social structure have perpetuated certain stereotypes and myths about women. Although their virtues and merits have at times been extolled, the principal social role assigned to a woman is essentially one subordinate to man. The social norms, attitudes, and values sustained by such stereotypes are deeply entrenched. To eradicate them would need determined and purposive effort. Education and the mass media of communication could be important in bringing about changes in attitudes, but both have limitations. Like education, mass communication is a necessary but not sufficient condition of change.

The role and influence of the mass media on the status of women can be considered from the following angles:

(a) a content analysis of the media and their treatment of women;

(b) the influence of the media on their audience;

(c) the influence of the media on women themselves.

Studies have revealed that the mass media have made and make a great impact on social change. Changes in a society's attitudes, are the result of historical growth, the gradual spread of education, the work of social reformers and charismatic leaders and so on. However, modernizing societies have come to rely increasingly on the mass media for spreading messages.

The media provide information and guidance and create awareness. They can assist changes in attitude by reinforcing ideas and providing real or ideal models or behaviour and can raise aspirations for better standards of living. The media can thus contribute towards the development of skills, tastes and images current in a society.

The content of communication at any given time reflect the pattern of values of a society. The way subjects dealing with women are treated indicates to a great extent, the prevailing attitudes of that society towards its women. This could work both ways, to improve, or lower women's status in the society by introducing new, or reinterpreting old ideas.

In any country, women who are half the total population are often half the audience. The success or failure of development plans, in education, family planning, community development, health and nutrition depends upon the involvement and participation of women. Our investigation shows that compared to men, women are underprivileged in many ways and suffer from serious disabilities. Since formal education is a costly and a long-term process, it is essential to harness the mass -media for the eradication of illiteracy and to speed up the spread of basic education among women and girls. The National Council for Women's Education emphasized the potential significance of the mass media to generate public opinion in rural areas in favour of girls' education. The Family Planning Programme is making intensive use of the mass media to inform and create awareness among the people.

Incidental studies on the impact of mass media indicate, however, that women's exposure to the media is often very inadequate, and unsatisfactory. It appears that the mass media has not been an effective instrument to inform and prepare women to play their new roles in society. The committee's investigations indicate a general lack of awareness about rights, problems, opportunities and responsibilities among both men and women. Since the government controls a significant section of the mass media, it should set the pace. May be there is little that the private sector can be forced to do, but there is need for pressure groups within society itself to spearhead changes in the role of the media.

A proper assessment of the present role of the media in regard to the status of women will require detailed surveys and studies. Due to the want of empirical data, our comments on the influence of mass communication media on the status of women is, based mainly on expert comments and views, and discussions with individuals in various walks of life.

The most significant factor in mass communication is that in India, where 80 per cent of the total population is still rural, the mass media is concentrated in urban areas and emanates from there. The themes are mainly urban and are concerned largely with the educated elite. The communicators themselves are from the urban areas. Starting with the Press, which has a powerful role to play in moulding public opinion, almost all the newspapers are published from the major cities and towns and give emphasis to political and urban news.

Role of the Press

The serious press in India has by and large not degraded the status of women. News items highlighting the role of women have been published whenever possible. Some noteworthy achievements by women in different fields appear in daily newspapers from time to time and the major dailies and almost all the Indian language dailies carry a weekly women's section. A content analysis of this section would be needed before any comment can be made on the subject matter of the sections and their views on the role and status of women.

A citizen should be able to appeal against misuse of his or her name by the press. For instance, in report about rape, abduction or other such incidents, the press should not mention the name of the girl, or of her relatives. The press is supposed to exercise restraint and not publicize news which may affect a woman's reputation.

Recently there has been some protest against the use of the female figures in advertising. As far as the press in India is concerned, the revenue from advertisement sustains a large number of dailies. The discretion, if any, in the selection or rejection of advertisements is exercised by the owner or staff of a paper and could be heavily influenced by financial considerations and not the subject matter of the advertisement. The present tendency of advertising agencies to over-emphasize the female form has resulted in number of complaints to the Press Council of India about exploitation of sex in advertisements.

Among the powers and functions of the Press Council, the following two have bearing on the status of women:

(a) To build up a code of conduct for newspapers, news agencies and journalists in accordance with high professional standards.

(b) To ensure the maintenance of high standards of public taste and foster a due sense of both the rights and responsibilities of citizenship.

An examination of the complaints made to the council during 1972-73 showed that there were quite a few from individuals complaining against the photographs of female figures in advertisement and otherwise.

It is interesting to note that out of a total of 103 complaints made to it in 1972, the Press Council considered 24 complaints about objectionable writing. Of these 9 dealt with obscenity. One ruling about the publication by Blitz of two photographs of women said that, as they served no purpose, "they could easily have been avoided by the Blitz, which was a serious paper". A number of other complaints dealt with undue exposure of the female figure in advertisement and film journals.

The debate on the use of the female figure in advertisement continues unresolved. While the Board of Advertisers are supposed to maintain high standards, it is the responsibility of the general public and particularly women's organizations to complain or protest against obscenity. The Press Council has already given a ruling on this subject and until there is more vigilant watch on advertisements, hoardings and posters, the present stress on near nudity and sex to sell goods and attract cinema audience may continue. It is commonly complained that cinema advertisements tend to use for display scenes cut out by the censors.

On a complaint that a soap advertisement was exploiting sex, the Press Council observed that such complaints reflect the confusion in values and attitudes prevailing in our society, because the woman in the picture was not less modestly dressed than several modern women one might see in the streets, at parties and at shopping centres. On saying this, the Council was not oblivious of the fact that many women appeared in public fully clad, without exposing anything below the neck, or above the ankle, with blouses up to the elbow. However, the norms of dress followed by a large number of other respectable women might not measure up to the requirements of the puritan.

The Council had this group in mind when it referred to the dress of the modern women, since in judging contemporary society it had also to consider the more prevalent among this section. They were an integral part of Indian society, and "signified the contemporary ethos."

Referring to this controversy in the foreword to the Seventh Annual Report, 1972, the Chairman of the Press Council observed, "The next aspect of journalistic propriety I wish to refer to is the increasing number of papers resorting to the publication of barely clothed female figures. These appear in advertisements and are sometimes published even when they seem to serve no apparent purpose. This criticism copied from the other societies which are more permissive, hardly, if I may say so, fits in with our culture." While the Press Council can fulfil a watch dog function it cannot lay down any positive guidelines to form new attitudes towards role of women.

Role of Radio

By its reach and impact the radio provides the most powerful mass communication. It is specially important as a medium of information and education in a vast country like India where the coverage of the press is not extensive. All India Radio operates under the administrative control of the Ministry of Information and Broadcasting and is the sole broadcasting organization in the country. Its special women's programmes are broadcast regularly from all stations of the AIR, at least twice a week. In 1971, women's programmes occupied a total of 3729 hours and 06 minutes, i.e., 1.4 per cent of the total broadcasting time and in 1972, they took 3,746 hours, i.e., 1.5 per cent. Special broadcasts are also put out by the Farms and House Units of AIR for rural women. These programmes, specially meant for rural women, provide education and entertainment and are broadcast in the regional languages at a time most convenient for women to listen. In each State, women's welfare organizations of the State Governments organize listening clubs with follow up discussions in the Mahila Mandals. Two mass communication researchers, Mathur and Neurath, who studied village radio broadcast in India found that such broadcasts had effect where listening clubs were organized and suggestions were followed.

Nutrition is a subject of recent interest to wives and mothers in villages and towns. UNICEF has provided 5,000 transistor sets to enable Mahila Mandals to listen to programmes about nutrition. Women also participate in broadcasts of cultural and entertainment programmes. Programmes for women range from 30 to 45 minutes twice or thrice a week. Discussions and talks on the topic of interest to women are also included.

Under the commercial services of AIR, started in May 1970, radio programmes are used for advertising. A code of conduct guides the staff and advertisers and ensures that commercial programmes are not only in good taste, but also in conformity, with the national interest and with public welfare. The Family Planning Units of AIR plan and produce family planning programmes for rural areas, industrial workers, women and youth, projecting a broad based social movement closely linked with maternity and child health and nutrition. While the Government of India has laid stress on family planning instruction, national integration, nutrition, new agriculture practises, just how much has been achieved in a positive way to emphasize the new role of women in present day society remains unsure. The Audience Research Unit might be able to provide some feedback. It is important to study the existing programmes and their impact which may indicate gaps in programme content and coverage and indicate guidelines for future women's programmes. It is important to remember that with the high percentage of illiteracy, higher among females, radio is the medium with a vast potential for educating the illiterate. An administrator with long experience of work in the AIR said at the Asian Region Seminar for the International Alliance of Women, New Delhi in November, 1973 that, "Village housewives have been badly neglected. AIR's programmes for women are for the urban middle-class women and have no relevance to the working women in the village. Programmes on family planning have to be directed to peasant women, along with programmes on hygiene, nutrition, etc., through those in the village whose voice can command respect.

Role of Television

The development of television as a medium of mass communication is still at a pioneering stage. Apart from the Delhi Television Centre set up in September, 1959, television facilities have recently been extended to Mumbai and Amritsar and will also start functioning in Calcutta, Madras, Jallandhar and Lucknow with relay centres at Pune, Bhatinda, Kanpur, Karnal and Mussoorie.

Two relay centres to be set up in Calcutta will serve Kharagpur and Durgapur/Asansol areas.

Apart from special educational and farm programmes, the television service from Delhi provides a varied programme mix to viewers including programmes for women and children. Few specialized programmes so far have been aimed at popularizing better agricultural practices under the 'Krishi Darshan' programme. The total duration of the transmission is more than three and a half hours daily apart from the school television broadcasts.

The weekly women's programmes include discussions about social problems, but the typical programme is likely to contain subjects of interest to housewives only. An assessment of the number of these women's programmes and their impact will have to be made before ways and means of utilizing this medium can be recommended.

Role of Literature

In the early part of the twentieth century, a large number of books on fictions were written. The aim of authors like Rabindranath Tagore, Sarat Chandra, Prem Chand and others was definitely social reform. They dealt with a number of social problems affecting the status of women and attempted to portray even prostitutes in a sympathetic light. A cursory glance at popular book stalls of fiction which is voraciously consumed by college students and others these days, however, shows a depressing lack of taste. In adherence to the western trend of sex and violence, modernity in Indian fiction seems to mean imitation of western themes. While a few playwrights have attempted to highlight social and economic problems, their books are still not best sellers. Romance and pornographic literature is still popular, perhaps because it is cheaper in price and readily available. Gandhiji criticized distasteful descriptions of the female form in popular fiction and condemned writers for dwelling on them with the "sickly sentimentality". Political leaders have also from time to time expressed their views on the new role of women in a developing society but these have not been adequately publicized. The Publications Division of the Ministry of Information and Broadcasting has brought out a few books on women of India.

Role of Youth Magazines

There are a number of recent publications of magazines aimed at youth. A brief examination of typical youth magazines shows that they do not provide much food for thought. They imitate their western counterparts and the emphasis is on fashion, music, films and sex. It remains to be assessed what that impact of such magazines may be on the minds of impressionable boys and girls and whether they are, in any way, preparing the future generation for accepting the new role women are expected to play in society.

Role of Films

Film exerts a tremendous influence on the audience because of its vivid and powerful impact. All cultural media like theatre, art, architecture and films project a pattern of moral values as well as reflect established patterns. The influence of these media on social values and modes of behaviour is thus a two-way process. The cinema makes a much wider and deeper impact because in the modern industrial and mechanized State, the cinema is more easily available.

India is one of the largest producers of films in the world. In 1971, India produced 433 feature films and 414 in 1973. Out of these respectively 146 and 134 films were produced in Mumbai, 250 and 243 in Chennai and 37 in both years in Calcutta. The Film Division of the Ministry of Information and Broadcasting, produces a large number of news and documentary films annually. The Division has produced more than 3,000 films in the last 25 years. Most of the films are in English and 14 regional languages. In 1971-72, Films division produced 90 documentary films through its own units and 23 through outside producers. In addition, 65 newsreels and 43 documentary films were produced by State Governments. These figures indicate the enormous scope of the film industry in India. An interesting fact is that out of the total number of feature films produced, as many as 283 in 1971 and 273 in 1972, were on social themes, the next highest category being crime films, which have shown a steady increase since 1961 when 30 crime films were produced as compared to 82 for 1972.

The Government appointed an Enquiry Committee on Films Censorship in April 1968 to enquire into the working of the existing procedure for certification of films for public exhibition in India. The Cinematograph (Second Amendment) Bill 1973, was prepared after taking into consideration the recommendations of the Committee. The report highlights the attitude of the film maker and film goers. The average Indian film goer is well aware of what usual themes in the films are likely to be and the box office usually demands a star-cast and dances and night club scenes, though not all witnesses and members of the Committee agreed with this observation. The contents of the bulk of Indian movies are sex and crime and "they follow the base motive of the lower type of American movies with inartistic plots, vulgar dances and songs and dialogues in a disgusting tone. Even the titles of the films are objectionable and the posters which advertise them are improper and vulgar." The sole aim of the film industry is to make money. The Vice-President of the South Indian Film Chamber commented, "The Chamber did not award any prizes for films of outstanding merits, nor did it discourage the production of low quality and vulgar films. The aim of the Chamber was solely to protect the industry." A film critic and social worker said that we knew instances of some girls who had deviated from the path of moral rectitude on seeing excessively erotic films. A lady member of an examining panel thought that producers should come to some kind of mutual agreement not to project on screen scantily dressed girls and women. The general opinion appears to be that there is a rapid increase in the emphasis on sex themes in films. The ambivalent attitude of the Indian film producer is illustrated in his projection of the heroine who is supposed to embody all the virtues but is usually immodestly dressed and the hero, who is otherwise a good man behaves in a very vulgar fashion on meeting the heroine. The usual Indian film has by and large exploited sex to attract audience and has degraded the image of the Indian women.

The cinema exercises a tremendous influence on the juvenile and uneducated mind. In 1957, a survey was made covering Greater Bombay, and large number of young persons and adults were questioned. The investigators noticed a marked tendency particularly among adolescents to imitate patterns of behaviour shown in the films. Four types of unhealthy influences noted were in habits of living and spending, manners and mannerisms including fashions in clothes, hair dressing, speech and behaviour towards the opposite sex and immoral and anti-social practices like stealing, prostitution, etc.

Another survey conducted by the Indian Institute of Mass Communication for the Enquiry Committee on Film Censorship in 1968-69, revealed that out of the total sample, nearly 88 per cent were film goers, with youths forming the majority. Categories of films preferred and generally viewed by women were: (i) films on family life, (ii) musicals and (iii) devotional films. Girls preferred: (i) Western films (ii) musicals (iii) romantic and (iv) tragic films. The least preferred films were on contemporary themes. Questioned as to what should be the chief aim and purpose of films produced in India, 31.11 per cent of the men said that it should be to educate. 42.40 per cent of the women emphasized the development of social, cultural and religious values in society. 37.65 per cent of the college boys laid emphasis on entertainment. As regards the treatment of sex and love in films and details of reactions to the nude human form in painting or sculpture, 36.60 per cent women regarded it as objectionable and 38.40 per cent as indecent, 34.47 per cent of the college girls regarded it as unobjectionable and 25.88 per cent as aesthetically satisfying. In regard to objectionable and undesirable elements in films, one out of ten adults considered a film undesirable when it dealt with violence, crime and horror, while one in twenty youths said so. Nearly half of the men and one-third of the youths considered films dealing with sex and violence to be undesirable, while seven out of ten women considered such themes as objectionable. 41 per cent of the adult sample and the 36 per cent of the youth sample agreed with the statement that 'sex and violence' are the predominant themes of a large number of Indian and foreign 'films' and that there was a growing tendency to expose the artists' body for either aesthetic purpose or dramatic purpose or merely for commercial exploitation. 71.67 per cent of the men and 36 per cent of the women agreed that this exposure served only commercial exploitation. The study indicated further that 32.90 per cent of the sample did not agree with the statement that the present day film goer will lose interest in Indian films if these did not have cabaret or night club scenes showing scantily dressed girls.

Among the grounds on which a film may be refused a censorship certificate are those involving 'indecency and immorality'. The Central Board of Film Censorship has headquarters and regional offices which review and censor films. This is one measure of possible control, though there is a great deal of debate as to the extent of control in censorship particularly regarding sex and violence. The legal aspects of film censorships have been discussed in the report of the Enquiry Committee on Film Censorship. Article 15 Clause 3 and Article 39 (f) which empower the State to make a special provision for women and children and to protect childhood and youth against exploitation, are thought to be wide enough to authorise any law or regulation to protect children and young persons from the influence of certain type of film.

In 1960, Government of India set up a Film Finance Corporation, which provides loans for films with valid cinematic values, which eschew the box office formula. The Government also gives national awards to films of high ethical and technical standards and of social, educational and cultural values.

Reviewing the role and influence of the Indian films, it may be observed that in its content and treatment of women, it has laid more emphasis on sex to draw audiences. The stress is on the physical attributes of the heroine. In most social films she is invariably assigned a subordinate status in relation to men in all spheres and thus continues to perpetuate the traditional notion of a woman's inferior status. Very few films have endeavoured to project the new role of women in present day society. These films have not attempted to educate women regarding their rights, duties or responsibilities and have ignored reality. A few film makers have made films on contemporary themes and problems. But even these have not attempted to change traditional or conventional images of women and tend to perpetuate the status quo.

Images of Heroine

In the earlier thirties, film themes were largely based on adventure, religion or myth with emphasis on a virtuous heroine who remained devoted to her love. During the period between 1939 and 1945, escapist films with light music, stunts, plenty of dances and physical display, made the heroine more a symbol of sex rather than devotion. Elements of crime and adventure were also thrown in.

This period was followed by revival of interest in moral and social themes and films by young directors like Raj Kapoor, Guru Dutt, Chetan Anand and others dealt with problems like casteism and prostitution. "The liberal inclusion of love and sex, dance and music and humour as concessions to the requirements of the box office have led to the vulgarization of serious themes in such films". Love and sex form a dominant theme in most Indian films and there is a full quota of amorous sequences. Women are treated only as an object of sex. The 'other girl' is a stock character who is responsible for disturbing the development of a love affair between the hero and the heroine and is usually portrayed as a 'vamp' or woman of easy virtue. The other stock character is older woman, who maybe the mother-in-law and she depicts the conflict between the younger and the older generations. She is usually of a shrewish temperament. Recently, western cinemas have greatly influenced Indian films, particularly in the physical display of love and of the human body especially female.

Part - V

Analysis

Fifteen

The Perspective Plan

Fro the Indian women, the Perspective Plan for Women is an effort at a long term overall policy. Guided by those constitutional principles and directives relevant to the development process. It is linked to the national targets determined for the end of the century in respect of certain basic indicators especially of health, education and employment. The Plan views women not as the weaker segment of society or as passive beneficiaries of the development process, but as a source of unique strength for reaching national goals.

The Plan aims at:

Economic development and integration of women into the mainstream of the economy.

Equity and social justice for all women.

These are critical goals for the all round development of women not merely as producers and providers, but also as individuals with a right to human dignity in a society where 'culture', 'caste' and 'class' tend to discriminate against gender.

The overall purpose of this plan is to find the highest common denominator for all national endeavour, running across the spectrum of class and religion; functions, sectors and disciplines; to harness the resource represented by the people-both the women as well as the men. This renewal of efforts, from the fifth decade of political independence, will have meaning only if the full potential of the silent half-comprising the 331 million women and girls of India, (about 150 million of them in material poverty and many more close to it) is harnessed. The direction and design, priorities and pace of national development, must have direct relevance to their lives and future. Every dimension of development-political, economic and cultural, not just social-has to assist and hasten their generation.

If the results and lessons of the past are any guide, a larger allocation of resources for women within the prevailing patterns and structures of development, does not promise a reversal of trends. A parallel sub-stream of women's development even if possible, will only perpetuate discrimination and subordination. An alternative strategy of national development which will provide not just some additional space for women, but create a democratic, egalitarian, secular, cooperative social structure has to be defined and tried. In such a scheme, it will be necessary to accelerate the women's component of composite programmes, to ensure the integrity of the enterprise as well as a measure of compensatory justice. The goals of holistic human development must not be at the expense of one another and the ascent to equality must be collective.

Situational Review

For outlining a development perspective, a review of the existing situation of the Indian woman is an essential prerequisite. Both, positive indicators as well as negative indices that are a growing cause of concern to policy makers, planners, administrators and activists are projected to present her overall status. A brief review of the Five-Year Plans and the programmes for women launched in the last few decades, is also included.

Among the positive developments affecting women are:

The expectation of life at birth has improved from 44.7 years in 1961-71 to 52.9 years in 1971-81.

The sex ratio has registered a slight rise-from 930 women per thousand men in 1971 to 933 per thousand men in 1981. The average age at marriage for girls has reached 18.3 years in 1981 as against 17.2 years in 1971, achieving for the first time an average higher than the minimum prescribed age for marriage.

The focus in the programmes for women has shifted from welfare to development. This shift can be perceived in the creation of a separate department for the development of women.

The Programme of Action of the National Policy on Education (1986) lays stress on women's equality and has identified for the first time three areas for special attention, viz. (i) review of school textbooks to remove sexist bias and developing approaches to promotion of the value of equality through school curricula; (ii) reorientation of teachers to promote gender equality through their teaching and (iii) increasing the coverage of women and women's issues in the research and teaching activities of higher education.

Women's Studies and Development Centres have been set up in constituent colleges of several universities with the objective of using students and teachers as resource groups for creating social awareness and bringing about attitudinal changes in society.

There is an effort to sensitize administration to the women's perspective in development programmes, through the introduction of a women's component in training programmes for senior administrators conducted by the Department of Personnel in the Government of India.

There is a special effort launched to involve women at all levels in the planning and implementation process of programmes for women.

There is an increasing emphasis on professionalizing women's programmes by providing technical expertise for their implementation.

For the first time since Independence the elected

representation of women in Parliament has gone up to almost 10 per cent of its total membership.

The Prime Minister's office has now identified 27 beneficiary oriented schemes exclusively for women. These schemes though falling under various Ministers are monitored by the Department of Women and Child Development, Ministry of Human Resource Development.

A National Advisory Committee on Women has been set up with the Prime Minister as Chairman.

Several legislative enactments/amendments have come into force to protect the interests of women.

Overshadowing the positive indicators, there are certain distressing negative indices as follows:

Though a marginal improvement has been registered in the sex ratio, the projected ratio for 2000 AD is depressing with 500 million males to 480 million females.

Amniocentesis tests are being misused to determine the sex of the child in the womb, resulting in the female foetus being aborted.

Age specific death rates indicate higher rates for female children and women up to 35 years of age.

As per the 1981 Census, 75 per cent of women are illiterate. This is compounded by the high drop out rate for girls which is estimated at 55.5 per cent at the primary stage and 77.7 per cent at the middle school stage. Enrolment of girls in higher education has been almost static from 1975 to 1985. There are also substantial disparities in the enrolment of girls and boys at the university stage, and in technical and professional colleges.

The work participation rate for females declined in the census decades up to 1981. In 1981, it recorded a marginal improvement.

The fertility rates in 1981 showed only a very marginal decline-average number of children born to a woman during her lifetime being 4.6. There are in addition many incomplete pregnancies. Over 50 per cent of women suffer from anaemia in pregnancy, which accounts directly for 15-20 per cent of all maternal deaths.

Approximately 90 per cent of the women workers are engaged in the unorganized sector. Of these over 80 per cent are in agriculture and allied occupations. In the organized sector women constitute only 13.3 per cent of all employees. In the public sector, they account for 11 per cent of total employment and in the private sector for 17.8 per cent.

The number of female job seekers through employment exchanges increased from 11.2 lakh in 1975 to 51 lakh in 1986. After showing an increase between 1975 and 1982, the percentage of placements declined in the subsequent years, i.e., 1983-86.

Studies show that modernization and mechanization are tending to marginalize women in many sectors. They are either pushed down or out of the workforce. There are also indications that agricultural modernization/ industrial growth policies have tended to widen gender disparities.

Estimates of the average hours of unpaid work done by women outside their homes vary from 6.1 and 7.5 hours per day, with some women working up to 10 hours and more. Apart from their domestic duties, women are engaged in agricultural operations for an average of 12 hours a day. Despite this, their access to ownership of land, credit and other productive resources remains negligible.

Recent surveys indicate that, 30-35 per cent of rural households are headed by women due to male migration, neglect, abandonment.

Only 994 women hold senior management/administrative

> posts as against 15,993 men in similar jobs in the All India Services, constituting only 5.8 per cent. There are only 21 women officers in the Indian Police Service as against 2418 men (0.9 per cent). In the Indian Administrative Services, there are 339 women against 4209 men (7.5 per cent).
>
> Women comprise only 7.5 per cent of the membership of registered trade unions and approximately one per cent of the office bearers and executive committee members.
>
> Proportional representation of women in elected offices either remained stagnant or declined in the last decade. This is not withstanding their increased voting turnout in the general elections.
>
> Crimes against women continue unabated, there were 6668 reported victims of rape in 1987 and 1517 dowry deaths including by burning (provisional figures).

The *First Five-Year Plan* (1951-56) envisaged welfare measures for women. To spearhead welfare measures, the Central Social Welfare Board (CSWB) was established in 1953 which symbolized the welfare approach to women's problems. The CSWB was also reflective of the community development approach, which envisaged for the first time, the need for organizing women into Mahila Mandals or Women's Clubs. A number of studies have shown that the community development (CD) worker, perceived more as a harmonizer of interests rather than a stimulator of awareness, worked closely with the rural elite. Moreover, although rural women came within the purview of the CD programmes, they were not specifically catered to as a target population based on economic or other specific class related criteria. A large majority of poor rural women thus remained untouched.

The *Second Five-Year Plan* (1956-61) was closely linked with the overall approach of intensive agricultural development. The welfare approach to women's issues persisted. The plan recognized the need for the organization of women as workers. It also perceived the social prejudices/disabilities they suffered. The Plan stated that women should be protected against injurious work, should receive maternity benefits and creches for children. It also suggested speedy implementation of the principle of equal pay for equal work and provision for training to enable women to compete for higher jobs.

The *Third Five-Year Plan* (1961-66) pinpointed female education as a major welfare strategy. In social welfare, the largest share was provided for expanding rural welfare services and condensed courses of education. The health programme concentrated mainly on the provision of services for maternal and child welfare, health education, nutrition and family planning.

The *Fourth Five-Year Plan* (1969-74) continued the emphasis on women education. The basic policy was to promote women's welfare within the family as the base of operation. The outlay on Family Planning was stepped up to reduce the birth rate from 40 to 25 per thousand through mass education. High priority was accorded to immunization of pre-school children and supplementary feeding for children, expectant and nursing mothers.

The *Fifth Five-Year Plan* (1974-79) emphasized the need to train women in need of income and protection. It also recommended a programme of functional literacy to equip women with skills and knowledge to perform the functions of a housewife (including child care, nutrition, health care, home economics, etc.)

This Plan coincided with the International Women's Decade and the submission of the Report of the Committee on the Status of Women in India (CSWI). The overall task of the CSWI was to undertake a comprehensive examination of all the questions relating to the rights and status of women in the context of changing social and economic conditions in the country and problems relating to the advancement of women. The report stressed that the dynamics of social change and development had adversely affected a large section of women and had created new imbalances and disparities such as:

- The declining sex ratio;

- Lower expectancy of life;
- Higher infant and maternal mortality;
- Declining work participation;
- Illiteracy; and
- Rising migration.

The CSWI Report led to a debate in Parliament and the emergence of a new consciousness of women as critical inputs for national development rather than as targets for welfare policies. A second significant outcome was the recognition of women as a group adversely affected by the processes of economic transformation. It was realized that constitutional guarantees of equality would be meaningless and unrealistic unless women's right to economic independence is acknowledged and their training in skills as contributors to the family and the national economy is improved. A major outcome of the CSWI report was the National Plan of Action (1976) that provided the guidelines based on the UN's World Plan of Action for Women. The National Plan of Action (1976) identified areas of health, family planning, nutrition, education, employment, legislation and social welfare for formulating and implementing action programmes for women as called for planned interventions to improve the conditions of women in India.

An immediate outcome of the National Plan of Action was the setting up of the Women's Welfare and Development Bureau in 1976 under the Ministry of Social Welfare, to act as a nodal point within the Government of India to coordinate policies and programmes and initiate measures for women's development. The Women's Welfare and Development Bureau was charged with the nodal responsibility of:

(a) Co-ordinating and collaborating with multifarious programmes in other Central Government Ministries;

(b) Initiating necessary policies, programmes and measures;

(c) Collecting data to serve as a clearing house;

(d) Monitoring programmes for women's welfare,

(e) Servicing the National Committee on Women;

(f) Following up on the recommendations of the CSWI by formulating proposals and providing guidelines;

(g) Working out financial and physical targets;

(h) Liaising with multinational /UN agencies in the field of women's welfare;

(i) Legal issues and problems concerning women; and

(j) Implementing programmes and schemes.

In 1977-78 as an exercise for the Sixth Plan, the Government appointed the Working Group on Employment of women. Two other critical reports on village level organizations and participation of women in agriculture and rural development were prepared as part of the exercise. This plan was undoubtedly influenced by the CSWI Report of 1975. It devoted a whole chapter to Women and Development. For the first time a shift was perceived from welfare to development approaches for women. Influenced by the era that heralded concepts of social justice, the Sixth Plan recognized women's lack of access to resources as a critical factor impeding their development and, among others, the programme providing joint *pattas* (titles) to men and women was initiated. However, though the plan defined the magnitude of women's problems and suggested development strategies, the 'Family' rather than the 'women' remained the basic unit of development programming.

The *Seventh Five-Year Plan* operationalized the concern for equity and empowerment articulated by the International Decade for Women. For the first time, the emphasis was qualitative, focusing on inculcating confidence among women; generating awareness about their rights and privileges; and training them for economic activity and employment. In keeping with the spirit of the decade which aimed at integrating women into mainstream national development, the Plan emphasized the need to open new avenues of work for women and perceive them as a crucial resource for the development of the country.

The access of women to critical inputs and productive resources such as land (joint title on *patta* scheme initiated in the Sixth Plan period) were expanded in the Seventh Plan period to include support through credit (or small scale capital), marketing, training in skills/ management and technology. At the same time, it was emphasized that technology that causes unemployment or displacement of women must be resisted. Another salient and crucial recognition was the need for organization of women workers and unionization that could:

(a) Make demands for improving legal services to safeguard rights; and

(b) Reduce occupational and health hazards.

The Plan acknowledged the long hours spent by women in activities within the household especially in the collection of fuel, fodder, water, etc., as well as their labour on the family farm or in family business. While the Seventh Plan did not call for the computation of women's work in these two areas as part of women's contribution to the GNP, the identification of these hitherto invisible areas was a significant beginning. Complementing the productive endeavour were the supportive services offered to women, especially maternal and child care facilities as part of the total package of services for women.

Existing Programmes

Currently, the Government of India has over twenty-seven schemes for women, some women specific and others both for the male and female population. These schemes are located in different departments and ministries of the Government of India such as Rural Development, Labour, Education, Health Science & Technology, Welfare, Women and Child Development, etc. The total outlay on the women-specific schemes in the Seventh Plan is 2.4 per cent of the total while a gender break-up of beneficiaries or targets is unavailable for general schemes (RLEGP, NREP, etc.)

In 1985 the Government of India constituted a separate Department in the Ministry of Human Resource Development, for the development of women and children. This Department funds the Central Social Welfare Board that has developmental and welfare programmes for women. The Department also plans and executes programmes for women besides monitoring programmes for women in other Ministries /Departments. A number of these programmes were envisaged in the Sixth/Seventh Plan period-viz., Women's Development Corporations, Support to Training and Employment Programme (STEP), Training-cum-Production Centres for Women, Awareness Generation Camps for Rural and Poor Women, Women's Training Centres or Institutes for Rehabilitation of Women in Distress, Short Stay Homes for Women and Girls, Voluntary Action Bureau and Family Counselling Centres, Free Legal Aid & Para Legal Training, Working Women's Hostels, etc.

Women specific programmes implemented by the Department of Women and Child Development include:

(i) Strengthening and improvement of women's work and employment in agriculture, small animal husbandry, dairying, fisheries, handlooms, handicrafts, khadi and village industries, and sericulture;

(ii) Economic rehabilitation of women from weaker sections of society in the form of training and employment on a sustained basis;

(iii) Better employment avenues for women to bring them into mainstream national development;

(iv) Providing Short Stay Homes for women and girls in moral danger together with counselling, medical care, psychiatric guidance and treatment and services, and development of skills; and

(v) Preventive and rehabilitative services to women and children who are victims of atrocities and exploitation.

The thrust of these various programmes is to provide five principal categories of services:

(a) Employment & Income Generation Services;

(b) Education & Training Services;

(c) Support Services;

(d) General Awareness Services; and

(e) Legal Support Services

Holistic Perspective

Poverty is a consequence as well as a cause of several factors that limit life. The obstinacy of this self-perpetuating cycle needs to be broken before its grip can be loosened and overcome in the measurable future. The poverty-induced cycle affects all the people but impinges hardest on girls and women. Material poverty starts a chain of consequences, namely, infections, nutritional deficiencies, ill-health, growth retardation, slow learning, small body size, low productivity, repeated child bearing, excess of unpaid and unrecognized work, low earning capacity, unemployment and perpetuation of poverty. The strategic response need not tax the nation's resources and can yield decisive social benefits if it spans the spectrum of needs through the life cycle-the girl's education, food, security, safer environment in the home and neighbourhood, vocational training, support services to save time and energy, income and employment opportunity, safe motherhood, breast feeding and proper weaning, immunity against childhood diseases, management of common illnesses like diarrhoea and respiratory infection, growth promotion and early childhood stimulation as educational foundation leading to full and equal participation in socio-economic life. The process of inter generational (and now intragender,) improvement, which is what development planning is about, has to ascend these steps in an unbroken sequence.

These may not necessarily cover women in specially difficult circumstances such as refugees and migrants, prostitutes and victims of atrocities, the mentally and physically handicapped, etc., as these would require separate and detailed studies as has been done in the case of women in custody. However, for the majority of women, especially the rural poor, an integrated and decentralized approach to planning is envisaged. While the plan perceives main-streaming as long-term goal, it also realizes that some sector-specific measures will have to be undertaken to elicit higher participation of women in the development process during the interim period.

Recognizing the need for a holistic approach, in the new millennium, the Perspective Plan offers sectoral reviews of the situation of women in rural development, employment, supportive services, education, health, legislation, political participation, media and communication and voluntary action, while suggesting inter-linked and converging strategies towards a holistic development of women.

Sixteen

Issues at Stake

There are many an issue at stake. Issues involving women are closely related to supportive services. These refer to the gamut of services and amenities that make the women more functional and productive, while at the same time reduce the overburdening drudgery of the daily chores which she is expected to perform for the survival of her family. The major supportive services that require attention are fuel, fodder, water, creche and housing services. One of the major hurdles to women's development activities is the difficulty of providing economically viable means of releasing them from day to day drudgery and survival activities which are neither awarded an economic value nor are shared by men. Data indicate that women are unable to avail of tubectomy services in the absence of a substitute who can care for the children while the woman is away. Similarly, the education of girls is impeded because they are invariably required to help the mother to look after younger children. It is well known that besides adult women, children are also expected to fetch fodder, fuel and water. Cooking also accounts for a large chunk of the woman's time. The use of inefficient smoky chulhas affect their lungs, eyes and health in general. This also interferes with social interaction.

The factors affecting women's advancement are thus critically linked to the socio-cultural environment. In keeping, with her sex stereotyped role as a housewife and home maker, an Indian woman irrespective of clan, creed, region, religion, spends, most of her time on household chores. While the actual time distribution would vary from place to place, undoubtedly many women are subjected to the drudgery of a day to day subsistence working up to 16-18 hours per day. Unfortunately, such 'shadow work' brings her no monetary returns nor does it enhance her prestige in the family or society which is necessary for her to participate in decision making.

In addition, women are often left to fend for the household's basic needs and sanitation, especially in the rural context. The Seventh Plan notes that women play an important role in agriculture, animal husbandry and other related activities such as storage, marketing of produce, food processing, etc. About 54 per cent of rural women and 26 per cent urban women are engaged in marginal occupations in order to supplement family income by collection of fodder, firewood, cowdung, maintenance of kitchen gardens, tailoring, weaving, teaching, etc. It is not easy for a woman to take up employment, unless there are alternative ways to saving time at home and sufficient remuneration to justify her employment outside. Thus all programmes for women, be it education, health, family planning, nutrition, social welfare or legislation are necessarily interrelated support structures for reducing the household drudgery.

Since drinking water, fuel and fodder are the basic requirements especially in the rural areas, a major portion of women's time is spent on collecting these. Strategies which help overcome such problems by providing the necessary support services need to be carefully devised and effectively integrated in development strategies/ plans for women.

In the previous plan periods, the emphasis was mainly on issues concerning education, employment and social aspects, without giving commensurate attention to supportive services. For example, the section dealing with the 'Infrastructure for Women's Participation in a Modernizing Economy', the Report on the Status of Women, touched only upon childcare services. The National Plan of Action (1976) was also silent on the structuring of various supportive services. However, the Sixth Five-Year Plan recommended separate Science and Technology (S&T) inputs for women (Item 19.35) as a part of Science & Technology for Human Resource Development. The Plan suggested the setting up of special cells for promotion of Science and Technology for women under the aegis of different organizations such as the University Grants Commission (UGC, Council of Scientific and Industrial Research (CSIR), Indian Council for Medical Research (ICMR), Department of Adult Education (DAE), etc. Although it was proposed to apply Science and Technology for the improvement of the living conditions and status of women, support services were not specifically discussed. The Seventh Plan is more emphatic on women's development and has a separate section on 'Socio-Economic Programmes for Women'. It notes that in giving Science and Technology inputs for women, special efforts have to be made to reduce their drudgery.

The interlinkages between various sectoral and support services have to be fully understood so that an integrated purposeful view is taken of women development. The programmes have to be planned on the basis of a detailed analysis both at micro and macro levels. The analysis should identify critical factors including resource availability, appropriate technologies, skill constraints, public awareness and organizational, institutional and policy supports.

Fodder and Fuel

Fuel and fodder are best taken up together since they are bio-mass based and often the same plant provides both. This system also integrates with food which, in turn, is linked to fuel through cooking. Hence the discussion here also touches upon forestry and wasteland utilization for growing a variety of biomass in the broader perspective.

Women participate in fodder production as a part of their activities in agriculture and in cutting and fetching fodder for feeding the animals. Generally green fodder is raised as one of the crops or in grasslands and is gathered from the fields as and when required. Alternatively a variety of straws and other agricultural residues are collected and stored as fodder or converted into silage or hay. Often women also have to visit the nearby forests to cut fodder from trees and bushes. This is generally done along with fuel collection. The harder biomass like twigs and firewood are used as fuel and the palatable leaves, as fodder. As for fuels, as indicated by a number of studies, cowdung (gobar) and agricultural residues and firewood form the major fuel for cooking and are gathered and stored mainly by women. The act of making and storing cowdung cakes has developed into an art, with 'bitodas' (cowdung storage structures) prominently standing out in the rural landscape. Cowdung cakes are preferred for slow cooking on low fires or heating milk, while firewoods and agricultural residues serve to produce more intensive heat. Depending on resource availability, the utilization pattern varies with cowdung being more prominent in the northern regions. The major portion of total energy, consumed is through such 'non-conventional' sources which, in rural areas, accounts for 90 per cent of the domestic energy expenditure.

The three plans (Fifth, Sixth and Seventh) had generally discussed the fodder under 'Animal Husbandry', fuel under 'Energy', and biomass under 'Forestry'. The Fifth Plan observed that the 'forestry' development has assumed a significant dimension as a source of timber and fuel and for the maintenance of the natural ecological system. Special plantations have been given high priority. Under the section 'Energy' it has been proposed to adopt a multipronged approach to develop biogas technology and tap new sources such as solar energy, tidal and wing power. The Sixth Plan noted that feed and fodder constitute 60 to 70 per cent of the cost of production of various livestock products and that the area under fodder crops has remained more or less static during the last two decades. It also stated that emphasis will continue to be placed on the promotion of fodder production as an integral part of crop husbandry through a mixed farming system, particularly, on the small landholdings. Effective farmer-oriented extension programmes will be taken up by the Government for evolving and popularizing high yielding varieties of fodder crops, and introduction of leguminous fodders in existing crop rotations. Production and distribution of high quality fodder seeds will also receive priority attention. Accordingly, a Central Fodder Seed Production Farm and Centres for Forage Production and Demonstration were set up during this plan. The development of extensive grasslands and creation of grass reserves were taken up by the State Forest Departments. Under the social forestry programmes marginal and degraded forests were allocated for cultivation on fodder trees.

As for fuel, the Sixth Plan (item 9.248 under social forestry) proposed: (i) Mixed plantation of wasteland; (ii) Reforestation of degraded forests and raising of shelter belts. In the districts where shortage of fuel wood was particularly acute, new centrally sponsored schemes of social forestry including Rural Fuel Wood Plantation and Farm Forestry were introduced in selected areas. New thrusts in the form of Tree for Every Child Programme, Economic Development Force, Eco-development Camps and Agro Forestry programmes were devised during the Sixth Plan. The concept of organic recycling (Item 9.36) and the propagation of biogas technology (Item 9.40, 9.41) were also envisaged. Further, this plan dealt with the new and renewable energy sources and suggested that energy forestry, biogas and biomass conversion technologies have to be taken up along with solar and wind energy and a variety of other technologies. For example, item 15.95 on 'Energy Forestry' notes that firewood is the most important traditional fuel accounting for two-thirds of the total energy contribution from non-commercial sources and is becoming scarce. In view of the pressure on land, all available unutilized pockets of land could be used for energy plantations. Considering that rural communities will continue to depend heavily on such resources, it was proposed to decentralize energy production and distribution as a part of an Integrated Rural Energy System (Item 15.105) which considers all energy resources in a given area.

In the Seventh Plan also, emphasis has been given to social forestry, agro forestry and various renewable energy technologies and the necessity of creating awareness among people through mass media. The Plan notes that a proper implementation of some components of forestry programmes may be entrusted to local and voluntary bodies (NGOs). Concepts like 'social fencing' may be tested. Infact the revised 20-Point Programme (1986) has advocated a "New Strategy for Forestry" (Point No. 16).

In recognition of the importance of renewable resources, a Department of Non-conventional Energy Sources has been set up.

Also a National Wasteland Development Board was created with the objective of bringing 5 million hectares of land every year under fuelwood and fodder plantation.

In many of the above programmes, the role of women in the production, collection and utilization of fuel and fodder and the related problems are not adequately emphasized. However, it is heartening to note that the Department of Science and Technology set up a cell on "Science & Technology for Women" in 1982. This cell divided the various technologies required for women into the following four areas: Technologies for Drudgery Reduction; Employment Generation Technologies; Health and Sanitation Technologies; and Technologies for Minimizing Occupational Hazards.

Under the first category, the problems of fuel, fodder and drinking water were perceived from the point of view of women. Besides a number of projects funded through individual institutions, an All India Coordinated Project was also undertaken on 'Fuel and Cooking Aspects' through Science and Technology Department. More than 20 institutions from all over the country participated, analysing the data based on micro level surveys. The local specific and general problems of women in dealing with fuels were identified and the viability of a variety of technologies were field tested. Similarly, some of the selected technologies like the improved chulha, biogas solar cooking biogas based technologies, etc., are being taken to the people through the Department of Non-Conventional Energy Sources. Apart from various governmental institutions like Department of Science and Technology (DST), Indian Council of Agricultural Research (ICAR) Council for Scientific and Industrial Research (CSIR) and Department of Non-Conventional Energy Sources, a number of relevant State departments are also taking up the implementation of such projects. Some reports analysing the reasons for the success as well as failures of experiments undertaken are available.

It is encouraging to know that recently a number of NGOs have taken up programmes with funding support from the various Government bodies noted above. A Bio-energy Society of India has also been established with a view to promote research and development as well as public awareness. Bio-energy education dealing with the production, conversion and utilization of biomass with special emphasis on fuel aspects is being given prominence. People's participation is being promoted through social forestry and other programmes. However, the linking of women with these activities is still weak. A few movements like 'Chipko' stand out, emphasizing that much can be achieved by organizing women at the local levels.

The agricultural universities, dairy development institutions and forest institutes undertake research in fodder and fuel production and have a network of extension centres such as Krishi Vigyan Kendras for taking these technologies from the lab to land. While agriculture provides fodder crops, special attention is also paid to trees and plant species like 'subabool' which can cater to both fuel and fodder needs. Researchers on social forestry and agro-forestry all over the country now recognize the need for integrating the food, fodder, fuel, fertilizer, fibre and other biomass based production and utilization aspects.

The various technologies developed are being compiled into suitable directories for dissemination, e.g., the Science and Technology Women's Cell has listed a number of technologies for women. Council for Advancement of People's Action and Rural Technology (CAPART) has undertaken the publication of several volumes of *National Directory of Rural Technologies*, the first volume titles '*Post-Harvest Technologies*' has already been printed.

However, the scope exists for designing and developing more technologies appropriate to women taking into consideration the agronomy, ease of handling, economics, etc. A special mention must be made of Agricultural Tool Research Centre at Bardoli, which has tried to make efficient agricultural tools especially suited for women.

Drinking Water

Although India is one of the wettest countries in the world with an average annual rainfall of 1170 mm, it still faces and is expected to face in future the threat of acute water shortage. Among the various usages of water in rural areas, drinking water followed by irrigation, sanitation and agriculture are of importance for the overall developmental process.

Water resources are generally dealt with as a part of irrigation in agriculture. In addition to this, the Sixth Plan laid special stress on rural water supply as a part of the 'Minimum Needs Programme'. As in the Sixth Plan, the Seventh Plan also highlights the importance of drinking water. The supply of drinking water to all problem villages features at Point 7 of the Twenty-Point Programme (1986). A 'Technology Mission on Drinking water in Villages and Related Water Management' was established in 1986-87 under the Department of Rural Development, Ministry of Agriculture, Government of India. The collaborating agencies identified were Council of Scientific and Industrial Research, Ministry of Science and Technology, Department of Environment and Forests, Department of Defence Research and Development, Ministry of Health and Family Welfare, Ministry of Water Resources and State Governments. The 'problem' villages were identified as those with: (i) No source of water; (ii) Water sources more than 1.6 km. distance, 15 km depth and 100 metres elevation difference; (iii) Biological contamination (guinea worm, cholera, typhoid); and (iv) Chemical contamination (fluoride, brackishness, iron). The number of such problem villages amounts to 39 per cent of the total villages (2.27 lakh out of 5.57 lakh).

Apart from these, the strategy has focused on 50 project areas (Mini missions) to evolve new, cost effective science and technology techniques, to apply and replicate these techniques in the rest of the problem villages and to implement an integrated approach to water conservation.

A booklet outlining the project objectives, background, strategy, management structure, targets, methodology, milestones, accomplishment, resources and policy needs, has been brought out by the Ministry of Agriculture. Already this mission has started working with the State Departments concerned. In addition, universities, research institutions and voluntary organizations are also being involved. A first Regional Seminar to focus on these issues for Southern States and Union Territories was held at Gandhigram in Tamil Nadu in July 1987.

Most of the above efforts, however, are not directly addressed to women. Although in the Sixth Plan, special mention has been made about assuring the weaker sections of their due share of water, only a few organizations like the Science and Technology Women's Cell have looked at this problem from the women's development angle. In addition to sanctioning some institutional level projects on various aspects of potable water, an "All India Coordinated Project on Drinking Water" has also been proposed by this department.

Ideally, as in the case of urban services, the Government should be in a position to supply potable water to all households through pipelines and taps right at the doorsteps. However, considering the current constraints of finance and non-availability of suitable water sources, problem terrains, etc., this may not be feasible in the near future. Hence constructing and maintaining smaller water sources like wells, water tanks, hand pumps, etc., are to be given due consideration.

As with the implementation of any project, there is always the problem of ensuring people's participation in both maintenance and the distribution systems. Merely installing different kinds of units and equipment does not lead to sustained water supply. Thus, organizing women to adopt different technologies is a key issue. In this context, a successful experiment by a voluntary agency in Rajasthan could be considered as a model for replication. In this case, the people were involved in identifying the locations for tube-wells. A few persons were then trained in their actual construction and maintenance. The system of giving due remuneration for subsequent management to these trained personnel was also evolved. This ensured sustained working of the pumps/tube-wells and equitable distribution of water. Other case-studies worthy of note are the "Water Harvesting Systems" employed at Banwasi Sewa Ashram and the "Water Sharing System" evolved at Sukhamajari.

Although a number of technologies are available, only a few have reached the villages. More research and development is needed on issues like devices for carrying water in hilly terrain, water purification techniques suitable for different problem areas, storage at home levels, and rapid methods of water testing.

A list of available technologies have been compiled in a volume brought out by the Cell on Science and Technology for Women. The CAPART has also brought out publications on drinking water and the third volume of its National Directory of Rural Technologies will be on Drinking Water. The Technology Mission on Drinking Water has brought out two publications entitled *Sub-Mission on Desalination of Water and Sub-Mission on Eradication of Guineaworm*.

Creche/Daycare

With the advent of industrialization and modernization, and with the gradual disappearance of the traditional joint family and with its in-built security system, the problem of working mothers has become increasingly serious. Although it is mainly an urban phenomenon, rural India is beginning to experience it too. With increasing economic pressures more and more women have to take out of home jobs. The situation is serious because the majority of women who need daycare for their children are from economically backward strata of society.

Working mothers of low-income groups need day care most as they cannot afford to hire or pay for labour-saving devices. Thus, in addition to the general need for child care for all working mother's, there is also a more specific and strong need for child care for those belonging to the poorest sections of the society.

Rural mothers struggle hard not only in the fields but also to collect fuel, fodder and water. Thus their time 'out of home' is much more and the majority of them are forced to either take their infants along or to leave them under the 'supervision' of elder children who stay at home, or even alone. This situation not only keeps older children away from the educational system, but endangers the health of infants and small children. The need for childcare services had already been accepted, but the legal provision exists only for women in the organized sector, which comprise approximately 10 per cent of the working women.

After the submission of the CSWI report (1974), and the International Women's Year, childcare has been recognized as an important and essential support service in women's development. The CSWI report has stated that despite the laws and ILO Convention, maternity and childcare benefits are available only to 3-5 per cent of Indian women workers in the organized sector. The other 3-5 per cent of the organized sector (mainly in services) do not get creche facilities because they are not covered by labour laws. To the 90 per cent of women workers who are in the informal sector, these facilities have so far never been provided as highlighted in the report of the National Commission on Self-Employed Women and Women in the Informal Sector.

In 1950, creches were run by four national level voluntary organizations - The Indian Council for Child Welfare, Bhartiya Grameen Mahila Sangh, Bhartiya Adimjati Sevak Sangh and Harijan Sevak Sangh. The then Ministry of Social Welfare launched a scheme of creches/day care centres for children of working and ailing mothers in February 1975. The aim of the scheme was to promote healthy all round development of such children. The scheme caters to the basic needs of young children of poor working and ailing women in the unorganized sector. The services under the scheme include health care, supplementary nutrition, sleeping facilities, immunization, entertainment and nursery school facilities for children. Starting in 1974-75 with 247 creches to cover 6175 beneficiaries, the scheme has been considerably expanded since then. In the year 1987-88 there were 3,137 agencies running 10,210 creches in the country which included both permanent and mobile units. The Department of Women and Child Development which now deals with the scheme had on its plan that by the end of 1988-89, 12,000 creches would cover 2,82,800 children. The training of creche workers under this programme commenced from September, 1986.

Grants-in-aid to certain all-India level institutions were released for conducting training courses. In the statutory sector, around 55,000 children are taken care of in creches/day care centres.

The Balwadi Nutrition Programme is another programme being implemented since 1970-71 which looks after the social and emotional development of children in the age group of 3-5 years, apart from providing supplementary nutrition to them. About 5,045 balwadi centres are functioning in the country covering about 2.29 lakh children.

The Integrated Child Development Services (ICDS) scheme launched by the government in 1975 is designed both as a preventive and developmental effort. It extends beyond the existing health and education systems to reach children below six years and their mothers in villages and slums and delivers to them an integrated package of services - non-formal pre-school education., immunization, health checkups, supplementary nutrition, medical referral services and nutrition and health education for women. As on 31 March, 1988 information received from 1,455 ICDS projects indicate that 1,46,693 Anganwadis were providing supplementary nutrition to 96.10 lakh children. In these Anganwadis, 18.40 lakh nursing mothers were receiving supplementary nutrition. Though focused on the all round development of the pre-school child, it is also the largest scheme providing part time creche facilities to children in rural and tribal areas and in slums. As an employment generation scheme for women, it employs nearly 2,00,000 women at the Anganwadi level.

The National Policy on Education' 1986 (NPE), for the first time took note of the growing awareness that the performance of household chores, specially care of younger siblings, is a major reason for the stagnation in enrolment of girls in schools. At two, places in the policy document, (vide para 5.2 in Early Childhood Care and Education (ECCE) and para 4.3 in Education for Women's Equality, reference is made to the need for child care, attached to or near primary schools, as a support service to encourage and allow girls to attend school.

Housing

The rapid rate of urbanization in India, coupled with large scale migration of people into the metropolitan cities, has created a tremendous pressure on the housing situation in the country. On the one hand, is the ever increasing shortage of housing which is estimated to be to the tune of 5.1 million dwelling units in urban areas alone (NBO 1981), and on the other, is the steep cost of housing and new construction which is unable to keep pace with the increasing demand and is beyond the reach of the urban dwellers.

In the successive Five-Year Plans, the Government of India has launched several social housing schemes for different income groups under which, loan/ subsidy is given to the low income and economically weaker section families. The implementation of these schemes on a countrywide basis has created great awareness of the desirability of improving the housing and environmental conditions among all sections of the populations including women.

Several other measures which have been taken include providing house building advance, housing finance at low rates of interest through financial institutions, fiscal incentives, bulk acquisition and development of land and ceiling on land, land use regulations, promotion of housing through cooperatives, setting up of Housing Boards and City Development Authorities and Slum Clearance Boards to augment the housing stock.

A Central Scheme of assistance for construction of hostel buildings for working women was initiated in 1972. The scope of the scheme was widened in 1980 by including a provision for daycare centres for children. Financial assistance is given to voluntary organizations for construction/expansion of hostel buildings for working women. Local bodies are also eligible for taking up these programmes. The total number of hostels sanctioned so far is 429 with a total capacity of 27,292 working women with day-care centre facilities for 2,920 children, since the inception of the scheme in 1972. It has been decided to reserve 5 per cent seats in the hostels for widows and other women in distress who are otherwise, eligible for hostel accommodation.

Under the Minimum Needs Programme to ameliorate housing and environment conditions, the Government of India has been implementing various schemes, viz., Slum Clearance Improvement Scheme, Scheme for Environmental Improvement in Slum Areas and the Schemes for Provision of House Sites to landless workers in rural areas and other social housing schemes for improving the living conditions of the urban and rural poor. The benefits of the schemes accrue to women also.

In the Twenty Point Programme (1986) high priority was accorded to provision of drinking water supply (Point No. 7), improvement of housing conditions for 14.6 million rural landless families (Point No. 14) and those living in slums and squatter settlements (Point No. 15).

Large-scale housing programmes were taken up in different states under the National Rural Employment Programme (NREP) and Rural Landless Employment Guarantee Programme (RLEGP). Housing schemes with employment as the main feature have also been taken up in many States. For implementing the Indira Gandhi Grih Nirman Awas Yojna, an allocation of Rs. 125 crore annually has been provided in the Seventh Five-Year Plan to build one million houses for Scheduled Castes and tribal families.

Improvement in the quality of life of people depends to a great extent on the quality of housing and related facilities which determine the physical environment. It is in recognition of this fact that the world conference of the International Women's Year adopted a World Plan of Action in 1975 which included aspects related to housing amongst its recommendations. The Plan suggested that settlement planning and policies should be formulated keeping in view the trend to recognize women's role in the development process and should prioritize investments in infrastructure therein according to the needs of women. Subsequently, following the declaration of 1987 by the United Nations as the International Year of Shelter for the Homeless, the Ministry of Urban Development of the Government of India formulated a Draft National Housing Policy (March, 1987) with a view to ensuring every family a shelter by the end of this century. Nowhere in its text, however, had the draft acknowledged that housing and women's needs required to be closely linked. Passing references to women were made only at page 12 para 13.4 of the draft wherein it stated that special efforts would be made to improve women's skills and working conditions in the housing sector.

For women, housing has a wider meaning. It implies their working and living environment to which they are confined for a greater portion of their lives, performing their multiple roles that of production which is often home based and therefore implies the use of the shelter and its environs as the working space; that of reproduction which is traditionally viewed as their primary role and includes child rearing activities linked to domestic chores; and that of management of resources and assets within the family unit which includes activities such as storage, managing domestic provisions, processing, etc.

Women's housing needs, arising from their multiple roles, have been listed as follows; as child bearers, they need access to sanitary facilities and a healthy living environment; as child rearers, they need space for childcare and recreation within or outside the house; as managers of households, they need water, fuel, waste and garbage disposal, proper light and ventilation and space to perform domestic chores; and as producers, they need a working space as well as space for storage of raw materials and finished products, besides space for processing of materials. In addition, women also need privacy and security as well as facilities for education, recreation, production and training within the housing space. Housing thus, implies space beyond the confines of the immediate shelter.

An effective public distribution system for essential commodities like rations and cloth is a necessary support for women, especially women workers in the unorganized sector. Poor women are denied ration cards which forces them to purchase basic necessities from the open market at exorbitant prices. Even women with ration cards are often denied rations due to understocking or diversion of stocks.

Each of the above roles indicates that women's efficiency and effectiveness in performing the productive and reproductive tasks are linked to the quality of housing. Since they are in effect the primary users of housing, women must have a role to play in decisions regarding housing as well as ensure that they have access to ownership of the same.

In planning for women's development, priority needs to be given to creating access to assets for single women and female headed households. An estimated 30-35 per cent of households in rural India are headed by women according to available micro studies. Women have hitherto had no rights to ownership or inheritance of property within the framework of customary law. Recent legislative provisions have tried to remedy this situation but ancestral property still remains inaccessible to women. By and large, the patriarchal patterns of land ownership and transfer have implied that land is transferred to males. This pattern has been adopted by the planners in formulation of housing programmes so that men are recognized as heads of: households and land is distributed in their names. Although distribution of land deeds or pattas has been legally sanctioned for men and women jointly, in effect, women are not given land titles. Where women are able to gain access to land or assets, they are often required to have a man stand surety for the same, as also for loans and credit.

Within the patriarchal norm, women may not customarily claim ownership of the matrimonial home. This has often denied women access to shelter in times of crisis. In cases where women have been deserted and are destitute, they have not had any legal right to claim access to shelter, housing or any such assets. Only recently have policy makers and legislators realized that, it is imperative to accord priority to the provision of housing for single and women headed households.

Various strategies have been evolved to augment the housing stock in the country by urban planners and specialists especially for economically weaker sections. The target groups have however seldom been involved in planning for such housing. The norms applied to make such houses affordable for the identified target groups have ignored women's needs for space in the dwelling unit. It is necessary to scrutinize established standards and develop norms in housing especially for economically weaker sections, and to determine their adequacy for women. There must also be visible participation of women in the planning and execution of housing programmes in order to ensure that women's needs are adequately considered in the housing designs.

Women have had no traditional access to capital assets or to institutional finance and credit for housing. They have had to resort to borrowing from traditional credit sources at exorbitant rates of interest. Institutional sources of credit such as banks have not recognized women as credit-worthy individuals in their own right so that they may borrow through existing schemes at differential rates of interest. Various agencies have tried to play an intermediary role in creating access for women to institutional credit but their out reach has been limited. It is essential, therefore, that institutions such as HDFC and HUDCO recognize women in their individual capacities as beneficiaries for housing credit and finance.

The housing market also offers a vast potential for employment, especially in the rural areas. Expanding construction activity in housing would ensure that greater opportunities for employment are created, while also creating shelter for the rural populace.

Problems and Remedies

Problems specific to women have to be highlighted in considering issues like fodder, fuel and drinking water. Since these directly concern women, their involvement in the programmes related to such issues must be given prominence. The interlinkages among fuel, fodder and drinking water with other aspects of the development of women such as education, employment, food and nutrition, health and sanitation must be recognized and integrated programmes worked out on a holistic basis for optimal utilization of personnel and financial inputs.

As had been stressed by the Seventh Plan, the government must ensure public participation and draw upon the resources of voluntary agencies, educational (especially Science and Technology) institutions, industries and financial organizations in implementing various programmes for the development of women. Various funding agencies may consider sponsoring All India or regional projects on a coordinated basis wherein, Science and Technology experts could collaborate with the NGOs and the people in designing and implementing programmes based on micro-level surveys.

Women must be specifically organized by involving the NGOs wherever necessary to participate in the implementation of social forestry programmes, water sharing projects and in the maintenance of various gadgets and devices. The necessary formal and non-formal education has to be appropriately matched with their time schedules, seasonal occupations and socio-cultural constraints.

In training programmes, in addition to NGOs, educational institutions could play an important role. Agricultural extension centres, home science colleges, and youth forums like NSS should be purposefully involved. Science and Technology institutions can take up the task of training and provide the technical back up in technology transfer as well as monitoring and evaluation.

A data bank may be set up with such resource centres, where information may be made available not only on technologies but also on manufacturing availability of training facilities, etc. These centres must have working models readily available for demonstrations, and requisite resource persons. Interaction among the centres will enable them to serve as a national network.

Research must be undertaken both in improving and developing hardware and software systems. All the necessary technologies on collection, processing, storage and utilization of fodder, fuel and drinking water may be carefully analysed and gaps identified. Many issues are regional and location specific and tackled best at the micro level. For example, carrying water is more problematic in hills than in plains and fuel problem is more acute in arid zones. The choice of fuel and fodder generating plants would depend on the agroclimate and terrains. The type of improved chulha required depends on the food and cooking practices. Perhaps an area based approach can be taken combining locations with similar type of problems into groups or clusters.

The necessary industrial support in the manufacturing of various small equipments should be created, e.g., manufacture of small water storage systems, forage harvesting system, etc. Women and small entrepreneurs should be involved in such ventures with suitable subsidies.

The decision makers both at the bureaucratic and political levels should be sensitized to the importance of programmes specifically targeted for women in the context of national development.

The socio-cultural and traditional practices must be suitably modified for conservation of various resources and more efficient utilization of time, energy and capital. For example, cooking recipes which require more fuel and time in cooking have to be pointed out and corrected. Where possible, community kitchens should be encouraged. Especially in the periphery of towns, the food prepared in neighbouring areas can be brought in packages. This would reduce the load on fuel, provide employment to women in the surrounding areas while benefiting many working women.

Many of the local hardware and software problems especially with respect to fuel and drinking water are not easily solved at the household level. The right level of scaling has to be planned, keeping in view both the economic viability and the consumer's convenience. For instance, in a biogas system, a 80m' community biogas plant is more economical than a 2m' household plant but the former calls for a more elaborate management system. Perhaps a subcommunity biogas plant of 15-20M3 for 15-20 families could be a solution. Thus for each problem, a suitable community or sub-community system has to be worked out.

Some of the above recommendations have been noted both in

the 'Country Report of 1985' presented at Nairobi and "Forward Looking Strategies for the Year 2000". However, at the level of implementation, the programmes of various governmental departments tend to get superimposed. Hence it is important to identify one of the Ministeries as the 'Nodal Ministry' for coordination and keeping abreast of all programmes related to women. The Ministry of Human Resource Development could perhaps take this up so that a Master Table could be prepared of all action/projects having a bearing on women, noting the time schedules - for implementation, and the agencies involved in planning and action at the central, state, regional local levels. This "Nodal Ministry" for women may constitute sub-committee with members drawn not only from government but also from other participating agencies to discuss the various issues and evolve strategies.

Supportive Services

Creche services must be universally provided to all women, especially in the poverty sector. This would enable some of them to augment their family income and, at the same time, ensure proper care of their children. The children's health, sanitation, nutrition and early stimulation would get attention. Increasing the number of creches would also generate more employment opportunities for women. In view of the above, it is recommended that in rural areas, wherever ICDS infrastructure already exists, creches should be opened and attached to the Anganwadis. These creches should make provision for babies below 3 years age. The timings of Anganwadis which provide pre-school services for children of 3-6 years, should be adjusted according to the working hours of rural women. These creches will help in containing morbidity and mortality rates and malnutrition of infants and small children. They will also relieve the children in the school going age group from child care responsibilities, and give an opportunity to them to utilize the ICDS pre-school services.

The existing law that stipulates provision of a creche for employment of thirty or more women should be changed to thirty persons (men and women). This would ensure that employers do not use loopholes in the law to their advantage and would extend creche facilities to children of men workers whose wives, if they are not in the organized sector do not otherwise have access to such facilities.

The Government of India, being an employer of a large number of women, must provide creche facilities in or near all workplaces.

Creche service must follow an integrated approach to childcare.

Creche workers should preferably be local women to whom appropriate skill-oriented, on the job training should be imparted.

Technical institutions and home-science colleges should be utilized to train creche workers and also provide inputs for systematic monitoring and supervision of the creche programmes.

Organizations running creches should be given flexibility to adopt timings suitable to the needs of the working mothers.

Local women's groups and mothers of the children attending creches must be given training in preparation of toys, play materials out of low cost/no cost indigenous material. Employment for women can be generated by employing local women to prepare the midday meals, etc.

Action research projects, such as, a study of the impact of day care services on the education of girls should be initiated.

Domestic Management

Traditionally, women have had a significant role in resource management including housing management. It is important to recognize this role and provide for women's participation in development programmes, and for incorporating their needs in schemes for improvement of housing and environmental conditions in the following manner:

Identify the needs of women in relation to housing and community facilities and build them in an integrated manner into housing development programmes.

Integrate environmental factors into development planning for women including their requirements in settlement planning.

Involve women at all levels of decision making and bring about their participation in programme implementation so as to ensure that the benefits of housing, essential services, and community facilities are directed to women in general and to the poor and vulnerable among them in particular.

The special needs of women should be identified and adequately catered to while formulating minimum housing standards.

Necessary facilities in homes should be provided to lessen the burden and drudgery of women in performing productive and reproductive roles.

Priority investment in infrastructure such as water supply, sanitation, energy, transportation, working women's hostels, public distribution of basic needs, etc., should take into consideration the needs of women.

Provision of housing for working and/or single women is recommended on priority basis. In addition, women in difficult circumstances such as widows, refugees, destitutes, victims of social oppression, seasonal migrant workers, victims of natural disasters, etc., must be provided shelter as part of an integrated rehabilitation programme.

The National Housing Policy which has been formulated, must pay adequate attention to the special needs and roles of women in the implementation of housing programme.

The social and economic constraints which come in the way of women's participation should be removed and their active involvement in housing should be promoted by:

- Allotting house-sites in the joint name of wife and husband;
- Mobilizing savings of women for housing;
- Organizing self-help in undertaking house construction work;

- Imparting training so that women could become skilled labour (including masons and other skilled labour); and
- Ensuring access for women to institutional credit at low rates interest without collateral.

In India, rural women constitute nearly 80 per cent of the female population. They contribute largely to the country's economy which is mainly agriculture based. Although distributive justice has been categorically underlined in all the development plans, the needs of women have not been adequately addressed. While laying emphasis, on enhanced agriculture production in which the involvement of women is high, the plans have fostered a target group and area oriented approach to reduce regional and ecological imbalances disregarding women's equality as embodied in the Constitution. Rural development programmes for women have only in recent decades recognized the crucial role of organization and mobilization as strategies for women's empowerment and development. Rural women's organizations are also mechanisms for restructuring and redistributing power and have been utilized pressure groups that influence and/or bargain on behalf of rural women.

Situational Analysis

The launching of the Community Development Programme in 1952 was a landmark in the history of India and ushered in an era of development with the participation of the people. The Community Development Programme adopted a systematic integrated approach to rural development with a hierarchy of village level workers and block level workers drawn from various fields to enrich rural life. Agriculture, animal husbandry, public health, women's development, rural industries, etc., found a special niche in the framework cast for this purpose. Five thousand National Extension Service Blocks were created under the Community Development Programmes by the end of the Second Five-Year Plan. During the Third Five-Year Plan the momentum was maintained through a series of developmental schemes though allocations under the NES programme tapered. This was succeeded by the Small Farmers Development Agencies followed by

Marginal Farmers Development Agencies, Crash Schemes for Rural Employment, Food for Work Programme, Drought Prone Areas Programme and Desert Development Programme in the early seventies. The contents of all these programmes were to strengthen the rural base of the economy, specifically the primary sector comprising agriculture, animal husbandry, etc., and employment through labour intensive works that would create the infrastructure of roads and other community assets for the benefit of the rural people.

It was recognized that the skewed pattern of landholdings stood in the way of creating an egalitarian society and obstructed modernization and intensification of agriculture. Land reform measures for abolition of intermediary tenures, tenancy reforms, imposition of land ceiling on agricultural holdings, distribution of surplus land to the landless agricultural workers and consolidation of landholdings were introduced through a series of State Legislations under Central guidelines.

Certain areas of the country are characterized by soil-erosion, water stress and environmental degradation. The Drought Prone Areas Programme was started in 1973 aiming at an integrated area development for optimum utilization of land, water, livestock and human resources through a watershed management approach to mitigate the effects of drought. A few years later the Desert Development Programme, a wholly centrally funded scheme, specifically to cover extremely arid areas for controlling desertification restoration of ecological balance, was also started.

The emphasis shifted to fulfilling minimum needs of the people during the Fifth Five-Year Plan.

A systematic analysis and examination of the status and role of women within the agriculture and rural development strategies in India started with the National Plan of Action (NPA) for women which followed the report of the Committee on the Status of Women in India (CSWI). Subsequently, efforts of women activists, social science institutions and researchers produced enough documentary support to persuade the Sixth Plan document to include a chapter on 'Women and Development' for the first time in the country's history of planned development.

A strategy of direct attack on poverty was adopted in the Sixth Plan as the theory of trickle down benefits of general development programmes had not proved as a successful strategy for the removal of poverty. Forty-eight per cent of the population were found to be living below the poverty line at the beginning of the Sixth Five-Year Plan.

One positive outcome of these developments has been the recognition that rural women are not a homogeneous group to justify a uniform development strategy. The development plans in the case of women must be based on the assessment of their actual role and participation in socio-economic activities.

Women's employment has been recognized as the 'critical entry point' for Women's integration in mainstream development. The low and deteriorating status of rural women is attributed to their declining economic participation and other factors like the modernization of the agricultural sector. The need for giving a better deal to the rural women is beginning to be widely recognized. It is now accepted that the participation of women themselves in the development activities is the most effective tool for the promotion of the access of women to the benefits of development. A working group set up by the Deptt. of Rural Development, Ministry of Agriculture and Rural Development in 1978 recommended that the major objectives of the development plan for rural women should be: (i) The improvement of their economic status, and (ii) The promotion of women's organization to have the collective strength to articulate their needs and promote their participation in the development process.

The Integrated Rural Development Programme initiated in 1978-79 and extended to all the development blocks in the country in 1980-81 was conceived as one of the instruments for a direct attack on poverty. It dealt with individual rural families below the poverty line. Credit from banking institutions and subsidy from the

Government were given to the families for self-employment and income generation. Under IRDP, a special place was accorded for training rural unemployed youth for employment with the introduction of TRYSEM. An exclusive scheme for the social and economic uplift of women belonging to families below the poverty line, DWCRA (Development of Women and Children in Rural Areas) was launched in 1982 as a sub-component of IRDR ·

The Sixth Plan accepted poor rural women to be targets of rural development strategies. The specific problems identified concerning rural poor women were:

(i) Marginality of attention and services to them in rural and agricultural development;

(ii) Special constraints that obstruct their access to available assistance and services such as, lack of training to develop their awareness and skills; lack of information and lack of bargaining power;

(iii) Low productivity and narrow occupational choices;

(iv) Low level of participation in decision making;

(v) Inadequate finance and expert guidance for promoting socio-economic activity of rural women and their participation;

(vi) Inadequate monitoring of women's participation in different sectors;.

(vii) Wage discrimination;

(viii) Inadequate application of science and technology to remove drudgery; and

(ix) Low health and nutrition status.

The Sixth Plan document stated that one of the most important means of achieving improvements in the status of women would be to secure for them a fair share of employment opportunities, to earmark a percentage of allocation for women, and to fix for them a quota in all the poverty alleviation programmes. The Seventh Plan reiterated the strategies suggested in the Sixth Plan with a sharper focus on the increased coverage of women in various rural development programmes.

Simultaneously, the National Rural Employment Programme (NREP), assuring wage employment to the unemployed rural population was introduced in 1980. Subsequently, concentration on the rural landless was attempted by the introduction of the Rural Landless Employment Guarantee Programme (RLEGP) in 1983. The Indira Awas Yojana was added as an important component of the programme in the Seventh Plan for constructing houses for SC/STs and free bonded labourers. Social Forestry was added as another component of the RLEGP with national emphasis on greening fuel and fodder.

The establishment of the Technology Mission on Drinking Water and Related Water Management gave a new thrust to the Rural Water Supply Programme. Safe and adequate drinking water is to be provided to the entire rural population by the end of the Seventh Five-Year Plan.

The impact of the poverty alleviation programmes coupled with the development in various sectors reduced the rural population below the poverty line to 37 per cent by the beginning of the Seventh Plan. The target is to bring this down to 28 per cent by the end of the Seventh Plan Period.

Agriculture and allied fields provide the largest sector for women's employment. It largely determines the rural women's socio-economic status. This is the sector where women's role as unpaid labour in productive activities is most prominent and is responsible for conferring women a non-working status. In case of both agriculture and animal husbandry, development strategies have provided very little attention to women in comparison to their active involvement in both the sectors. Some training is imparted to women in agriculture and animal husbandry under the programmes for

Farmer's Training and Krishi Vigyan Kendras. But the Farmers Training Programme has lost much of its importance after the introduction of the new extension system of Training and Visit (T&V). Though women constitute a major work force in agriculture which with regional variation is estimated to be around 60 per cent, they are invisible in the T&V system. Currently there is one major extension programme for women in Karnataka and 2-3 such programmes on the anvil in other states. There is an in-built resistance observed in them in viewing women within their home making role. Even the visual presentations (slides, filmstrips and films) which are used for the orientation of the functionaries, often depict the women in the field and the extension agent talking to the contact farmer on the same field, fail to project the full dimension of women's role.

While rural women have become marginally visible in the anti-poverty programmes, they have not been adequately recognized in agricultural development, land reform, or rural industrialization. Non-recognition of women in agriculture has many implications. Intensive agriculture and the green revolution have reduced women's participation in farm activities but the work load related to the home based farm activities has increased considerably. That has only reduced them from the 'working' to a 'non-working' status. Limited employment opportunities created by technology resulting in the means of production being concentrated in the hands of a few, and increased landlessness for the poor led to men replacing women in many of their traditional areas of employment. But women have had to work and survive. They are thus found to be gradually moving to the non-traditional sectors seeking employment for survival.

Following the Sixth and Seventh Plans, the Department of Rural Development issued directives to the State Governments to give priority to women headed households, enhance the share of women under the anti-poverty programme (IRDP), and the programme of Training for Self-Employment (TRYSEM). Guidelines for NREP and RLEGP envisage increasing participation of women in wage employment and creation of assets specific to the needs of women's groups. At present the share of employment generated under NREP for women is approximately 20 per cent. A special programme for women entitled DWCRA was also introduced in 1982, as a sub-component of IRDP to accelerate the process of integration of women in the rural development programmes. Up to 1987, there were 11,553 groups which were reported to have been organized in 106 districts under this scheme.

The Integrated Rural Development Programme meant for the poorest in the rural areas has been formulated for creating assets with a view to increasing the productivity and income generation abilities of the beneficiaries. Efforts have been made under this programme to select female headed households. The scheme of DWCRA could be strengthened and modified in order to ensure that the benefits reach more target groups. The National Rural Employment Programme (NREP) and Rural Landless Employment Guarantee Programme (RLEGP) would generate additional employment to women in the lean season. Under Training of Rural Youth in Self-Employment (TRYSEM), one-third of the beneficiaries were expected to be women and special attention was to be given to improve existing skills of women and imparting to them new skills under the programmes of farmers training, fodder production, post harvest technology, application of pesticide, budding and grafting, training in horticulture, fisheries, poultry, dairy and social forestry, etc. The training of women under TRYSEM exceeded the target to 44 per cent in January 1988. Out of a total of 37.23 lakh families which received benefits under the IRDP during 1986-87, the number of women headed families was 5.67 lakh which amounts to only 15.23 per cent as against the target of 30 per cent. On assessment of the programmes, it is observed that considerable efforts are required to elicit the participation of women in these activities. The training provided under TRYSEM and DWCRA is not always viable and there is a tendency to limit to a few traditional crafts, though the Department of Rural Development is laying greater stress on taking up innovative activities too. Therefore, a fresh look is needed to be given to identification of trades and activities which may gainfully be taken up by women. Many income generating programmes have not succeeded due to full thought not being given to the input availability, training and marketing of products.

Special development projects linked to certain ongoing activities need to be taken up on a project basis to improve the effectiveness of the programmes related to women. Specific projects such as sericulture for tribals in certain states like Bihar and Orissa, development of dairy units linked to Operation Flood areas, fruits and vegetables cultivation linked to marketing through Mother dairy, prawn farming and fishing in the coastal region were commended. Agro-based industry schemes, etc., are essential.

The scheme of Training of Rural Youth for Self-Employment (TRYSEM) should be revamped with a view to organizing training in trades with assured employment potential to women in rural areas, as well as for wage employment in peripheral metropolitan and urban areas. State Emporia, marketing channels of KVXIC, etc., should be tapped to ensure elimination of middlemen and better prices.

The Accelerated Rural Water Supply Programme (ARWSP) and the Minimum Needs Programme (MNP) are of special significance to rural women who are the victims of drudgery, such as fetching water from distant locations. The Technology Mission on Drinking Water and Related Water Management lays emphasis on purification of water to make it potable, training in the use of water and maintenance of water sources. Women are the target of the awareness creation programmes as well as agents for creating awareness in conservation of water and maintenance of water sources. The low cost sanitation programme is also of great importance to women, who are otherwise subjected to a lot of privation due to lack of appropriate sanitation facilities. Rural Technologies and innovation promoted by CAPART aim at relieving the drudgery to women in several areas of their households and economic activities. They include the improved varieties of stone grinder, wheel barrow, ball-bearing pulley, groundnut shelter and smokeless chulhas.

The limited performance of the programmes introduced to achieve the integration of women in the development process suggests that only policy directives do not achieve the desired objectives. Programmes do not get implemented due to the lack of comprehension of the relevance of women's contribution to national development. Although a concern for development of women is well articulated at the central policy making level, an ambivalence is observed at the implementation level. The policy directives issued by the Government of India for the increased share for women in the development programmes and the promotion of a participatory approach, do not provide for corresponding development in the infrastructure, extension, training information support and a strong monitoring system which is particularly lacking at the State level. The programmes for rural women still continue as a separate exercise within the sectoral programmes with marginal attention, resources and inadequate monitoring.

The major shortcomings noticed in the implementation of the programmes for women with development objectives are:

(i) Perpetuation of the concept that women need only welfare services;

(ii) That the developmental benefits will automatically accrue to the women as a result of economic development of the family;

(iii) Inadequate knowledge and skills for designing socioeconomic activities for women and in group organizations; and

(iv) Lack of supportive services such as credit, childcare, marketing, training and technology for reducing the drudgery.

Methodological Issues

The approaches used for integrating women in the mainstream of development have raised some methodological issues. These relate particularly to the organization of groups, involvement of the voluntary sector, and the household approach in development programmes for rural women.

The organization of women's groups is considered to be one

of the most effective tools for integrating women in the development process. Yet it has raised several issues which are not fully resolved. Some of the questions which are being asked repeatedly are:

(i) Who will organize the groups (the role of intermediaries)?

(ii) What will be the size, structure and status of groups formal or informal?*

(iii) Should the groups be organized first and the choice of activities to be undertaken by the groups come next?

(iv) Should women be assisted individually under the IRDP, etc. or be formed into groups.

Apart from these unresolved issues, there are problems in selecting and working out economically viable group projects. Women activists argue against giving individual projects to be carried out within the household as it would only perpetuate their subordination in the household hierarchy. They claim that assistance to the voluntary agencies, which was expected to provide grass-roots structural support in this regard, is either not forthcoming or has not been sought.

It is logical that the size of the group to be mobilized should be such as to enable close interaction amongst the members which is only possible when they come from the same background and from one cluster of villages. It is also evident that poor women acquire confidence when they get organized. The delivery system will respond positively even if they are informally grouped. But in the interest of economic viability, and to strengthen their earning capacity, it is desirable for the group to be formalized. It is however, impossible or advisable to suggest one organizational model for all situations. The experience by and large is that the organization based on personal interface and on localized issues is more effective, more flexible and functional than the highly structured and impersonal form of organization.

Some of the processes under IRDP, such as identification of

beneficiaries/ productive activities, preparation of loan applications, sanction of the same and procurement of assets have not been given much attention in terms of proper planning, particularly of the linkage required after the asset is given, to make the same optimally productive. Such linkages include most critically the supply of raw materials and facilities for marketing. These processes and linkages are more effective when implemented through the group approach.

The crucial question in the field of land reforms is how rural poor women should get land and have access to land. Power structures in the villages are dominated by the relatively better off classes. Considering that implementation of land reforms measures leaves much to be desired, there is an urgent need for people's participation more specifically of the women, by promoting their groups organizations and through Panchayati Raj institutions. Each village should have a village plan which should include cultivable lands, *gochar* lands and forest lands with clearly demarcated boundaries.

The involvement of intermediaries in development programmes for rural women has been considered vital, particularly in demonstrating and promoting the participatory model and to provide support to the grass-root structure. Here too, there are basic issues which need to be carefully resolved. Among others, it is queried whether the role of the intermediary organizations has been understood by the Government, or whether it is feasible for the voluntary organizations to function in partnership with the government, given the differences in approach.

There is no uniform understanding and acceptance of the role of the voluntary agencies in the States. In some cases, there is a complete lack of rapport between the Government and voluntary agencies. In others, there is the tendency of associating the women's programmes entirely with voluntary action, showing a lack of initiative on the part of the, Government. There is little doubt that the voluntary agencies are committed to the cause of women and have expressed a real concern for the enhancement of women's status.

They have also demonstrated skills for mobilizing women, and in trying innovative projects. In view of this, the association of the voluntary agencies with the programmes is bound to enrich the programmes as well as the delivery mechanisms. Yet, they cannot be a substitute for Governmental action. To end women's isolation from rural development, the Government must work in partnership with voluntary agencies.

Currently debated issues in the context of women in rural development and in the anti-poverty programmes, is the household versus group approach; some argue in favour of ensuring a share of developmental resources and benefits to women in all sectoral programmes, while others argue in favour of having separate investments for women.

In India, the family is hierarchical, traditional and the status in the family is determined by sex and age. In the patriarchal society, it is the man who holds the position of the head of the family and the bread-winner. Therefore, it is the man who gets attention in the investment of developmental resources, training, extension and other supports. Women's contribution to the family's earnings goes unrecognized. This bias, in fact, is responsible for the earlier programmes not taking note of women headed households whose number is currently estimated at 30-35 per cent of all rural households. With mounting pressure on the government to give priority to this group, it has been convincingly argued that an improvement in the income of the household does not necessarily mean development for women. The household approach instead of creating equitable conditions, perpetuates the subordination of women and limits their opportunities for self-growth and self-expansion.

Having a special component within sectoral plans can stimulate action for women provided the components are monitored separately. The introduction of the scheme of DWCRA within the programme of IRDP was aimed at stimulating the response of the State Governments to integrating women into anti-poverty programmes. Therefore, in case of women, it can be contended that a combined approach is desirable. This would allow women to be adopted as a target in all sectoral programmes, with earmarked resources along with special component plans aimed exclusively at women. Such dual approaches can be continued until women acquire sufficient power to articulate their needs and demands, and until such time as women's concerns get to be internalized in the planning and administrative structures.

Access to Land

In the economic sphere and in particular in the rural sector, the empowerment of women relates mainly to their access to means of production and control over the fruits of their labour. The access to the means of production implies ownership of land, other productive assets, access to capital and access to technology and acquisition of various skills required to make labour power more productive.

The aspect of ownership of land relates to rights of inheritance which are governed by personal laws of different communities. These personal laws at present are discriminatory against women and have a bias in favour of the male heirs. The State Governments of Kerala and Andhra Pradesh have sought to remove some of these discriminations with a view to give daughters in the family, coparcenary ownership in the family property on the same level as the sons. But even these changes do not go far enough and still discriminate against a married daughter and a widow and do not apply equally to the separate properties of the father in the Hindu Customary Law. There is discrimination against women of different types in the personal laws of other communities also. In the customary law of certain tribes, only male agnates in the male line are recognized as valid heirs and an unmarried daughter is only entitled to usufructuary maintenance. It would be necessary to introduce correctives to overcome the discrimination, in order that the gap between the State's proclamation to achieve equality of the sexes and its laws which deny it, is bridged. Women's undiluted access to land, the most productive resource, would undoubtedly bestow on her necessary economic independence and power and would improve her social position in the family as well.

Regarding access of women to land, the land records do not incorporate the rights of women in the landed property shown in the name of the husband or the father. Only where a woman is a widow and happens to be the 'karta' of the family, her name may figure in the record of rights as the owner of property.

Co-ownership of property by women, should not merely be confined to land but also to other productive assets like house, family wealth, shops, factory or any other income generating establishment or asset. This would provide sufficient conditions for women to participate in and influence the decision concerning the use and disposal of such properties.

As regards access to capital, there is a general reluctance on the part of the public financial institutions to extend credit to women independently of the male head or guardian of the family.

The existing land ownership pattern in India is largely male oriented except in some areas of the North-east and a few other places where matrilineal system is in operation and inheritance of property passes through the institution of the mother. The land records, to the extent they reflect the ownership and other interests in land, only record the names of men. Similarly, where shareholders of such lands are recorded, it is usually the male shareholder who finds mention in the land records. The processes of preparation of land records, i.e., the survey and recording of rights also deal with such male holders of interests in land. The only exception would be in such cases where a widow with no other male person, manages the land. Her name is recorded as the owner and manager of land. Land reform measures have also not taken into cognizance interests of women as co-owners or cultivators of land, and to this extent land reform measures seem to have bypassed the women. The most prominent example where this inherent discrimination in land reforms has been noticed is the case of ceiling laws where most State laws have provided for a separate unit of ceiling for major sons in the family but not major daughters married or unmarried. Although from the point of view of implementation of such ceiling laws, addition of yet another unit in the name of major daughters would have further defeated its objectives, nonetheless, the discrimination cannot be denied. Further, in the matter of distribution and allotment of various lands, it is usually the male head of the family who gets the 'patta' in his name. Recently, of course instructions have been issued to give joint 'patta' on the name of both husband and wife while allotting land and house-sites. Similarly, in the matter of collection of minor forest produce and enjoyment of rights over common property resources, the rights of women are not focused, even though it is the women, who have to collect fuel-wood and fodder and minor forest produce from such lands.

Tribal social structures are more egalitarian and open and less stratified than social structures of larger and more advanced communities in India. The status and position enjoyed by tribal women in society is, therefore, in certain tribes, much better than their counterparts in other communities. This is on account of many reasons. Tribal society has a tradition of both men and women working on an equal footing whether in agriculture or in other vocations. Thus tribal women have access to income and are therefore, economically independent. There are also no restrictions on women going out for work independent of men, and not necessarily along with them. Usually tribal women go out for work in large groups. In social matters and family life also tribal women are far more emancipated. They have a much greater say in the decision making in family and community matters and are not subjected to the same degree of social control by male members of the family as women in other communities are.

Despite this, in matters of inheritance of father's/husband's property and in access to land, there is a certain built-in discrimination against women in some tribal communities. The customary law of some tribal communities excludes women from inheritance rights, such inheritance rights being restricted to "male heirs in the male line". These customs are even enshrined in tenancy laws wherever enacted and applicable to these communities. This discrimination against women has a harmful effect on their lives, rendering them economically and socially powerless and driving large numbers of them into destitution. Infact, in certain tribal communities, for example, the Ho Tribe in Singhbhum district of Bihar, a large number of women remain unmarried so as to ensure to themselves usufructuary rights available to them as unmarried daughters. Many of them are harassed by their husband's and father's male agnates who wish to deprive them even of this usufructuary right. A number of women are forced to migrate in order to earn their livelihood, since their hold over the family land is so insecure and dependent on the attitude of their male relatives even though these women do the bulk of agricultural work. Sometimes, the women are declared witches, the concealed motive being to drive them out of the village or even to kill them in order to usurp the family property.

The married women also enjoy limited usufructuary rights in the deceased husband's property. Even these usufructuary rights cannot be freely exercised by them since the husband's male agnates often harass them and try to get rid of them in the hope of asserting their inheritance claims to the land. If the married woman has a son, he inherits the land from his father, and she has no legal claim to it. If the husband has one or two or more wives, the sons of other wives have inheritance rights to the land, and she is dependent on them for maintenance. In case, the marriage breaks up, or a man remarries or deserts his first wife, the woman is absolutely without land rights, since she has, by marriage, lost the usufructuary rights in her father's house, and she is also deprived of rights in her matrimonial home. Since tribal communities have their customary laws, the Hindu Succession Act, the Indian Succession Act, or any other succession Act do not apply to them.

The discrimination against women in the customary law of tribal communities, historically speaking, may have evolved with a view to preserve the integrity of the tribe and to prevent land passing from the tribal to persons outside the tribe which would have the effect of disintegrating the tribal society. While, it is necessary to preserve the integrity of the tribe and to protect the interest of the tribals in land against any encroachment by non-tribals, it is also necessary to protect the interest of tribal women in land by giving them rights to inheritance in father's and husband's property. But safeguards will have to be provided in the event of marriages outside the tribe.

Therefore, provision in law and customary practices which discriminate against women in matters of inheritance of property and restrict such inheritance to male agnates in male line should be changed, while at the same time preserving alienation of tribal land to non-tribals.

Women, especially tribals, migrate in search of work. They are employed in large numbers in the unorganized sector like brick-kiln, road construction, irrigation works, agricultural operations, forestry operations, stonecutting, domestic labour, etc. They are subjected to brutal exploitation at places of work by contractors and the middlemen, who recruit them. The exploitation is not merely confined to payment of low wages, long hours of arduous work and other dismal working conditions. They are also subjected to sexual exploitation. It is necessary, that for each category of employment in the unorganized sector, specific institutional mechanism be built-in to protect women's interests.

Perspective for the New Millennium

Poverty alleviation in the rural sector remain central. It is targeted to bring down the percentage of rural poor below 10 per cent by 2000 A.D. The Department of Rural Development has already suggested that in case of women, poverty alleviation goals for the new millennium should be to:

(i) Bring all women-headed households (estimated to be 30-35 per cent) above the poverty line; and

(ii) Attain the target of having women constitute 30 per cent of all beneficiaries to be assisted under IRDR.

In addition, the endeavour should be to bring in the women's development dimension into the sectors particularly, agriculture and allied sectors which have hitherto not responded adequately to women's needs. Women's access to productive resources must also be ensured.

Political power and access to positions of decision making and authority are critical prerequisites for women's equality in the processes of nation building. Hence it is crucial that the representation of women in local bodies up to the district level be ensured.

Health and Family Welfare

Women's health status is basic to their advance in all fields of endeavour. Any serious attempt to improve the health of women must deal firstly with biased social customs and cultural traditions that have an impact on their health status. Though the health problems of women have been identified for priority attention and efforts made for maternal and child services since the beginning of planned development in India, much remains to be done to improve health care for women both in qualitative and quantitative terms. However, in subsequent plan periods it has been observed that resource allocations for health have been decreasing. There is need for a more comprehensive integrated approach to health issues if there is to be a significant impact on the present conditions of Indian women.

The cultural norms that specially affect women's health are the attitudes to marriage, age of marriage, the value attached to fertility and sex of the child, the pattern of family organizations and the ideal role demanded of women by social conventions. They determine her place within the family, the degree of her access to medical care, education, nutrition and other accessories of health. Improvements in female health status are, therefore, critically dependent on a number of non-health development components such as education, opportunities for skill-building, income generation and decision making and the availability of basic support services to carry out women's multiple roles. Thus it is essential to address the causes of women's ill-health. Measures to improve the social and health situation would have to form an integral part of a multi-sectoral package operationalized simultaneously, in complementary thrusts. Earlier analysis have emphasized this aspect. But gaps have existed in preceding plans and even more in the implementation of strategies.

Important Indicators

The demographic trends are important indicators of women's health status. The sex ratio which illumines the survival scene for women versus men was 933 females per 1000 males in 1981. Not only is this ratio unfavourable, but its steady decline from 972 in 1902 to 930 in 1971 is a cause for great concern. Marginal improvement has taken place in the last decade, but even today fourteen States and Union Territories have less females per 1000 males then the national average and in eleven States and Union Territories, the ratio has further declined.

Life expectancy has increased over the decade from 44.7 years in 1971 to 54.7 in 1980 for women. It was estimated to be slightly higher in 1980 for women than men: 54.7 and 54.1 years at birth respectively. A general reduction in female mortality, as well as the greater differentials in death rate was observed over 1970-82 in both rural and urban areas. However age specific death rates indicate higher mortality for female children and women for every five-year period till 35 years of age. This higher mortality experience of female children and younger adult women during the prime reproductive years is largely preventable through appropriate health and other interventions, and points to the continuing neglect of female health.

Women face high risk of malnutrition, retardation in growth and development, disease, disability and even death at three critical stages in their lives, viz., infancy, early childhood and adolescence and the reproductive phase. In old age, they face threats of cancer, breast cancer and uterus cancer and menopause related problems.

Infancy and Early Childhood

Discrimination starts even before birth in the form of sex determination tests misusing the high technology of amniocentisis, resulting in a new kind of femicide, i.e., abortion of female foetuses. A survey carried out in Bombay during 1984 revealed that out of

8,000 abortions 7,999 were of female foetuses. Considering that this test facility has spread to even small towns and people from rural as well as urban areas are utilizing it, the magnitude of the problem can be imagined.

Micro studies have shed light on the fact that sex is the main determinant of infant nutrition, irrespective of economic development. It is worse in a situation of poverty. Studies indicate that while both boys and girls get less than recommended daily dietary allowances, girls are more deficient and suffer more from related disorders and illnesses. However, more girls go without treatment when ill, than boys.

Boys are breast-fed longer, given more of weaning foods, and get a bigger share of whatever food is available. Consequently, although the female children are biologically stronger when born, their morbidity and mortality rates are worse than that of male children. Age specific death rates are higher for female children, as noted earlier. Whereas, no male/female break-up is available for immunization rates, the total figures themselves are low. By 1982, only 25 per cent of all children below 3 years were given DPT, 5 per cent of infants were immunized against Polio, and 65 per cent were given BCG.

The shadow of the girl child's deprivation looms throughout her later life, but most particularly increases her vulnerability to the risks of child bearing, which in turn create risks for the child to be born. Thus is set into motion the vicious cycle of deprivation, debilitation, disease and disability. Leading to greater deprivation and debilitation and often death. That is the depressing lot of a significant numbers of mothers and children today.

Adolescence

As girls attain puberty, they go through a second spurt of growth when their bodies grow much more rapidly to prepare them for child-bearing. But unfortunately, in addition to the poor economic conditions, their gender denies them proper nutrition. Even in situations where food is available, girls are taught to eat less so that they remain slim to rate better in the marriage market. Nutritional deprivation at all growth stages gets compounded during the inset of puberty resulting in severe growth retardation in girl children.

The half grown, uneducated, adolescent girl is married early and becomes pregnant soon. Teenage pregnancy interrupts the physiological growth spurt which brings a girl to her genetically determined maximum stature. As of 1981, 7 per cent of girls in the age group 10-14 and 43 per cent in the age group 15-19 were already married. They enter into sexual life and child bearing with no knowledge about sex and the reproduction process. As estimated, 10-15 per cent of all the annual births (around 25 million) are attributed to these teenage mothers. With their malnourished status, small pelvis, under-nutrition, and overwork during pregnancy, these adolescent mothers run a high risk of life. Their babies are of low birth weight and suffer risk of mortality many times higher than those of fully grown, well nourished, educated mothers.

Girls who marry before the age 18 are twice as likely to end up with a large family than those who marry after completing 20 years, and therefore not only face much higher risks in pregnancy when they first conceive, but also compounded risks and related ill-health over their lifetimes.

Maternal Health

The Indian woman on an average has 8-9 pregnancies, resulting in a little over six births, of which 4-5 survive. She is estimated to spend 80 per cent of her reproductive years in pregnancy and lactation.

Dietary surveys have shown that the intake of women in low income groups is deficient by 500 to 600 calories. The corresponding findings for pregnant and lactating women reveal daily deficiency of 1100 calories and 1000 calories respectively. Deficits in nutrient intakes have been observed in various occupational groups, particularly in those without land and are labourers. Women belonging to the lower socio-economic groups gain around 3-5 kgs. during pregnancy as against 10 kgs. in the developed countries. Over 50 per cent of pregnant women have a haemoglobin level of less than 10 grams. Anaemia in pregnancy accounts directly for 15-20 per cent of all maternal deaths in India, and indirectly for a much larger proportion.

With the fairly high fertility levels during the reproductive span prevailing in India, maternal mortality accounts for the largest to near largest proportion of deaths among women in their prime years. Official estimates place maternal mortality at 400-500 per 100,000 live births but figures as high as 1000-1200 have been reported from certain rural areas. A woman in the subcontinent runs a lifetime risk of 1 in 18 of dying from a pregnancy related cause. Anaemia, haemorrhage, toxemia, sepsis, and abortion are the major causes of maternal deaths in India. It has been estimated that 70 per cent of these deaths can be prevented. Multiparity increases maternal illnesses and deaths which rise significantly with the fourth pregnancy and reach very high levels after the fifth. In India, 38.4 live births in rural areas and 33.0 live births in urban areas are of the fourth order and above.

Accurate assessments of maternal morbidity are unavailable but evidence from available studies point to an appallingly high incidence of pregnant women not in contact with health services.. Around 71.1 per cent of deliveries in rural areas and 29.2 per cent of deliveries in urban areas are conducted by untrained personnel outside the health system. In Rajasthan, one-third of pregnant women reported illnesses lasting on an average for over two weeks. The maternal mortality rate was 592 per 100,000 live births; for every maternal death some 60 episodes were related directly to pregnancy and childbirth and together represented both the leading cause and over a quarter of overall morbidity.

Abortion has been legalized in India as a health measure since 1972 by the Medical Termination of Pregnancy Act, 1971. Even so, because of non-availability of MTP services within easy reach for most of the rural population and ignorance of the law, 'illegal' abortions continue to be performed by incompetent persons under unhygienic conditions. As a result, abortion-related mortality and morbidity remain major problems. Only 507,719 terminations were performed through the health services in 1986-87 which is around 9 per cent of the induced abortions that were likely to have been performed during the same period. Since the inception of the programme, 5.1 million abortions have been performed under the MTP programme, which is less than the total number of induced abortions likely to be performed in one year. Induced abortions indicate an unmet need of women for family planning, highlight a gap between the availability of services and their accessibility to those in need, and demonstrate women's inability to make use of the services they need acutely.

Respite from pregnancy, and rest and care during pregnancy emerge as major needs. Studies have clearly shown that women engaged in hard physical labour during pregnancy did not gain much weight, and delivered low-birth-weight babies, as compared with women doing less work but having the same food intake. One study on energy consumption and expenditure per household per day, found the energy expenditure to be 5.68 units for men, 9.69 for women and about 3 for children. The major part of domestic energy consumption was for survival-cooking, fetching water, firewood, etc. Technology for reduction of drudgery in women, and providing water, and fuel within the easy reach of all, could go a long way in energy conservation for women.

Hardly any information is available for the health hazards of women engaged in different occupations, in agriculture and industries, birth during pregnant and non-pregnant states. In agriculture, they are exposed to heat and rain and have to work in standing and bending postures for long hours, which are hazardous to health. They also work in large numbers in industries such as beedi, carpet, jute, coir weaving, slate, electronics, etc. Micro studies have indicated that workers of these industries suffer from several health hazards.

The health services for children and women, particularly during pregnancy, childbirth and after are inadequate. About 40 per cent of pregnant women receive tetanus toxoid. Although data are unavailable separately on the proportion of pregnant mothers receiving iron and folic acid, it is roughly estimated that around 25 per cent of pregnant and nursing mothers receive iron and folic acid. About 46 per cent of pregnant women are estimated to register for antenatal care. Facilities and basic equipment for mid-wives have been found to be grossly inadequate.

The situation regarding women's health may be summarized as:

(i) Major disparities in health care in population groups in rural and urban areas; remote, backward, hilly and desert areas; and in socio-economically deprived groups.

(ii) Social attitudes and prejudices inherent in our milieu which are unfavourable towards girls and women, effect their health and nutrition negatively.

(iii) Poor health of women due to the synergistic effects of high levels of infection, malnutrition and uncontrolled fertility extending over a prolonged span.

(iv) Inadequate basic health care facilities (including facilities for MCH, family planning, MTP and nutrition) for women and children, in terms of outreach, range of services, quality, availability, etc.

(v) Inefficient use of resources available for health care of women, resulting in a slower pace of health development for them.

(vi) Ignorance and lack of knowledge related to health nutrition and family planning, affecting self-help efforts in health; and resulting in underutilization of existing resources.

(vii) Absence or inadequacy of essential non-health facilities which affect health, such as potable water, sanitation; female education; food supply, etc.

Guidelines for Health Care

Health care has been accepted as an important intervention for women's development since the First Five-Year Plan. It was recognized that the high infant and maternal mortality would have to be reduced through the provision of maternal and child health services and family planning. The basic strategy for providing health care to the general population as well as women, in the 1950's during the first and second plan periods included:

(i) Expansion of physical infrastructure for health (including opening MCH centres);

(ii) Initiating the family planning programme;

(iii) Communicable disease control (for malaria, filaria, tuberculosis, leprosy and venereal diseases); and

(iv) Establishing facilities for training (attention was given to training female health personnel including nurses, auxilliary nurse midwives, health visitors and dais) and having more manpower.

The need to link hospitals at different levels into an effective coordinated hospital system, and correlate their functions with those of "clinics, domiciliary care services and public health activities", was recognized. The maternity centres which were established during the first two plan periods, were to be linked up with district and referral hospitals. MCH services in urban areas were generally provided through maternity and child health centres, in isolation from the rest of the services. 4500 maternity centres had been established, one-third of which were in urban areas; and about 2800 health units were also established in rural areas. In rural areas, the "health units" in the block were expected to provide MCH services in addition to other health services. During the decade 1950-60, female health personnel were increasingly trained and employed, which resulted in availability of 27,000 nurses (from 5,000 in 1950); 19,900 auxiliary nurse midwives (from 8,000 in 1950); 1,500 lady health visitors (from 52 in 1950) and 11,500 nurse-dais and dais (from 1,800 in 1950). From the First Plan itself, family limitation and spacing of children were noticed to be "essential steps for securing better care in bringing up children, and therefore, as an important part of public health." Though initially, family planning services were provided primarily through specialized family planning clinics, the need to integrate it with the general health services was realized; and when the fourth plan was put forth, maternity and child health services were stated to be integrated with family planning.

The basic strategies for health care in terms of expansion of physical infrastructure, training more female health personnel, communicable disease control and family planning were continued during the Third and Fourth Plan periods. Specific prophylaxis programmes were initiated to prevent anaemia in pregnant women, and vitamin deficiency in children 1-5 years of age during this period. Also, programmes were started to control smallpox were also formulated, which included a component for instruction of school teachers.

The primary objective of the Fifth Five-Year Plan was to provide minimum public health facilities integrated with family planning and nutrition for vulnerable groups - children, pregnant women and lactating mothers. The accent during this period was similar to previous plan periods - increasing the accessibility of health services to rural areas; correcting regional imbalances; development of referral systems for health care; and communicable disease control. The need for qualitative improvement in the education and training of health personnel was also recognized. Several schemes were initiated during this period to give increased emphasis to the health of mothers. The Integrated Child Development Services Scheme was accepted for countrywide application in 1977. Though primarily for child development, this scheme provides a package of health, nutrition and family planning services for pregnant women and nursing mothers who are socio-economically deprived. Since a large proportion of deliveries are conducted by traditional birth attendants (TBAs) particularly in rural areas, a scheme was initiated during this time to train them for safer mid-wifery practices; the target was to have atleast one TBA per 1000 population. In order to involve the community in health care, and to further promotive and preventive health care at village level, the health guides scheme was initiated. The norm of one health guide per 1000 population was suggested.

The guiding principles for the first two and a half decade of planned development in health in India included measures to:

(i) Make health services more accessible to the population;

(ii) Developing the needed human resources;

(iii) Provision of services for health, including maternal and child health, and family planning.

Over time, the need to interact more closely with people has been felt, and somewhat more emphasis was given to preventive and promotive aspects of health care.

Committee on the Status of Women in India

The Committee on the status of women in India highlighted the impact of social attitudes on the health of women, which clearly revealed the poorer lot of women, from the time of birth. The demographic analysis brought into sharp focus the deterioration in the condition of the majority of women despite the advances in medical care and the general improvement in health services, pointing to the criticality of the social conditions.

On the health side, it was pointed out that more resources were being spent for curative than preventive and promotive services; and that major rural/urban and regional disparities existed in health care was noted to be an unfortunate distortion. The report further underlined that lack of security and mobility are major problems of female health personnel in rural areas.

However, their recommendations, while emphasizing the need for an integrated thrust for MCH, nutrition and family planning, were limited mainly to upgrading the posts of MCH officers at Central and

State levels; the provision of a separate budget for MCH and separate units for MCH at primary health centres. Some modifications in the MTP Act were also recommended. However, while the legislative aspects were gone into detail, the main problems with medical termination of pregnancy, that is the wide availability of services and ignorance of the law, did not get sufficient attention. Altogether, while the analysis of problems was a powerful indictment of the existing situation, this was not matched by comprehensive suggestion to bring about the desired changes in women's health.

Plan of Action for Women

The National Plan of Action recognized that the health profile of women (and girls) in India was poor. While giving attention to the salient issues in the social and health areas, it did not however, develop the needed coordinated thrust for actions in each sector converging to achieve common goals. In fact, while emphasizing that the plans of action would have to cover a wide spectrum of programmes and needed to integrate with other strategies, it did not even attempt to provide any directions and made the action plans for health under six separate categories, namely: (1) Provision of Services; (2) Development of the needed human resources; (3) Mass Education Programmes; (4) Legislative Measures (5)Role of Voluntary Organizations; and (6)Areas of Research

Broadly, it stated that services for women, including mothers and female children, should be part of the general health system. It was recommended that the physical infrastructure be expanded and manpower for health care be augmented. However, their emphasis on the qualitative aspects of maternal care as well as training was inadequate. The necessary infrastructure strengthening at village, primary and secondary levels, linked by an affective referral system, did not receive much attention. Instead, they recommended the establishment of various types of clinics. The need to modify medical undergraduate curriculum, in order to cater to the needs of mothers and children in rural areas, was rightly stressed, so also, the need to orient doctors in services. The TBA was identified as one of the most important person, in the provision of maternity services, and steps to involve her were outlined. The Committee underlined the need to have mass education programmes for mother and child care. Several legislative measures were suggested.

They referred to the MTP Act, age of marriage, and provision of MCH services in municipalities and local bodies. However, the main issue remains operationalizing the law, ensuring that the necessary developments take place. This includes better services for MTP, specially in rural areas; more resources for MCH services through local bodies; and providing education as well as income generating opportunities to women to raise the age of marriage. Some legislative measures have been taken to ensure that advertisement of baby foods is curbed - this was also a recommendation. The committee suggested some areas, in which the voluntary organizations could be involved, such as school health services, MCH care in urban slums, training health workers and information dissemination. Though some efforts have been made to involve them, much more remains to be done on this aspect. Areas for research were suggested, on which only limited action has, followed.

Health Care for Women

During the Sixth and Seventh Plans, the major strategies for health care, including that for women, continued to be: (i)Expansion of physical infrastructure; (ii)Increasing the availability of trained health manpower; (iii)Strengthening services for communicable disease control, as well as other diseases; and (iv)Provision of family planning as well as MCH services.

During the Sixth Five-Year Plan period, in 1983, the National Health Policy was formulated and accepted for implementation. The policy for the first time, defined goals for women's health; reduction in maternal mortality, crude rate and crude birth rate; coverage with antenatal care and immunization of pregnant mothers, and the control of leprosy, tuberculosis and blindness (from which women also suffer), were specified. The levels to be achieved over time were also specified. The policy stated that:

"the highest priority" would have to be given to "efforts of launching special programmes" for the improvement of maternal and child health, with a special focus on the less privileged sections of the society. Such programmes would require to be decentralized to the maximum possible extent, their delivery being at the primary level, nearest to the doorsteps of the beneficiaries. While efforts should continue for providing refresher training and orientation to the traditional birth attendants, schemes and programmes should be launched to ensure that progressively all deliveries are conducted by competently trained persons, and that complicated cases receive timely and expert attention, within a comprehensive programme providing antenatal, intra-natal and postnatal care. Also, organized school health services, integrally linked with a general, preventive and curative services, would require to be established within time-limited programmes.

The Seventh Five-Year Plan clearly stated that primary health care will be the main sphere of action in health. It was stated that 'women would be organized around available economic activities to enable them to actively participate in the entire process of socioeconomic development, including health.' Care of pregnant and nursing mothers, young children and school-age children (both in and out of school) was stated to be a priority.

Matters Needing Attention

Some of the critical factors and issues related to women's health have evidently not received the necessary attention in the existing health programmes, Girls need adequate care so that they can enter motherhood without physical and social inadequacies. Optimal reproductive and child-bearing patterns (age of the mother at first childbirth - 20 years; interval between pregnancies at least 3 years; a small family; and no pregnancy after 35 years of age, which influence the health of mothers and their children) need to be advocated, and backed by policies that make them feasible for women. Measures to reduce the workload of women have to be promoted to conserve their energy. Adequate and appropriate information for decision-making, particularly during pregnancy and lactation, needs to be made available.

Recognizing that the renewal of the human race is the unique contribution that women make at considerable personal cost to the nation's existence and productivity, it must be taken as a national obligation to ensure that the fulfilment of this role occurs with minimum personal risk to women's lives and health. Control, over reproduction is a basic right for all women, as this right forms an important basis for the enjoyment of other rights. The enormous wastage of female life and well-being occurring at present has, however, been demonstrated to be containable within human capacity and existing resources.

Women are victims of possessive syndrome and many other kinds of neurosis. The majority of women face mental depressions due to family related problems which are the outcomes of the present social attitudes. Particularly, in the rural areas, such depressions are believed as "possessed by spirits". This encourages many cruel practices and treatment which often lead to physical harm to the women. The primary health centres are ill-equipped to deal with even simple mental disorders.

With rapid urbanization and commercialization, the nutritious foods produced in the villages like fruits, vegetables, milk and so forth are being exported to urban areas thereby denying them to the rural poor. Growing poverty in the countryside is also encouraging such exports. This results in a further drop of nutritional levels of the rural poor.

The Bhore Committee way back in 1946 recommended establishing one Primary Health Centre for each 30,000 population which has not yet been achieved.

Health for All goals and indicators have already accepted and accorded primacy to maternal and child health care inter alia including a halving of maternal mortality, hundred per cent coverage for ante-natal care and delivery by trained birth attendants by year 2000 A.D. The health services programmes are already committed to work towards the achievement of these goals. The Technological and Societal missions for eradication of illiteracy, immunization and safe water supply include certain critical indicators that will have impact on maternal and child care. However, as in the past, the present efforts lack in scale and systematic organization of the various components that together could radically alter the situation for women and children. Therefore, a comprehensive programme of health care of women needs to be developed with a special technological and societal mission to halve maternal mortality and morbidity and ensure optimum child bearing patterns by the year 2000. This mission, the details of which would have to be worked out by an expert working group, would need to, simultaneously gear the health services to reduce maternal, infant and child mortality and address the conditions that can assist women not to bear a child when this event will increase the risk to the health of the women and/ or the child to be born/already born. Inter alia, the observance of the small family norm through proper education of its impact on the health of women and children, will be an integral part of this mission.

Family Welfare

It is unfortunate that the family planning policy is oriented towards fertility control and not concerned with providing a means for women and men to have control on their own bodies. A reflection of this policy is the encouragement of injectable contraceptives like Net-en which have been banned in most developed countries.

Though the family welfare and planning programmes have been a part of development planning since the First Five-Year Plan, actual achievements are below expectations. By March, 1987, the effective couple protection rate was only 34 per cent. From the beginning, emphasis has been placed on sterilizations rather than on temporary methods. Whereas in the early phases more vasectomies were performed, during the last decade, female sterilizations have been promoted at a very high rate. With the introduction of laproscopy, female sterilizations have reached high numbers amounting to almost 90 per cent of all sterilizations.

Research studies have shed light on the fact that the knowledge regarding family planning/methods is low despite the huge amounts of money spent on propaganda. The only method known to all is sterilization. The higher rates of abortions show the desire and need of the women for family planning and the failure of the family planning information and services to reach them in time. Laproscopic operations are being performed in several family planning camps without proper care and follow-up. Consequent problems tend to create apprehension among people. More intensive propagation of spacing methods together with innovative strategies for delivery of supplies has to be, taken up and spread of information about temporary methods accorded high priority.

The shift towards female sterilizations has to be reversed. Ironically, while that programme mainly provides female centred methods most of the women using these are not really happy due to the side effects. Hormonal reactions to oral pills, pain and heavy bleeding due to IUD, etc., are common complaints. In many areas women suffer from post-operative problems following tubectomy. The health personnel also concentrate most on' sterilization (female) as it helps them to realize their target and earn cash rewards.

Recommendations

Infancy & Early Childhood

1. Using amniocentesis for sex determination tests should be banned as in Maharashtra. Practitioners indulging in and abetting such acts should be punished severely and their medical licenses should be revoked.

2. Incentives should be considered to encourage parents to have female children. A couple who opts to limit their family to one female child may be given a regular monthly cash subsidy to attend to the girl child's needs. The amount must be given to the family over a period of time and not in a lump sum, as this might result in misuse of the female child as an instrument for getting easy money and later to neglect the child.

3. Infants and small children's growth and development should be monitored by recording their weights and heights at regular intervals. Proper corrective interventions should be made wherever necessary.

4. Universal immunization should be enforced to encompass all children.

5. Oral Rehydration Therapy (ORT) should be widely disseminated. ORT salts in packed form should be made available at a large scale in order to reduce the mortality from diarroheal diseases.

6. The ICDS should be strengthened and priority access should be provided to the girl child. Higher participation of women would also result from expansion of the programme.

7. Efforts should be made to bring a qualitative change in the attitudes against girl children. Media should be used for this purpose aiming to get the girl child to be accepted in the family and the society as an equal to the male child.

8. Focus is needed on the adolescent girl (12-18 years), so that she attains her maximum physical and mental capacities. It is necessary to provide alternative options to an early marriage. This can be ensured by a mix of education and employment opportunities and enforcement of the law on minimum age of marriage (18 years). The younger girl child needs to utilize health and education programmes more fully. It has been proposed that the ICDS will also address this issue in specific areas.

9. Adequate nutrition should be ensured for adolescent girls during the pre-puberty and pubertal growth phase to ensure 'catch up' on physical development by providing supplements to deprived groups.

10. Health and nutrition education should be promoted to ensure that preventive and promotive measures are adopted. The

necessity of safe water, sanitation and personal hygiene also should be advocated.

11. Immunization against tetanus and rubella should be introduced for this age group.

12. Linkages with basic health care must be developed at the village level in the view of the special problems of mobility faced by young girls.

13. A massive communication campaign to create widespread awareness of the law prohibiting the marriage of the girl before 18 years and boys before 21 years and generate consciousness on the severe health implications in children and women of such early marriages must be launched.

14. The aim should be to implement the present legal minimum age of marriage effectively by creating a social consciousness for the desirability of marriage for girls only after 20 and for boys at 25. Preferential employment for unmarried males and females and priority in other developmental schemes for such youth, need to be seriously examined.

15. The comprehensive school health scheme which is being formulated, should be speedily implemented. Special efforts must be made for the health services to reach girls of the school-going age who are out of school. Each child should be examined and screened at least three times at primary school entry, before leaving primary school and at completion of high school. Similarly, a girl child out of school should be examined and screened three times - at around 6, 10 and 15 years of age. Screening kits and medicines should be made available. School teachers and non-formal education functionaries should be trained in the required areas of health care. The health programme for school and non-formal education systems should be integrally linked with the general health services.

16. It is necessary to impart information about reproductive

processes, ways to prevent conception, need for spacing between children, optimum age of child bearing, necessary care for pregnant women and lactating mothers and small family norm, etc. This may be introduced as a part of the regular curriculum in school, colleges and universities. For girls/boys who are not in school, Anganwadi workers/ female CHWs may impart this knowledge.

17. To improve women's health status, there is no doubt that the general health services have to be made to respond to women's specific problems. A strategy for improving the health of women in the reproductive age group would be to reduce the risk of death and illness associated with pregnancy as well as to reduce the exposure to pregnancy itself. Comprehensive minimal care during pregnancy, childbirth and thereafter, steps to ameliorate malnutrition as well as decrease the workload of women, and improved access to health services, particularly family planning services, should be the salient instruments for improving the health of women.

18. Since women are severely restricted in their mobility, basic health care services must be made available to them as close as possible to their homes. Therefore, resources should be allocated as a priority to health services at the village, as well as at the first level of referral. The services would be provided by the female health workers, supported by the functionaries and the community from the village, as well as supervisory echelons within the health sector. Measures should be taken to reduce the incidence of low birth weight babies.

19. A minimum package of services should be available for pregnant women at village level. This should include at least:

- Facilities for early detection of pregnancy, with low cost pregnancy detection kits;
- Antenatal registration;

- Minimum of three antenatal check-ups in the second and third trimester;
- Screening of high-risk cases;
- Anaemia prophylaxis with iron and folic acid tablets; Tetanus toxoid coverage;
- Prophylaxis against malaria in high endemic areas; Advocacy of adequate rest;
- Health and nutrition education;
- Priority attention to locally endemic diseases affecting women; and
- Adequate safe drugs for her illness.

20. ANMs should be trained to assess pelvic proportions of pregnant women to identify the high risk cases and refer them to competent institutions. This will help in saving women from maternal deaths and also to reduce the incidence of still births.

21. The emphasis will have to be on providing better care to the pregnant woman in her home, as well as to ensure that adequate facilities are available at the first level of referral to deal with obstetric emergencies such as toximias, sepsis, obstructed labour and haemorrhage. In order to improve village level care during childbirth, the following are suggested:

- Continuous training, supervision and support for better mid-wifery practices to the TBA and female health workers;
- Provision for sterile delivery kits to the TBA, health workers and even to mothers;
- Stocking adequate drugs and supplies with the health workers, and providing a restricted number to the TBA; and

- Pre-arranged transport (or reimbursement of transport costs) for any emergency, when a woman has been registered for antenatal care.

22. Post-natal services should be available as close to the homes of mothers as possible. In rural areas in several, parts of India, women do not leave their homes for 40 days after delivery. Post-natal care should include:

    - A minimum of three contacts with the mother by the TBA and/or female health worker within the first 10 days after child birth;
    - One massive dose of vitamin A within one month after delivery to all mothers;
    - Iron and folic acid for 50 per cent of mothers:
    - Adequate drugs to deal with puerperal sepsis;
    - Education for the mother's nutrition and contraception as well as for infant feeding and health care, particularly immunization.

Women's Health Care

23. The health of women who are not pregnant or nursing, is an area which has received inadequate attention so far. Interventions thus made can cause a significant difference to women's health status not only between pregnancies, but also improve the outcome of future pregnancies. Moreover, the woman's right to health care as an individual must be promoted.

24. Women with chronic or serious illnesses, such as tuberculosis, leprosy, viral hepatitis, anaemia, sexually transmitted cases, etc., should be promptly treated and advised to postpone their pregnancy for a suitable safe period.,

25. High priority should be given to women for treatment/control of all endemic diseases, specially those which have a harmful effect on the next generation (for example, goitre, sexually transmitted diseases, etc.)

26. Doctors of the Primary Health Centres be given in-service training to handle the cases of possessive syndrome and neurosis. Mass education programme be taken up to change the negative attitudes prevalent against mental illness.

27. Nutritious foods produced in the villages should be primarily utilized to cater to the nutrition needs of the rural poor. Only the surplus should be allowed for export to urban areas. A widespread public distribution system would be essential to make basic foods available at affordable costs.

28. Emphasis should be placed on Science and Technology research pertaining to sex linked diseases, occupational hazards, and indigenous methods of family planning as affecting women. Undergraduate level programmes should introduce courses relevant to women, i.e.

    (i) Work physiology (ergdonomics) as related to health, and occupational hazards.

    (ii) Basic tenets of genetics, related to family studies, genetic disorders and environmental effects.

    (iii) At the postgraduate level and above, research needs to be conducted in ergonomic abnormalities in women such as spinal strain after carrying loads. Also, work is needed on sex-linked, genetic disorders like muscular dystrophy and haemophilia, where women are the carriers.

29. More Primary Health Centres should be set up in the rural areas to achieve the target of having one Primary Health Centre for each 30,000 population as recommended by the Bhore Committee.

30. The timings of the dispensaries and hospitals should be fixed in a way which would be convenient to working women.

31. There should be a 24 hours creche facility for women patients with children in every hospital and PHC.

32. There is a need for a humane Drug Policy and check on the pharmaceuticals industry that at present operates on the profit principle like any other industry.

33. It is necessary to provide safety equipment including powerful exhausts to remove harmful dust from the work environment and, personal protective equipment like masks, feet protectors, eyeglasses, ear muffs and gloves and strong contraceptions for the safety of women workers.

34. There should be Refreshers /Orientation courses for the doctors on the subjects of women's work and health.

Family Welfare

35. Family planning policy should be such that it will help women have greater control over their bodies and enable them to make conscious choices on having or not having children and declining the number of children they want.

36. Injectible contraceptives as well as other contraceptives banned in developed countries should not be permitted in the country.

37. More research needs to be carried out to develop contraceptives that can be used by men and they should be propagated more widely.

Bibliography

Altekar, A.S., *The Position of Women in Hindu Civilization*, Varanasi: Motilal Banarsidas, 1962.

Anshen, R.N., (ed.), *The Family: Its Functions and Destiny*, New York: Harper & Row, 1959.

Arora, K.K. et. al: "*Women and Career*," Group Project Report, Bombay. Tata Institute of Social Sciences, 1963.

Asthana, P., *Women's Movement in India*, Delhi: Vikas Publishing House, 1974.

Badel, Auguste: *Women: Past, Present and Future*, New York, Bone and Liveright, 1918.

Baig Tara Ali: *India's Woman Position*, Delhi: S. Chand and Company Pvt. Ltd., 1976.

Bala, Usha: *Indian Women freedom Fighters*. New Delhi: Manobar Publication, 1986.

Barot, Jyoti: *The Indian Family in the Change and Challenge of the Seventies,* New Delhi: Sterling Publishers, 1972.

Bebel, August: *Women in the Past, Present and Future*. ed. By Mukerjee. Subrata and Rama Swami, Sushila, New Delhi, Deep and Deep Publication, 1996.

Bhasin, K. (ed.), *The Position of Women in India*, Bombay: Leslie Sawny. 1971.

Bhushan, Jamila Brij: *Muslim Women,* New Delhi: Vikas Publishing House. 1980.

Billington, Mary Frances: *Women in India*, Delhi: Amarka Book Agency. 1973.

Blalock, H.M. and Blalock, A.B., *Methodology in Social Research*. New York: McGraw-Hill, 1969.

Bose, Moni Mohan: *Female Education in India*. Kanpur. B.B. Gupta

Publication, 1921.

Caplow, T., *Sociology of Work*, New York, Mc-Graw Hill, 1954.

Carden, Maren Lockwood: *The New Feminist Movement*, N.Y. Russall Sage Foundation, 1974.

Carstairs, G. Morris: *The Twice Born*, Bloomington: Indiana University Press, 1958.

Chakrapant, C. Kumar-S. Vijaya (editors): *Changing Status and Role of Women in Indian Society*, New Delhi, M.D. Pub., 1994.

Chattapadhya, Kamladevi, et. al: *The Awakening of Indian Women*, Madras: Everyman's Press, 1939.

Chaturvedi, Geeta., *Women Administration in India: A study of the socio-economic background*, Jaipur, RBSA Publication, 1985.

Cofer, C.N. and Appley, M.N., *Motivation Theory and Research*, A Wiley International Edition, John Wiley and Sons Inc., 1964.

Cormack, Margaret: *The Hindu Women*, Bombay: Asia Pub.. House. 1961.

Das, Ram Mohan: *Women in Manu's Philosophy*, Jalandhar, ASB Pub.. 1993.

Deckard, B.S, *The Women's Movement*, Harper and Row, New York, 1979.

Desai Devangana: *Erotic Sculpture of India: A Socio-Cultural Study*, New Delhi: Tata McGraw Pub., 1975.

Desai, Neera and Patel Vibbuti: *Indian Women*, Bombay: Popular Prakashan. 1975-85.

De'Souza Alfred: *Women in Contemporary India and South Asia*, Delhi: Manohar Pub., 1980.

Devasia, L. and Devasia, V.V: *Empowering Women for Sustainable Development*, New Delhi, Ashish Pub. House, 1994.

Drucker, P.F., *An Introductory View of Management*, Harper College Press, New York, 1977.

Engineer Asghar Ali: *Islam and Liberation Theology*, New Delhi- Sterling Pub., 1990.

Evan, M. William, *Organizational Theory Structure, Systems and Environments*, Wiley Interscience Publications, John Wiley and Sons Inc, London: 1976.

Everett, J.M.: *Women and Social Change in India*, Heritage Pub., 1979.

Friedan, Betty, *The Feminine Mystique*, N.Y., W.W. Norton, 1963.

Gandhi, M.K.: *The Role of Women*. Bombay: Bhartiya Vidhya Bhavan. 1964.

Ghadially, Rehana: *Women in Indian Society*, New Delhi: Sage Pub..

1988.

Good, W.J., *World Revolution and Family Patterns*, London: Collier MacMillan, 1963.

Goldstein, Rhoda L.: *Indian Women in Transition: A Banglore Case Study*. New Jersey: The Scarecrow Press Inc., 1972.

Gorwaney, N., *Self Image and Social Change: A Study of Female Students*, Delhi: Sterling Publishers, 1977.

Gullahorn, J.E.: *Psychology and Women in Transition* New York: John Wiley. 1979.

Gupta, A.K.: *Women and Society*, New Delhi: Criterion Pub., 1986.

Gupta, A.R.: *Women in Hindu Society*, Delhi: Jyotsna Prakashan. 85.

Gupta, J.L.: *Challenges to the Fair Sex*, Delhi: Gyan Pub., 1988.

Hasan, Zoya (ed.): *Forging Identities, Gender, Communities and the State*, New Delhi : Kali for Women, 1994.

Hate, C.A., *Changing Status of Women in Post-Independence India* Bombay: Allied Publications, 1969.

Hate, C.A. *Hindu Women and her Future*, Bombay: New Bombay Co., 1948.

Horney, I.B.: *Women in Farly Buddhist Literature*, Kandy: Buddhist Publication Society, 1961.

Horney, Karen: *Feminine Psychology*, N.Y.: W.W. Norton & Co., 1967.

Indra Prof. *The Status of Women in Ancient India*, Lahore: The Minerva Book Shop. 1940.

Inkeles, A. and Smith, D., *Becoming Modern*, London: Heinmann Educational Books Ltd., 1974.

Jain, D: *Indian Women*, Delhi: Publication Division, Government of India. 1975.

Jain, P.C., Jain. Shashi and Bhatnagar, Sudha (eds.): *Scheduled Caste Women*, Jaipur: Rawat Pub., 1997.

Jain, Pratibha and Mahan, Rajan: *Women Images*, Jaipur: Rawat Pub., 1996.

Jayal, Shakambari: *The Status of Women in Epics*, Delhi: Motilal Banarsidas, 1966.

Jayashree: *India and Indian Women*, Aligarh: Granthayan, 1980.

Jogdand, P.G. (ed.): *Dalit Women, Issues and Perspectives*, New Delhi: Gyan Publishing House, 1995.

Kalarani: *Role Coriflict in Working Women*. New Delhi: Chitra Pub.,

1976.

Kapur, Promilla: *The Changing Status of the Working Woman in India*, Delhi: Vikas Pub., 1974.

Kapur, Promilla. *Marriage and the Working Woman in India*, Delhi: Vikas Pub., 1975.

Keeton Kathy and Basrin Yvonne: *Woman of Tomorrow*, N.Y.: Harvard Univ. Press, 1985.

Khanna, G: *Indian Women Today*, New Delhi: Publishing House, 1978.

Kidwai, Shaikh M.H.: *Women under Different Social and Religious Law*, New Delhi: Seema Pub., 1976.

Kirpal, Viney (ed.): *The Girl Child in 20th Century Indian Literature*, New Delhi: Sterling Pub., 1992.

Kishwar Madhu: *Off the-Beaten Track Rethinking Gender Justice for Indian Women*, New York: Oxford, 1999.

Kumar Ashok, *Women in Contemporary Indian Society*, New Delhi: Anmol Pub., 1993.

Kuppuswamy, B., *Social Change in India*, Delhi: Vikas Publishing House, 1972.

Lateef. Shahida: *Muslim Women in India, Political and Private Realities: 1890-1980s*, New Delhi: Kali for Women, 1990.

Law, Bimla Churn: *Women in Buddhist Literature*, Ceylone: N.E. Bastian, 1927.

Lederer, Wolfgang: *The Fear of Women*, N.Y.: Arun and Strattan, 1968.

Marshall, Katherine, *Employed Parents and Division of Housework, Perspectives*, Autumn, 1993.

Mehta, Hansa: *Indian Woman*, New Delhi: Butala & Co., 1981.

Mehta, Rama: *Socio-legal Status of Women in India*, Delhi: Metropolitan Book Co., 1982.

Mehta, Raman Lal: *The Western Educated Hindu Woman*, N.Y.: Asia Pub. House, 1970.

Mehta, Raman Lal: *Thesis on the Legal Rights of Women under Different Communal Laws in Vogue in India*, Bombay: The Advocate of Indian Press, 1933.

Mehta, Sushila: *Revolution and Status of Women in India*, Delhi: Metropolitan Book Co., 1982.

Menon, M. Indu: *Status of Muslim Women in India*, Delhi: Uppal Pub. House, 1981,

Meyer, Johann Jakob: *Sexual Life in Ancient India: A Study in the Comparative History of Indian Culture*, N.Y.: E.D. Dutton & Co., 1930.

Mies, M., *Indian Women and Patriarchy: Conflicts and Dilemmas of Students and Working Women*. Concept Publishers, New Delhi, 1980.

Minault, Gail: *Secluded Scholars, Women's Education and Muslim Social Reform in Cobaial India*. Delhi: Oxford Univ. Press, 1998.

Misra, Rekha: *Women in Mughal India*. Delhi: Munshiram Manoharlal.

Misra, R.S.: *Women Education and the Upanishadic System of Education*, Allahabad: Chugh Pub., 1993.

Mittal Mukta (ed.): *Women in India. Today and Tomorrow*, New Delhi: Anmol Pub., 1995.

Moddie, A.D.: *The Brahamanical Culture and Modernity*, Lond.: Asia Pub. House, 1968.

Mohanty, Jagannath: *Education for All*, New Delhi: Deep and Deep Pub. 1994.

Moneil, Elton B. and Rubin Zick: *The Psychology of Being Human*, San Francisco, Canfield Press, 1977.

Montagu, Ashley: *The Natural Superiority of Women*, N.Y.: The Macmillan Co., 1968.

Mujtaba, Sayid, Lari, Rukni Musawi (Translated by Goulding, F.J.): *Western Civilisation Through Muslim Eyes*, Qum, Iran: Ansariyan Publication.

Myrdal, A. and Klien, V., *Woman's Two Roles*, Routledge & K. Paul, London, 1968.

Nanda, B.R.: *Indian Women*, Delhi: Vikas Pub. House, 1976.

Pal. B.K.: *Problems and Concerns of Indian Women*, New Delhi: ABC Pub. House, 1989.

Pandey, Rekha: *Women from Subjection to Liberation*, New Delhi, Motilal Pub., 1989.

Pandit, S. K.: *Women in Society*. Delhi: Rajat Pub., 1998.

Paul, Diana Y: *Women in Buddhism*, California: Asian Humanities Press, 1979.

Phandis, Urnifla: *Women of the World*. Delhi: Vikas Pub. House, 1978.

Pinkham, Mildreth Worth: *Women in the Sacred Scripts of Hinduism*:

N.Y.AMS Press Inc., 1941.

Prakash, G., *After Colonialism: Imperial Histories and Post Colonial Displacements*, Princeton University Press, Princeton, 1995.

Pujari, Premlata and Kaushik, Vijay Kumari: *Women Power in India*, Delhi: Kanishka Pub., 1994.

Rajgopal, T.S.: *Indian Ideal of Womanhood*, Calcutta: Ramakrishna Mission, 1969.

Ramabal, Saraswati Pundita: *The High Caste Hindu Woman*. Philadelphia: Jas. B. Podgers Printing Co., 1888.

Ranganathan, Sarala: *Women and Social Order. A Profile of Major Indicators and Determinants.* New Delhi: Kanishka Publishers, 1998.

Rani, K., *Role Conflict in Working Wives*, Chetana Publications, New Delhi, 1976.

Rege, Y.M.: *Whither Women*, Bombay, The Popular Book Depot, 1938.

Rehman, M.M. and Biswal. Kantala Kanta: *Education, Work and Women: An Enquiry into Gender Bias*. New Delhi: Commonwealth Publishers, 1993.

Roby, Pamela, *Women in the Work Place*, M.A. Schenkrnan, Cambridge, 1981.

Rohibaugh, Joanna Bunker: *Women: Psychology's Puzzle*, N.Y.: Basic Books Inc., 1979.

Ross, Aileen D.: *The Hindu Family in its Urban Setting*, Toronto: Univ. of Toronto Press, 1961.

Sachidananda and Sinha, Ramesh P.: *Women's Right: Myth and Reality*, Jaipur, Printwell Pub., 1984.

Sengupta, Padmint: *The Story of Women of India*, New Delhi: Indian Book Co., 1974.

Sharma, Anuradha: *Women and Work, Human Resource Management Perspective*, New Delhi: Gyan Pub., 1999.

Sharma, S. Ram. (ed.): *Women's Education in Ancient and Muslim Period*, New Delhi: Discovery Pub. House, 1996.

Sharma, Usha and Sharma, B.M.: *Committees and Commissions on Women Education*, New Delhi: Commonwealth Pub., 1995.

Shridevi: *A Century of Indian Womanhood*, Mysore: Rao and Raghavan, 1965.

Sikkri. Rehana: *Women in Islamic Culture and Society: A Study Family, Feminism and Franchise*, New Delhi: Kanishka Pub.. 1999

Singh, Indu Prakash: *Women, Law and Social Change in India*, New Delhi: Radiant Pub., 1989.

Singh, Uttam Kumar and Nayak, AR: *Women Education*, New Delhi. Commonwealth Pub. in association with Dr. Zakir Institute for Non Formal and Continuing Education, Discovery Pub. House, 1996.

Sinha, Anjana. Maitra: *Women in Changing Society*, New Delhi, Ashish Pub. House, 1993.

Srinivasan. M.N.: *The Changing Position of Indian Women*, Delhi: Oxford Univ. Press, 1970.

Subbamma, Malladi: *Women, Tradition and Culture*, Delhi: Sterling Pub.. 1985.

Suguna, B: *Working Women and Religion*, New Delhi: Discovery Publishing House, 1994.

Tandon, R.K.: *Women, Nature, Education, Teaching and Rights*, Commonwealth Pub., 1996.

Thomas, P.: *Women and Marriage in India*, Lord: George Allen and Unwin, 1939.

Thomas, P.: *Epics, Myths and Legends of India*. Mumbai: D.B. Teraporevala, 1961.

Thomas, P.: *Indian Women Through the Ages*, N.Y.: Asia Pub. House, 1964.

Tikoo, Prithvi Nath: *Indian Women*, Delhi: B.R. Publishing Corporation, 1985.

Tolman, E.C., *Principles of Purposive Behavior*. In S. Koch (ed.)

Trivedi, Harshad R: *Scheduled Caste Women Studies in Exploitation, with Reference to Superstition, Ignorance and Poverty*, Delhi: Concept Pub. Co., 1976.

Upadhya, Bhagvrat Saran: *Women in Rigveda*, Delhi: S. Chand and Co., 1983.

Usha, Rao N.J.: *Women in Developing Society*. Delhi: Ashish Pub. House, 1983.

Vashishta, B.K.: *Encyclopardia of Women in India*, New Delhi: 1976. Parveen Encyclopaedia.

Vitels, M.S., *Motivation and Morale in Industry*. New York: Morton 1953.

Vreede de Stuers.: *Girl Students in Jaipur. A Study in Attitude towards Family Life, Marriage and Career*, N Y.: Assen, Van Gorcum and

Co., 1970.

Vyas, Anju and Singh Sunita: *Women's Studies in India*, New Delhi. Sage Pub., 1993.

Watson, T., *Management Organization and Employment Strategy*, Routledge and Kegan Paul, London, 1986.

Whyte, F.W., *Money and Motivation*, Harper and Row. Inc., New York: 1955.

Yaqin, Anwarul and Anwar Badr, *Protection of Woman under Law*, Deep and Deep Publications, New Delhi, 1982.

Zeitlin, Irving, M. *Rethinking Sociology: A Critique of Contemporary Theory*, Appleton-Century Crafts, New York, 1973.

References

Aruna, Asaf Ali: 'Women's Suffrage in India," *Our Cause*. edited by Shyarn Kumari Nehru, Allahabad, Kitabistan, 1937.

Bhushan, Jamila Brij: "The Unassertive Sex," *The Hindustan Times*, Jan. 11, 1976.

Blau, P. (ed.), Focus on Social Structure, and Introduction to the Programme of the ASA Meeting in Montreal, 1974.

Blau, P.M., A Macrosociological Theory of Social Structure, *American Journal of Sociology*, 1977.

Brayfield, A.H. and Crockatt, W.H., Employee attitude and employee performance, *Psychological Bulletin*, 1955.

Burke, P.J. and Reitzes, D.C., An Identity Theory Approach to Commitment, *Social Psychological Quarterly*, 1991.

Carstairs, G. Morris: "Village Women of Rajasthan," in *Indian Women*, ed. by Devaki Jain, New Delhi: Pub. Div., Ministry of Information and Broadcasting, Govt. of India, 1975.

Dubey. S.C: "Men's and Women's Role in India:* a Sociological Review," in *Women in the New Asia*, ed. by Barbara Ward, Paris: UNESCO, 1968.

French, Elizabeth, G., Effects of Interaction of Achievement Motivation and Intelligence on Problem Solving Success, *American Psychologist*, 1951.

Gender Indicators of Developing Asian and Pacific Countries, 1993, Asian Development Bank.

Government of India: *Fourth World Conference on Women, Beijing 1995. Country report*. Deptt. of Women and Child Development, Ministry of Human Resource Development, New Delhi. 1995.

Human Development Report, UNDP, New York: Oxford University Press, 1996.

Kusum: "Can Wife be Made to Give Up Job? *The Hindustan Times*, Jan. 4, 1976.

Mead, M., Adolescence Issue, *UNICEF News*, 1974.

Noditch, Murray, P. and Demaw, T., Locus of Control and Competence. *Journal of Personality*. Dec. 1975.

Report of the Committee on Status of Women in India (1974), *Towards Equality*. Department of Social Welfare, Government of India, New Delhi.

Rotter, J.B., Generalized expectancies for internal versus external control or reinforcement. Psychological Monographs. General Applied, 1966.

Safilios-Rothschild, C., *The Influence of the Wife's Degree of Work Commitment upon Some Aspects of Family Organization and Dynamics, Journal of Marriage and the Family*, 1970.

Status of Women in India, A Synopsis of the Report, National Committee on the Status of Women (1971-74). New Delhi: The ICSSR. Allied Pub.. 1975.

Taylor, Ronald, N., Age and experience as determinants of managerial information processing and decision making performance. *Academy of Management, Journal*, 1975.

Index